Personhood and Christianity

Personhood and Christianity

in Psychodynamic and Corporate Perspective

Oliver Forshaw

The Lutterworth Press

The Lutterworth Press
P.O. Box 60
Cambridge
CB1 2NT

www.lutterworth.com
publishing@lutterworth.com

ISBN: 978 0 7188 9229 6

British Library Cataloguing in Publication Data
A catalogue record is available from the British Library

First published in 2010

Contents

Tribute

to

Frank Lake, MB, DTM, MRCPsych, DPM
1914-1982

Written in tribute to one of the most remarkable Anglican laymen of the twentieth century, this book commends his learning and reforming wisdom. I dedicate it to my grandchildren because so many who now carry most influence in society, and in their several professions, are at much disadvantage in being frequently deflected by current assumptions from even considering Lake's insights and discoveries. Because of widespread reluctance to face the personal nature of the human organism growing in the womb, it may be for my generation's grandchildren to investigate with open-mindedness and courage what seems to be going on in the life of the foetal child.

Frank was trained at Edinburgh (1932-37) and in Liverpool at the School of Tropical Medicine (1937-39) specialising in parasitology. He served as a missionary doctor in India (1939-50) where he worked first under the famine conditions then prevailing in Bengal. When appointed Superintendent of the Christian Medical School at Vellore he began to turn his attention to mental illness, through the influence of Dr Florence Nicholls, its Head of Psychiatry.

Returning to England he retrained in that field, as he worked in the hospital at Burley in Yorkshire. Towards the end of that period he met Donald Coggan, then Bishop of Bradford, and from that meeting sprang Frank's decision to leave NHS work and devote the rest of his life to what became the Clinical Theology Association in 1962.

For Zachary, Hannah, Henry and Jessica

Acknowledgements

The support and encouragement I have been given in writing this book has been great, leaving me with a long-lasting sense of thankfulness. In particular I want to thank the distinguished theologians who responded to an obscure unpublished author with extraordinary courtesy: John Bowker, Nicholas Lash and Mike Higton, bearing in mind that I have not met any of them. To each I express my gratitude and my high regard for their work. Dr Roger Moss has given me much encouragement to persevere. I am grateful to him and for ready help from two other professors of theology, Tim Gorringe and Basil Moss with whom I have had contact through my daughter and my present parish priest respectively.

Most remarkable of all has been the unstinting kindness and generosity of the Revd Chris Cook, the consultant psychiatrist and Honorary Professorial Fellow of Durham University, who over many months has given me time to discuss the substance and form of the book. To have his advice in the context of his own work on the theology and spirituality of mental health has been a privilege. In this respect I thank Professor Ann Loades who first introduced me to Chris.

In addition I am truly grateful to Aidan Van de Weyer and Adrian Brink of Lutterworth Press for enabling my argument to appear in print and to Ian Bignall for an immense amount of patient work in editing. I cannot put on paper my indebtedness to my wife, Jean, for her long-suffering devotion at the computer and her critical advice and wise help throughout.

I am most grateful to all the authors I have quoted or referred to, and wish to acknowledge that the publishers of the following have kindly granted permission to reproduce passages from the books concerned as specified in the endnotes. In many cases I have been able to contact the authors personally and in each case they have generously agreed to the way I have taken advantage of their writing. In particular I wish to thank the family of Dr Frank Lake for permission to use his unpublished material. In addition to the authors listed below I have been given the kind agreement of Mrs Carol Christian, Rt Revd Christopher Cocksworth, Mr Nick Earle, the Revd John Foskett and the Revd Jane Leach.

I have not been successful in tracing the present copyright holders of the work of Dr Richard Noll, Professor Anthony Storr, the Rt Revd Arthur Vogel and the late Canon Harold Lockley.

Diogenes Allen by kind permission of T&T Clark International
John Bowker by kind permission of I.B.Tauris & Co Ltd London
Sarah Coakley by kind permission of Wiley-Blackwell Ltd
David L. Edwards by kind permission of Darton, Longman & Todd Ltd, London
Daniel W. Hardy by kind permission of SCM-Canterbury Press Ltd
Julian N. Hartt by kind permission of T&T Clark International
Edward H. Henderson by kind permission of T&T Clark International
Frank Lake by kind permission of Emeth Press, Lexington, Kentucky, USA
Nicholas Lash by kind permission of Cambridge University Press and SCM-Canterbury Press Ltd
Charles Marsh by kind permission of Oxford University Press, Inc.
Alice Miller by kind permission of Pluto Press and of Virago Press, an imprint of Little, Brown Book Group
James P. Mackey by kind permission of Cambridge University Press
Richard Norris by kind permission of SPCK
Oliver O'Donovan by kind permission of Inter-Varsity Press and Wm B. Eerdmans Publishing Co
Heinrich Ott by kind permission of Lutterworth Press, Cambridge
Wolfhart Pannenberg by kind permission of Continuum International Publishing Group
Christina Rees by kind permission of Darton, Longman & Todd Ltd, London
Steven Shakespeare by kind permission of SPCK
Tom Smail by kind permission of Darton, Longman & Todd Ltd, London
Charles Taliaferro by kind permission of Cambridge University Press
William McF. Wilson by kind permission of T&T Clark International

Rowan Williams by kind permission of Continuum International Publishing Group, SCM-Canterbury Press Ltd and both Darton, Longman & Todd Ltd, London, and Campus Evangelical Press, Taiwan.

N.T. Wright By kind permission of SPCK, London, and T&T Clark International

Ann Belford Ulanov by kind permission of Westminster John Knox Press

Jeremy Young by kind permission of Darton, Longman & Todd Ltd, London

Introduction
The dimensions of wellbeing

What is human wellbeing?
Christians understand that the universe is destined for resurrection, a conviction that rests on God's self-revelation. However, if they are faithful to the New Testament's theology they will also be clear that they hold this position on rational grounds. That rationality will be affirmed throughout my argument. For this reason the theological anthropology I expound here is important because new perspectives, opening up in recent years, confirm afresh that human nature itself is the location where God starts to reveal himself. I begin with the notion of wellbeing to indicate where psychology makes its contribution to Christian thinking.

Frank Lake used the words being and wellbeing in connection with the two input phases of his diagram that describes the 'dynamic cycle' of psychological life (see fig. 1). This four-sided diagram will be looked at further in chapter 2 but here it is sufficient to say that it concerns the continuous reception and expenditure of personal resources. As the body needs to inhale and exhale air so the self is resourced as person through others. The word 'being' refers to the first degree of support which is warm acceptance, and the second that Lake called sustenance is needed to build up the self with some degree of assured strength from which satisfying interpersonal living is possible for a time. The cycle is continuous because activity is always followed by depletion. Wellbeing therefore stands on being, and if the latter has been deficient the former also will be less secure. Both these input phases in the cycle of the self's enduring existence refer to resources given through the personal presence of others. This resourcing is vital because, as Lake wrote, without access to relationships the individual 'dies', and the one who

> *enjoys* relationships of a generous and gracious kind is enhanced by them in his power of 'being'. The quality of 'wellbeing', good spirits, courage and personal vitality is a

> reflection of what has been communicated from others....
> [T]he person who responds to this donative experience
> [has] a worthwhile spiritual 'essence'. (*CT orig.* p.133)

The complete cycle of two input and two output phases indicates a series of truths about the development of the growing individual and his participation in community. One of these is the connection between the quality of sustained emotional support that the child has been given, and the quality of reliable, responsible citizenship that the same individual can contribute as an adult. In this perspective of long-term outcome we can appreciate that the distinction between being and wellbeing is not just a matter of degree, for they refer to two levels of personal engagement in life. At the second level, the person has not only been accepted but is gaining a stability of shared life that enables him to enjoy being himself as one who belongs and contributes to a creative community. Where repeated input phases of a child's nourishment and cherishing have given rise to sustained periods of enjoyable *wellbeing* the consequent confidence of the person concerned will enable him to bear the hardship of times when these resources are not being palpably received. After a time of satisfactory growth the sense of wellbeing does not need to be continuous, because it is now adequately stored in the memory of good times. Then there will be some expectation that the quality of life so far enjoyed should and can be restored when it breaks down. A person in that state knows that wellbeing is proper to his nature. It has been freely given and does not need to be earned or jealously guarded. Others who are seen to enjoy wellbeing do not need to be envied. Wellbeing is no longer in doubt and the danger of falling back entirely into the psychological state of mere *being* has passed. People in this state are usually stable enough to rest in their wellbeing, and so are sufficiently free to engage in the tasks and interests to which their personhood is being drawn. What they most value will include their relationships in which they enjoy their wellbeing but very often they will also have an increasing desire for the One who is the source of that wellbeing.

When wellbeing is not secured
But what of the person who has not begun to experience wellbeing in the earliest period of embodied life? His will be the condition of *being*. It will have some positive features and several negative

ones. There may be little predisposition towards deeper emotional disorders but the person will be liable to depression in some degree. There may also be a tendency to the paranoid condition if a period of warm acceptance has been followed by the sense that such support is being wilfully withdrawn, leaving him deprived. Broadly speaking, being is the kind of condition in which many people always exist, especially in industrialised western societies. They maintain high levels of psychological defence in order to manage their lives and succeed in their chosen projects. In this state there tends to be a considerable rigidity of thought and practice whatever style of life is adopted. The emotional tone of life in work and play can be a combination of interior resignation with aggressive and phrenetic activity, and this tone may dominate the culture of a society as well as its individual members. Enthusiasms are contrived both individually and collectively to subordinate the negativities of existence so that awareness of them is either tolerated or suppressed. The prevailing experience is often one of expected but only partially enjoyed emotional support in which case people are likely to find themselves unable to enjoy life without heavy reliance on stimulants or narcotics.

In contrast, those who have been adequately supported will have reached a stage of interpersonal experience where a different kind of horizon has opened up than the one that is possible on the basis of being only. This is the state of wellbeing that is sufficient to enable psycho-spiritual growth in the direction of mental health. People whose early make-up obliges them to live largely at the level of being, will not be aware that there can and should be a quality of emotional wellbeing, proper to human nature, which is markedly different in quality from what they can experience with the help of drugs. If that is a correct perception, psychodynamic study of personhood and of emotional healing should start from this recognition, with a psychological and theological search for the origin of personhood in the life of every individual. Beginning at conception, I shall argue, a person's wellbeing can grow steadily with the confidence that he is esteemed and acknowledged as a member of the caring community to which, in a non-conceptual way, he knows he belongs. But in the case of a person who lacks wellbeing, the original assurance (at conception) will have been too quickly obscured, requiring effort to be expended to bolster self-confidence. All these remarks are generalisations, for there are no hard boundaries between being and wellbeing.

Wellbeing in response to divine presence

Psychotherapists and academics in this field increasingly agree that mental wellbeing largely depends on good interpersonal relationships in the earliest periods of life. In view of that common ground, the psychodynamic thinking that I am commending can be perceived today, as it should be, in a non-religious, non-sectarian perspective. In moving towards understanding the Christian mission, the theological perceptions that Frank Lake pioneered in relation to psychotherapy are particularly relevant. The theology demonstrates the accuracy of Christian orthodoxy and in particular its communitarian understanding of human nature. The Christian gospel points to what God is doing, and where its non-possessive meaning is recognised the Church becomes a place of emotional healing and human maturing. On this basis I seek to show that all people share a capacity to constitute in community a creaturely embodiment of God's trinitarian relations as the Spirit moves them in responding to other people. Through their healing and maturing they can develop in being fellow-agents with the Creator, and as their sensitivity increases, that joint-agency will lead eventually to the transformation of communities in the properly secular way that God intends.

I hope the book will be read by fellow Christians but also by those on all sides of the religious-secular debate who may be ready to ask whether Christianity has a meaning and a future for the wellbeing of all people, a future that would leave behind as far as possible the tired, self-protective ways of religion which we notice so widely at present. Is there a mysterious core of gospel within all the various Christian traditions that is even more promising than has been apparent in the best days of the Church's history so far? That ancient thread of faith goes back to Abraham and finds its very strange and still growing culmination, initially in Jesus only and then in the community he established. Does this faith actually hold out the prospect of developing wellbeing everywhere, including those areas where communities are most subject to interpersonal disharmony and deprivation? I am proposing that it is not over-optimistic to think so, because underlying the diversity and the internal tensions of the Christian scene, the Church's faith does have a universal significance which takes it beyond the category of religion as commonly understood. The prospect of justifying that claim is now opening up through psychological research and practice, yet it has always been evident in the NT. Taking this seriously does not imply disrespect of the religious cultures and traditions which now exist, and are still needed, but it does challenge the Church to be true to her calling to be the meeting place where the corporate Christ is formed in the midst of human diversity.

The composition of the person

Much of the discussion to which this book attends concerns human motivation and what constrains it. The psychological side of the enquiry cannot go far, however, unless it is supported by attention to the philosophical aspect of faith and its theology. Because every person needs to be nurtured emotionally and intellectually, I shall be contending that no one moves towards faith in Jesus, or in God, without in some measure recovering the primitive 'knowledge' or experience of the divine presence implanted at the start of the individual's personal existence. Growth into adult faith nearly always involves a measure of heart-healing to enable people to develop beyond the emotional difficulties that tend to prevent them from seeing the world as it is and experiencing themselves as God intends them to be. The world-view I describe in chapter 1 uses the term duality in contrast to dualism. I think of this duality being the-world-and-its-enlivenment with God's own self-giving. Creation, as Christians understand it, is designed in such a way that it will be transformed eventually into a form that is entirely radiant with the Creator's personal life. Meanwhile, the universe as now experienced is recognised to be the place in which God is explaining himself, as well as the arena in which we can learn to receive the resources we need.

The discussion will focus on the centrality of personal need and suffering in the divine strategy, and also on the way God's activity, through which human lives are changed, is operating within the constraints of a community and its culture. So much are we social creatures that the self is always more than the individual, for a "*person* ... is not an individual but a plural being ... the identity of each person is spread across the whole extent ... of human personhood ... not hidden in a monadic internal place without extension".[1] The individual subject is rooted in the physical organism, but from conception onwards she is being composed as a person, and the personhood that is being built up is corporately extensive within forms of spiritual life to which people commit themselves in their diverse community groups. This concept of personhood is fundamental to the understanding of humanity, and, as we shall see, it helps to explain how people grow towards good or ill under the influence of others, and also how they can become reflectors of God's love and participants in his creativity.

Humanity intrinsically receptive

Although the dynamic cycle is evident most clearly in babies, it operates perpetually because in the gradually deepening satisfaction of personal neediness lies the fulfilment of humankind's deepest desire. The fact that we are made so helpless and dependent in infancy sets the growth of human creatures in the direction that leads eventually to their maturity. The original formation of the individual through the Creator's presence, which I propose in chapter 1, provides the foundation on which the creature's destiny is reached in a community of relationships. If I am right in this, the spiritual growth process advances by way of need and dependence because receptivity in the created person is intended to be paramount. For this reason I shall suggest that there is in humanity a fundamental priority of the feminine, though it should be noted that this is a distinction of psychological character and not narrowly one of gender and sex.

The hypothesis is strengthened further in the Christian tradition because the doctrine of God's Trinity in its properly orthodox and monotheistic form indicates that the Holy Spirit is constantly at work to facilitate the openness of people to each other and to God. His gracious influence helps them to restrain their anti-social impulses. The receptive side of their nature needs fostering in order to overcome the traits in both men and women, which dispose towards control, possessiveness, and eventually withdrawal from communal engagement. In identifying the trinitarian character of personhood, Christianity makes its basic contribution to the understanding of well-being for individuals and for communities.

The priority of self-questioning

In his book *Lost Icons*,[2] Rowan Williams affirms the fundamental point in Christian anthropology that I am concerned with in this book: "doctrine and exhortation are meaningless" unless we understand the nature of our humanity. To recover a true engagement with others and with ourselves "we must build a selfhood radically unlike what we take for granted as the modern norm of subjectivity" (p.149). He identifies two ways of becoming more deeply open to God's gracious initiatives, setting "some strands of psychoanalytic" practice alongside the "more primitive" kind of psychotherapy through falling in love (pp.150, 155), for being in love exercises the transcending function which can lift one or both lovers beyond the satisfactions they yearn for. Both therapy and love can enable people to see themselves afresh in a process of learning through frustration and yearning. I am "being shown to myself" as a person "in ways I couldn't have realised by myself" (p.156): that I am not here in this life for myself or for the one I love. If either the discipline of psychoanalysis or that of being in love are limited to meeting short-term needs, "what is lost in both cases is that vision of the self as *not* there to be possessed" (p.160). In pursuing his theme of human incompleteness, Williams borrows the terminology of Jacob Needleman,[3] who writes of the need for a "profound self-questioning". In the same vein, I discuss personhood in relation to contemporary problems of Church and society as a matter directly relevant to Christian discipleship. To put it in its briefest form, my proposal will be that human growth towards maturity occurs when people start attending, directly or indirectly to those difficult sayings which, in their everyday and social context, Jesus repeatedly addressed to his compatriots as children of Abraham.

Method
In presenting this thesis on personhood and its significance for community, psychologically and theologically, I have drawn on a number of contemporary authors and also on the earlier twentieth-century theologians Dietrich Bonhoeffer, Austin Farrer and Donald McKinnon. In order to show how I have benefited from the more recent writers and where I differ from some of them, I have, in some cases, quoted them at length. This I hope makes the argument clearer, especially for those in busy ministry who may not have easy access to these sources. This comparative way of discussing the subject has also seemed desirable in order to encourage a genuine seeking of common mind and to support the growing tendency for Christian leaders to venture beyond the segregated party positions to which we have become accustomed. My exposition of Christian faith stresses God's healing and redeeming initiatives in all human situations, as well as the implications for change in the Church. It is a theology of divine presence and activity within a suffering world.

Concerning pronouns for God
I have decided to remain reluctantly conventional and keep the masculine pronouns for God, simply to avoid any clumsy alternative. God is undoubtedly Mother as much as Father, but I shall argue that the Spirit is characteristically masculine. In that regard only the conventional usage is logical. With reference to the first and second persons of the Trinity the language does not provide a satisfactory pronoun.

Chapter One
Persons in dependence
on God's presence

A. Resources and consent for self-criticism

Reflection on my experience, as a parish priest since the fifties and in being involved in Frank Lake's Clinical Theology work since the mid-sixties, has convinced me of the need to bring the insights of psychodynamic study and practice to the full range of the Church's life and work. Lake believed his teaching and practice could be applied in the Church in two ways. The first is in guiding pastoral care and training in relation to the psychological imbalance of all kinds and degrees to which everyone is subject in some way. But secondly the outlook of his psychotherapy can enable the Church to develop a discipline in the Holy Spirit through which to discriminate between what in spirituality is unhelpful or even pathological and what is pointing towards the holy and the true. Following such a discipline is not something that is strange to the Church's tradition – the Bible's prophetic tradition is concerned with focusing on the deceitfulness of the human heart and on listening to God's Spirit who 'searches the heart and examines the mind' of humankind (Jeremiah 17:9,10). The practice of self-criticism leading to personal change has always been integral to the Christian way, and so it is appropriate to bring psychological knowledge to bear on the process and tasks of spiritual growth, both individual and corporate. In this the Church's God-given resources are intended not just for believers to mature in Christ but for the mission to be fruitful in society. While traditional Christian disciplines were in decline for much of the twentieth century welcome new developments have begun to appear. This has been particularly notable in relation to the mental health professions where there is now growing psychiatric and psychotherapeutic interest in and literature on the dimensions of faith and spirituality. This change, occurring over the years since Lake died, has in some cases been in direct continuation of the research into pre-and peri-natal psychology to

which he devoted the last years of his life. In that context of fresh
interest in the therapeutic and theological aspects of spirituality and
of ministry in the Church's congregations I offer the thinking essayed
in this book. Its thesis is that human personhood is strikingly communitarian even though rooted and displayed in the remarkable variety
and potency of individual lives.

I argue in this chapter that what gives humanity its privileged status
in the natural order is that people have the capacity to discern the
creative and redemptive presence of God and live in conscious relation to him. By his presence he makes it possible for people to change
in character and eventually be transformed within communities that
will express his Triune being beyond present expectation. The chapter
as a whole tackles questions about the theology and psychology of
experience, but I begin with an example of a practical dilemma (in
this case about worship) where the Church is challenged to be faithful
to the One who makes extraordinary demands on ordinary people.

As the discussion proceeds we shall see how prone we are to
be controlled by motives we barely recognise, the origin of which
may be partly or wholly hidden from ourselves. Here the issue is domestic for the Church and yet typical of behaviour generally, namely
a common response to the eucharistic meal. For those who have
found it the centre of their Christian experience, sharing in the Lord's
Supper, in any of its forms, is an obligation inherent to being 'in
Christ' and a straightforward privilege to be enjoyed. But for a good
many, in today's climate of individual choice and heightened self-
consciousness, the prospect can be something to avoid. It is partly
a matter of psychological make-up, but not only so. It is likely to
be complicated to a large extent by peer pressure and by inaccurate knowledge of the Christian faith, all these within the intimately
particular events of a person's family history or previous Christian
experience. Often the problem is made more acute because clergy
have not taught, or have not realised themselves, that by his body
and blood Christ meant the specific earthly character of God's actual
incarnation.

Mission to the unchurched and disaffected
Christian leaders are understandably afraid of antagonising the individuals for whom they have been given pastoral care, and of disturbing
the cohesion and assurance of congregations and of the wider community that the Church serves. It is a matter of proper concern. But along
with this immediate anxiety, there is the greater responsibility to be
the Church. How are we to adjust the Church's practice in a way that

will both enable her to communicate the gospel to the unchurched, and at the same time preserve the continuity of the tradition in ways that deepen the witness to its authentic character? People who feel the Church has failed them, and those who in the current climate are disaffected by orthodox Christianity, often turn to a spirituality which disdains a sacrament involving bread as a sign of this man's particular embodiment and wine as a sign of his actual dying. From their perspective the decision is not perceived as an unfaithfulness or even as a lack of cooperation, for everything they know from outside the Church's life, and sadly very often from within it as well, has encouraged them to suppose that they are within their 'rights' to be a Christian in this way. Their thinking can be further strengthened since they may well know that the Church locally, and in part more widely, has accepted the idea that non-sacramental worship is an adequate alternative either in the long-term or as a step in the individual's personal growth.

In this situation the Church's leaders at local level are in a dilemma that can, unfortunately, be easily escaped by not facing the underlying fears at work in individuals. It is just that avoidance of the problem that the Church of England has chosen to a very large extent – to its shame. The difficulty of finding the eucharistic elements an embarrassment has encouraged the idea that non-sacramental services provide a suitable intermediate stage towards full commitment in Christ. It continues to be regarded as plausible that the policy provides a way of advancing the Church's mission, especially in easing the difficulties involved in achieving 'all-age' worship. This supposed plausibility is then greatly strengthened, as many may see it, by the knowledge that the Church of England has behind it such a long history of non-eucharistic worship in which Matins and Evensong were the general diet.

Desiring satisfaction in community
With this problem in mind, it is worth noting what Charles Taylor was saying in his study of William James under the heading 'The new individualism'.[1] Having referred to 'post-war consumerism (and) the self-understandings that went along with' it, he writes of an

> understanding of life that emerged with the Romantic expressivism of the late 18th century, that each of us has his or her own way of realizing one's own humanity.... But it was only in the era after the Second World War that this ethic of authenticity began to shape the outlook of society in general. Expressions like 'do your own thing' became current....

Therapies proliferated that promised to help you find yourself, realize yourself, release your true self, and so on.

Taylor shows that the world of fashionable style and behaviour operates at different levels of consciousness with powerful effects in the culture as a whole.

> The space of fashion is one in which we sustain a language of signs and meanings, which is constantly changing, but which at any moment is the background needed to give our gestures the sense they have.... My gesture can change it, and then your responding stylistic move will take its meaning from the new contour the language takes on.... It matters to each of us as we act that the others are there, as witnesses of what we are doing, and thus as co-determiners of the meaning of our action.
>
> Spaces of this kind become more and more important in modern urban society, where large numbers of people rub shoulders, unknown to each other, forming the inescapable context of each other's lives. As against the everyday rush to work ... where others can sink to the status of obstacles in my way, city life has developed other ways of being-with.... Here each individual or small group acts on its own, but aware that its display says something to the others, will be responded to by them, will help to build a common mood or tone that will color everyone's actions. (pp 83-86)

This insight describes the situation in which we have to consider *experience* in relation to a much clearer understanding of our human nature as revealed through Christ. Taylor's analysis reminds us how necessary to our humanity is the drive for self-satisfaction in relations with others. Contemporary culture may be more widely hedonistic than its predecessors, but from the standpoint of Christianity this is not wholly wrong – as traditional asceticism has often assumed. The fulfilment of natural appetites is an important part of the divine purpose and is sacramental of God's holiness. But what is essential to Christianity is that the enjoyment of life's goodness is found most fully in a shared life directed towards God himself. In contrast to other religious traditions Christianity, as Nicholas Lash puts it, is:

> dedicated rather to purification and fulfilment than the 'suppression' of desire.... patterned to discipleship, to the following of Christ.... [O]bedience to the Word made flesh ... seeks not to stifle or suppress desire, but to release

it from the chains which bind it in egotism's nervous and oppressive grasp.[2]

Living out such discipleship, however, requires an acceptance of different priorities. Today it is being pointed out that opinion in the affluent world is complacent about its culture of excessive greed because the brain of modern humans still has the inbred drive of their ancient forbears who never had enough to eat.

Individualism over 1000 years

Individualism, as the prevailing outlook of both modern and post-modern cultures, which Charles Taylor's words bring into focus, has very deep roots in European history. Sarah Coakley has emphasised this, quoting Colin Morris to the effect that

> [i]t was neither the Renaissance nor the Enlightenment, that invented the 'individual' but rather the rich period 1080-1150, which developed a peculiar 'self-awareness and self-expression', a freedom from 'excessive attention to convention or authority'.... In sum, and to quote Morris, 'Twelfth century society was thus disturbed by the rapid emergence of a whole series of new groups or classes, all of them requiring an idea on which to model themselves.... They created a conflict of values, and faced the individual with choices which in the year AD 1000 would have been unimaginable'.[3]

I bring in Coakley's longer historical perspective to stress that the subjects of this chapter – concerning experience and selfhood – need to be viewed in terms of history as well as creative process. Individualism, being such an obstacle to the Church's mission, is also a necessary one. It tends to block what God is doing, but without their ability to resist God, human beings could never become the children of God. Only through the development of each individual's aims and capacities, with all the frustrations, conflicts and resolutions involved, can the corporate life, for which humanity is being created, move towards its fulfilment. Within that complex of individual energy the Spirit works to prise people out of their isolation and heal their disease into union with God in a process painful as well as slow.

I have titled this section 'resources and consent for self-criticism' because it is not enough for the Church and its ministers to be more objectively aware of the psychological characteristics of human nature. Research and practice in psychotherapy, neuroscience, and the observation of child development are bringing better awareness of the human condition. But that carries with it responsibility to apply the knowledge and sensitivity in every area of ministry and that can be costly in terms of deflated self-importance, first for those who minister but in the longer term also for those to whom they minister. Church leaders, like those in secular professions, may still persuade themselves that emotional disorders are only of marginal significance for their work. As we see in the more extreme instances reported in the media, turning a blind eye to blatant physical and sexual abuse has very serious consequences, but complacency does harm far more commonly in milder cases of misdirected power. So the 'self criticism' I refer to concerns our need in the Church and beyond it, to be persuaded that it is not just the few obviously disturbed people we come across who require psychological understanding and appropriate care, but *all of us*. As far as the Church is concerned, one essential implication of this is that these insights should be applied, with real thoroughness, to all who are called to ministry *before* they are commissioned to positions of responsibility for others, and in their supervision *afterwards*. Much of the difficulty the Church faces in commending the faith and helping members of the congregation to grow stems from deeply rooted refusals to face the truth about ourselves. Yet we know that the need for self-criticism belongs to the essential context in which the good news is preached. Without the willingness to judge ourselves guilty, the gospel is never heard. Often some substitute is chosen which claims to be Christian, but which serves only to strengthen mere self-satisfaction and group gratification. We need to challenge each other in this respect.

Resources of the Spirit in renewed congregations
An ambitious strategy is needed to meet the situation I have outlined, a strategy which can be described as submitting to the leading and discipline of the Spirit. There needs to be a deliberate marshalling of resources undertaken ecumenically by the Church in her present divided state, with the acknowledgement that unless that cooperation leads to increasing unity the effort will be largely wasted. After too many years of drifting with less than adequate theological resources, the Church may now be somewhat better equipped to change her ways and respond to God accordingly. Where people put real trust in God he raises up prophetic teaching ministries, enables processes of re-education, and inspires experimental community practice which, when taken seriously and applied *in combination together,* lead to widespread improvements. To strengthen the Church in this direction there are theologians who can help, some of whom I refer to

in this chapter. Taken together their work deepens our perspective on the human capacity to experience life in such a way that God can be known, not in an abstracted way but in the very midst of the created world, the world of which human beings are themselves the most significant part. In that perspective we can re-affirm that the human world's awareness of God implies a unitary concept of creation's destiny that is indeed hidden, but not impenetrably so. To develop and sustain that vision Christians will need to be nourished in a view of the Church's life which deliberately disavows the individualistic and denominational understanding of Christianity that is still so common. For that to bear fruit, existing barriers to intercommunion will have to be replaced by more sensitive forms of pastoral discipline, as a local catholicism is developed appropriate to the present age.

At the heart of this matter is surely the reality of personal conversion and its corporate reinforcement within committed believing communities. Conversion and incorporation into Christ, with the consequent *practice of trust in the guidance of God's Spirit,* involves a *decentring* of personal awareness and ambition from the individual to a corporate focus. By that deliberate turning away from much in the conventional outlook of religion, the personal presence and priorities of God can be truly acknowledged, and allowed to occupy centre-stage in the worship and mission of congregations. Here is the critical centre of the Church's crisis in our time and the reason why a better theological anthropology is our primary need. In order to pursue this end, we have to examine theological contributions which explore the nature of personal experience in more direct relation to God than between people only. A great deal is written these days about personal relations, in theology and in philosophical anthropology, but David Ford remarks that 'the language of relationship' is 'perhaps the main contemporary over-emphasis'.[4] Certainly talk of 'religious experience' must be related to the Christian doctrine of God the Trinity and not to a vague theism, if it is going to be of any help in enabling people to understand divine holiness. The universal resistance to self-criticism and the common focus on the individual's search for emotional assurance in religion are signs that any turn towards a de-centring of the self is unlikely to happen smoothly.

The secret of interpersonal fulfilment
During the early centuries the Fathers provided trinitarian resources for understanding humanity by reflecting on the Church's experience

of Christ. In the dark period that followed, Christians began communicating the faith in simpler and less adequate terms. John Habgood
points out that the definition of 'person' made popular by Boethius, as
an "individual substance of a rational nature" was much too narrow to
serve its purpose. Yet this notion became influential with 'disastrous'
consequences and was "to direct attention away from the concept
of persons existing always in relation to one another, and to give a
new prominence to their separateness".[5] From time to time I use the
word communitarian, but with the caution that Christian attention to
living in community is not collectivist. We should not turn away from
the strange secret at the heart of the universe – that each particular
human being is created to be the apple of the Creator's eye. Each is
created, not for his own private satisfaction, but to be drawn into the
joy of living with other people who are also receiving from God, that
together they may discover what the shared companionship of Christ
is like.

B. Critique of religious experience

In view of the considerations reviewed so far we are looking first for an understanding of human religiosity which will explain both its persistent fascination and its moral ambiguity. As so many contemporary commentators have pointed out, religion may have been driven from its traditional thrones by intellectual attacks and by emotional repudiation, but it continues to reassert itself, undoubtedly witnessing to deep needs in human selfhood. Consequently the Church at all levels needs to be more effective in unmasking the appeal of religious experience as it manifests itself in contemporary spirituality, and in showing how the world's individualism distorts what God is offering to the world in Christ. While that is the starting point for this chapter, its further purpose is to examine the weakest point of the European tradition in philosophy and theology, concerning human consciousness and selfhood, because it is there that the underlying confusion lies, giving further excuse for the prevailing habits of spirituality both in religion and in supposedly secular life.

Religion as private

Nicholas Lash drew attention, first in *Theology on Dover Beach (1979),* then in *Theology on the Way to Emmaus (1986),* and more extensively in *Easter in Ordinary (1988),* to a 'general consensus' that religious experience is 'by its very nature, 'private', 'inner', 'subjective',[6] referring there to words of Brian Hebblethwaite. He went on that such a 'notion of religious experience ... is parasitic upon a more general account of human experience ...' of which he gives an instance in Richard Swinburne's definition of 'experience'.[7]

> Behind the definition of experience as 'conscious mental going on' [Swinburne's phrase] there lurks the myth, at least as old as Descartes, that the *real* 'me', the essential person, lives somewhere inside my head. From within this private citadel, in which alone are certainty and security to be sought, I attempt (not without nervousness) to make contact, through sense or argument, with such other similarly sheltered egos as may surround and greet and threaten me.

This myth is of 'metaphysical dualism according to which all facts, events and things fall ultimately into one of two classes: the material and the spiritual, the physical and the mental, the bound and the free'. It appeals to people generally because on this basis religion can be kept under private control.

> What keeps religion going, especially in our day, is the
> attraction of and the quest for, religious experience ... often
> construed as an oasis of delight, wonder or reassurance, a
> warm, safe place in which the complexity and incomple-
> teness of argument, on the one hand, and the untidy and
> uncontrollable turbulence and terror of fact and flesh, rela-
> tionships and politics, on the other, are kept at bay.

But, Lash concludes, "all such dualisms profoundly distort and misrepresent our human, and hence our Christian experience.... [They]
express not simply a mistaken philosophy, but a pathological defor-
mation, a personal and cultural disease. That is why they are so
difficult both to diagnose and to heal".[8]

Experience and the individual
In *Theology on the Way to Emmaus* and then much more fully in *Easter
in Ordinary*,[9] Lash took the ideas of William James, the author of *The
Varieties of Religious Experience*,[10] as the outstanding example in the
English speaking world of how things were going, and going wrong,
in psychological thinking about religion. For James had defined religious experience as 'the feelings, acts, and experiences of individual
men in their solitude, so far as they apprehend themselves to stand in
relation to whatever they may consider the divine' (*The Varieties* p.50).
In contrast to that definition, we come now to the centre of this book's
concern to find a better statement of Christian orthodoxy concerning
human nature and the human awareness of God. Although modernity
has moved, both philosophically and theologically, in a systemati-
cally sceptical direction, there did arise through the humanism of the
age a very proper attention to the 'existential' sense of what it is to
be human. This experiential emphasis, the positive in modernity, has
been providential, and is in marked contrast to the generally negative
outcome of the Enlightenment as far as faith is concerned. On this
basis I consider what the *imago dei* doctrine means and concentrate
particularly on the origin of individual selfhood, outlining a proposal
for an orthodox Christian understanding of the relation between God
and the world in terms of duality and spirit.

Being open to recognise God's presence
To show why a philosophical theologian like Nicholas Lash has given
such thorough attention to the subject of 'religious experience' I take
his lecture in Canterbury Cathedral in September 1993, marking the
900th anniversary of Anselm's enthronement as Archbishop. The

whole lecture should be consulted,[11] but the essential points for my purpose are as follows.

> The best known phrase in Anselm's writings: ... [is] "I believe so that I may understand". If, when considering this phrase, you find yourself drawn into a discussion in which all sides take for granted that either 'faith' or 'reason', either received tradition or our individual attempts to make some sense of things, must gain the upper hand, then Anselm will stay a stranger to your world. If, on the other hand, you find yourself muttering, without pain or effort, complacent bromides about 'of course we need both "faith" and "reason"', then not only Anselm's writings, but those of all great Christian thinkers, will remain closed books gathering dust in the shuttered attic of your sleeping mind. (p.151)

Confronted as we are by the massive unbelief of our contemporaries, we must not diminish the significance of that unbelief by reducing it

> to a mere matter of finding no good uses for the small word 'God', whereas Anselm, who took serious things seriously, was interested in the unbelief that issued from the heart, not that which merely skimmed across the surface of the mind....

And under the sub-heading 'Experience and Expertise' Lash refers to words from Anselm's *Letter on the Incarnation:* 'One who does not believe, will not experience; and whoever does not experience, will not understand'.

> [W]here the knowledge of God is concerned, it is discipleship which furnishes the necessary context of experience. I say 'discipleship', rather than 'believing', because we will not hear what Anselm is saying if we indulge our pernicious modern habit of *contracting* the sense of words like 'faith', 'hope' and 'love' until they refer to individual, private, psychic states or attitudes, rather than to shared and public patterns of conviction and behaviour. For Anselm, 'believing' is living the life of a disciple: a life open to God's command, nourished (as he puts it) by the Scriptures in the way of wisdom. (pp.154-155)

Questing from the shared heart

By using the word discipleship, we are reminded that, not just as believers but simply as people, our life is corporate, and therefore both for the Church's wellbeing and for humanity's survival the character of personal reality should be made clear. Since society and its faith communities belong together especially at the level of personhood, there is an obligation on all to understand the heritage of community living which is upheld by shared belief in the value and potential of persons. As world citizens we need to be alert to the danger of seeing the act of believing 'through spectacles designed by the Enlightenment', rather than in being "bound together in a common project" that belongs to our humanity (p.157).

> The problems start when 'faith' and 'reason', heart and head, belief and understanding are taken to be antithetical, mutually exclusive ... In such a climate 'credo ut intelligam' rings out like a battle cry of obscurantism and irrationality. First take the leap of faith and then you will understand; first close your eyes and then, at last, you will see! Even quite sensible and educated Christians may be affected by this nonsense. (p.159)

My task now is to take the matter further with the help of James Mackey in *The Critique of Theological Reason*.[12] This complex study traces the roots of postmodernist positions in philosophy, with particular reference to human subjectivity, and then goes on to discuss research in developmental psychology in relation to this theme. The proposal from which he develops his argument is:

> that the most significant feature of postmodernism is not the apparently rampant relativism it is thought to entail, but the loss of the subject (to which some would add, the loss to view also of the rest of reality). (p.5)

In his long second chapter he refers to Heidegger, who 'encountered in his early years' the prevailing philosophy as one in which the

> still dominant subject is purely of the nature of mind, consciousness or spirit...as yet without any content from the material, empirical world. It is worldless, or other [than] worldly ... the transcendental subject that can only later, by some process or other, come to be or be seen to be related to this material world ... (p.54)

Mackey was pointing out that if the self transcends the body in the way our Creator has been held, in the western tradition, to transcend creatures, *our own existence can only be a matter of conjecture*, any knowledge of other persons that we seem to have can at best be a matter of inference. In contrast the Christian makes no such assumptions. Believing in resurrection as well as spirit, we can be confident that human consciousness belongs intimately to our embodied existence, and that its relative transcendence of the body's materiality needs to be defined differently from the way the transcendence of the Creator has been conceived.

Mackey explains how two philosophical streams of thought, the phenomenologist and the materialist, have formed the postmodern climate in which we live. His analysis of the phenomenologist thinkers Husserl, Sartre and Heidegger shows that a satisfactory account of reality is threatened in two separate directions. On the one hand it is difficult to establish the subject's 'relationship with the rest of reality; and in particular the relationship of knower to known'. On the other the loss is threatened of 'the real embodied subjects we ... seem to ourselves to be'.

> Heidegger's determination to rid us of a transcendent subject in the crude sense of transcendence ... tends to leave us rather too embodied in the world, with little or no transcendence of any kind.

Yet 'a 'Cartesian' dualism continues to be influential throughout Heideggerr's philosophy' (pp.78-79).

Some illumination in Sartre
What comes out particularly clearly in Sartre's kind of existentialism is an interpretation of human experience that has become more and more explicit among believers and unbelievers alike – the emotional sense that the human subject is alone and ultimately empty as if hanging over an abyss.

> The positive achievement of Sartre's opening aim begins with his distinctive analysis of the *Cogito.* Instead of defining the *Cogito* as a thinking substance, replete with ideas and *volontes* ... Sartre seeks to define something altogether more fundamental and originary, which he calls the 'pre-reflective *cogito*'. This is a consciousness which is a being; and being a consciousness, it is conscious of being conscious. Yet we must not then describe it as being conscious of itself, for that would be to suggest that of its own nature and essence it has a kind of content to be conscious of.... As Sartre puts it in *Being and Nothingness* p.349 ... it is of itself contentless, to the point where it can

be described quite accurately as the 'absolute nothing
which I am'. (p. 63)

It is that sense of personal emptiness to which I am pointing, for
although Mackey rightly concludes his thorough examination of
Sartre's thinking about the self by saying that 'his philosophy continues
to fail' (p.75), it seems to me that Sartre was right in his statements
about subjectivity if considered in isolation, that it is consciousness
of being conscious, yet *without content* in itself. We know, however,
that we are not obliged to identify the self in that disjunctive way at
all, for in being a certain individual, with a certain personality and a
great bank of memories, we know ourselves as embodied people in
relation to others and in the continuity of life in communities. How
then is it that so many people in real life share the feelings of isolation
that are the basis of Sartre's philosophical complaint? How, against
the background of such feelings, are we to account for our existence
as persons, being *in a real sense substantial*?

Personhood is raw material for resurrection
I shall argue that the apparent problem here in discerning the reality
of the individual's personal being requires a distinction between
individual subjectivity and personhood, although it will be different
from Sartre's distinction between For-itself and In-itself. What we
have to identify is the nature of our *dependence with other persons
on the Creator's personal being.* The distinction between subject and
person is needed because the substantiality of self which we tend to
identify closely with our subjectivity belongs rather to the order of
'intersubjectivity' (for which see section G below), since all created
spirit has its non-physical existence in relation to God the Triune
Spirit. This is the case for everyone whether obedient to God or not,
whether believing or unbelieving, because all personhood involves
the capacity to relate to others in the complementary way that we see
paradigmatically in God's Trinity.

Sartre, who did not perceive that we live in dependence on God,
could not solve the problem that his thinking had propounded.
He saw the reality of the In-itself on which personal continuity
depends, but could not conceive any prospect of being assured that
this was himself embodied in community. As Mackey represents
his position:

I *am* and can *be* (self-) conscious only in the process of
being conscious of something other than myself. The In-
itself affords me the very possibility of being, in both the

> ontological and ethical mode.... I depend upon it and act
> to try to make myself into an In-itself... at times trying to
> pretend I have already succeeded... (p.64)

We can all feel like Sartre cut off from our continuing reality, but in Christ we are able to see that this spiritual reality (In-itself), which I call our personhood, does remain through God's Spirit since our life as persons is sustained in God's Trinity who gives us our potential for healing and resurrection. This is why the NT affirms that all rise, either for salvation or for condemnation (John 5:29). Consequently Sartre's gloomy conclusion helps us to be realistic in recognising the need for this distinction between subject and person, and in understanding the belief in resurrection.

The individual's subjectivity does not encompass the wholeness of the person. Rather subjectivity is the place of access into personhood which is the dimension of each person's engagement with others and with the whole of spiritual or personal reality. The subject-self, as I shall call it, is in the first instance fundamentally physical; it mediates the encounter between persons and provides the individual with that identifying location from which he or she can both engage in the world of things and also participate in the interpersonal life of 'spirit'. The intersubjective life is one in which we absorb far more than we contribute. The input from beyond ourselves we absorb willingly or unwillingly, and with it we interact in active or passive response. Since we have only a little freedom to censor what we absorb, we often fail to appreciate how much we can be victims of the culture(s) and intersubjective climate in which we live. Consequently we have to stress that human life, which we tend to see in terms of separate individuals, is in fact deeply corporate and also dependent on God. We need a wider definition of personhood, and a perception of dependence on God's Spirit that has been part of the ancient wisdom of the biblical tradition (cf Job 12:10). When I agree with Sartre that human subjectivity itself is without content, I do not mean that the subject's mind is to be considered empty, as Locke does, a *tabula rasa*, for that would be to give the mind an essential aloofness and a self-contained constitution which I believe is to be expressly denied. Rather the subjectivity is empty in not being any kind of container. In my view the necessity of the subject-self concept lies in showing that the individual's consciousness exists in a participatory mode for feeling, for thought, for communication and in making decisions. The subject-self can stand out from the person's previous train of behaviour, and so is able to act with freedom from moment to moment. For that reason it can side with God or against him. This freedom, to change one's mind, and will, becomes the basis on which personhood can be healed and nurtured through repeated choices under the influence of the Spirit.

Weakness in personalist philosophies

Mackey's next section is intended "to observe what happened to…the (loss of the) subject, in the predominately personalist philosophies which have emerged in the course of [the twentieth] century; philosophies which … were welcomed with a mixture of relief and gratitude, and as much by Christian theologians as by moralists". (p.80) John Macmurray, for instance, was not able to take the critical step of realising that the human baby is a person, who knows and is purposeful even while she is largely helpless physically and has so much to learn. Because he has no concept of personhood that is much more than a knowledgeable subject, his thought remains individualistic and over intellectual.

> It is the parent who, for quite a long time in the case of humans, supplies the intentionality, the rationality; it is she who knows and understands and intends the successful outcome of the infant's 'random' movements and trial-and-error behaviour in general. The human neonate, one might say, is rational during these earliest years, but only potentially so, only by proxy.

At first Macmurray's account appears to be 'a totally intelligible and convincing explanation', says Mackey, but

> for all his talk about…being in relation with other persons from the outset…the child for all that time is…no more than a complex of very elementary feelings.… [T]he look, which for Sartre is itself the very paradigm of the conscious, knowing encounter with another person, falls for Macmurray amongst these random movements.… In consequence the newborn is only … 'potentially a person'.… (p.84)

Mackey's discussion of Macmurray's work leads on to the central question of this chapter: when and how does the human organism become a personal self? The answer has long eluded all enquiries, mainly because of assumptions that have prevented the search being directed to the right place. In showing that that was true in this instance Mackey has to conclude about Macmurray's work that he makes it impossible to understand how human neonates come to be rational-intentional agents.... So much that he said about the nature of persons in relation is so obviously heading in the right direction. But it would be fair to say ... that in the unstable philosophy of the time, his work shows the pendulum still swinging towards the extreme of the solipsistic mind.... (pp.85-86)

Transcendence with immanence
Going beyond the philosophical dilemmas of the twentieth century to find a 'better outcome', Mackey wrote:

the most promising approach ... would then begin with consciousness incarnate, subjectivity thoroughly ... embodied, in bodies and, through these, in the body of the material world. We can surely do this on the basis of our own immediate human experience.... (p.114)

He makes clear how we are to use the terms 'transcendence' and 'immanence' and be faithful to the nature of orthodox Christianity. All too often in the Church's history Christians have failed to use those terms properly.

A far more sophisticated account of immanence ... could correspondingly emerge ... Hence one would say of the mutual transcendence of subject and worldly reality that subject transcends worldly reality from within that reality, and that worldly reality transcends subject from within subject.... But this 'within' must not be taken in its spatial connotation, as is usual with the ghost-in-the-machine metaphor, but rather in the connotation of a kind of co-inherence which appears to be *sui generis* ... It follows that transcendence and immanence, in their properly sophisticated senses, turn out to be correlative terms rather than contraries; each calling for the other, rather than replacing each other, as happens when transcendence is taken in the crude sense of separation.... [Accordingly] subject and worldly reality could be described as correlative poles of the one inclusive being, rather than entirely separate regions of being. (p.117)

C. Duality not dualism

The discussion so far has implied that Christianity has to be firmly against a metaphysic of dualism, for although the world does have a two-fold character, we must be clear that God and the world are not two features of reality on a par.

The created world is dependent

The Christian public may be more or less familiar with the words transcendence and immanence in connection with the relation between God and the world, but perhaps a great deal less so when they are applied to the human subject's relation to her own body and the world. Since the terms transcendent and immanent are easily and frequently used in too loose a fashion, it may be that the concept of *duality* can be used in conjunction with them to sharpen up the ways in which we can think both about God's relation to his creation, and also about the human person's relation to her embodiment in it. Being used in the context of mind-body discussions about human nature, as Mackey does, transcendence and immanence point to a way of identifying what it is about the human being that cannot be expressed in the language of the physical sciences, that which the materialist is ready to ignore or explain away, and I use the notion of duality to reinforce Mackey's point.

If the world is *created*, as we sense it is, we have that intuition both because of the extraordinary intricacy of its design, and because the Creator is present to it in person. This latter perception, of divine personhood, enables us to say that being immanent (everywhere in the world), God is at the same time transcendent (beyond the world in the sense of embracing it). Thus the word duality emphasises that the whole universe has this dual character testifying by its own existence that it is created; that there is something about its being as we experience it which declares its dependence on God who is Spirit. It is fundamental to Christian faith not only that God is other than the world but also, consequently, that the way God acts in the world is utterly different from the ways in which created agents act. This is because God acts *from within and alongside* the processes that operate in creation as a whole without being himself an objective part of it. Such actions have been traditionally thought of as God's interventions 'from above'. It would be far better to think of them as 'from below', that is from God's immanence. Moreover, just because they are from transcendent immanence, they are *not* 'interventions'. We have to make it plain that there are not two objective elements in the world, the one a divine sourcing that penetrates the created part, as if God had to move around the world in order to advance his creative work. Rather it is the whole world that is dependent on his personal Being, a whole that rests in what is not itself. Thus the duality is of the world's two-fold reality – the finite in relation to God's infinity – in which the two orders of existence can in no way be placed on the same level, for the one is wholly upheld by the other. It is true this use of duality stretches the word's meaning. Another term is to be preferred, but is there one? At least duality is better than dualism, because the latter insists on division; here the word is being used to indicate a double character that precludes disunity but allows for God's priority, involving dependence and in the case of human persons a genuine partnership.

Subjectivity amidst duality
If it is appropriate to use the term duality in reference to the world's dependence on God, it follows that the way a person's mind transcends his body must be radically different from the way God transcends the world. We can say that transcendence-immanence language is primarily about God, and that any secondary usage of these terms needs careful handling. I think, however, we can add that, as our faith deepens, we perceive the personal being of creatures to be necessarily dependent on God's personhood in a way that is different from the physical dependence of created things. Although we never cease to have the status of creatures in both spirit and body, our spiritual being has an affinity with God's. In our nonphysical being we are bound to him in a closer way than in our bodily nature. With this in mind we should look again at the God-world relationship, but now in the context of the universe evolving as a creative *process*. Considering duality in the light of continuous creation rather than once-for-all creation, the notion acquires a fresh interest because God's relation to the world appears to be different from the point at which humankind became capable of bearing the divine image. The duality here is still that of the deeply uneven partnership between infinite and finite, between Creator and more or less recalcitrant creation, but now it is perceived at the point where human subjects are learning to be co-operators with the 'divine subject'. Despite the metaphysical contrast between God and the world, the human creature, being personal, participates in the divine life at the level of spirit to the extent that through being constituted in community every person is structured triunely by God's Spirit. Thus each is dependent on the Creator in a more intimate way than things and animals are, whether people

are living obediently or disobediently. We can therefore conceive the
duality taking on a more complicated shape at this level. Even before
the incarnation the spiritual or personal life of humanity has been
given a capacity to participate in the Trinity's activity in the world.

The notion of duality implies that the finite, visible world as
a whole is the site in which the infinite, invisible Creator can be
recognised by his human creatures. It is as if we are now looking at
the duality of Creator and world under the microscope at the point
where God is doing a new thing, by impinging on the world through
the consciousness of creatures. The radical nature of this idea is not
so surprising when we remember that it is exactly the outcome that
is to be expected on the basis of the New Testament gospel that God
identifies himself wholeheartedly with his creatures.

Duality of Creator and created people

This, my second proposal about the concept of duality, is with reference to God creating at two levels, the physical and the personal.
In the case of personal creatures who are conscious I use the term to
express the Christian's adventurous perception that God has bound
himself to be with his children, sharing their vulnerability and giving
them the opportunity to grow under the inspiration of the Spirit in a
strange union with the Father as members of the corporate Christ. On
this biblical view of the duality, the physical universe has ultimate
significance in partnership with the spiritual. Human life is grounded
and sustained in the physical so that we may not be overwhelmed
by God's awesome being, yet are able to live *in him* (cf Acts 17.28).
Whether we respond positively or negatively to the invitation, our
natural lives are entirely dependent on, and resourced by, God who is
pure Spirit. As a result the life of the human being is not free of God's
presence nor deprived of his personal resources. God is present to all
persons, though in being unaware that he is with them, they benefit
much less than he intends. I believe it is possible to discern that the
spiritual life of human creatures is constantly being instigated by God's
own being in subtle, interpersonal ways. That process has introduced
into the universe amazing degrees of creaturely achievement, creativity and sensitivity as people are stimulated by the Spirit while
remaining subject to their own wilfulness. In being nudged towards
God's life, morally, intellectually, and aesthetically, individuals and
communities have a finite potential to embody the infinite. Yet to
ensure that these personal creatures are free to choose their own
response to the Creator's influence, the physical exists to be, as it
were, the permanent theatre and medium in which the non-physical

is developed. Within the physical and social circumstances of their existence they will partly recognise and partly ignore God's presence as he invites them towards a more mature understanding of life in partnership with him and through him. How immensely important this duality of the world's existence is for Christian understanding is apparent in the way believers find themselves identifying God's presence in Jesus. Thus Mike Higton, in expounding Rowan Williams,[13] writes that the disciples

> did not meet in Jesus something that resembled God's love … they encountered God's love itself. They encountered, in Jesus, God loving them. (p.29)

Because of his personal immediacy the whole world is similarly close to God even though we need the incarnation if we are to engage with him fully. With that realisation in mind, I consider in the next chapter how and why humankind resists the attraction of God's Spirit so fiercely, and to a large extent frustrates his purpose. In those circumstances believers are tempted to be content with small religious alternatives to what the Creator continues to offer us through Christ and the Spirit.

Physical and non-physical
At this point we should recall how influential dualistic thinking has been and still is in the European tradition. Mackey has shown what great efforts have been needed to break the stranglehold of dualism in philosophy and theology during the late-nineteenth and twentieth centuries, yet its effects are still with us, persuading some scholars and to a large extent the general public to read Christianity along dualistic lines. To follow this I consider the thesis of Charles Taliaferro in his *Consciousness and the Mind of God*,[14] where he argues for 'integrative dualism', a version which at first sight takes into account most of the considerations nowadays presented in favour of abandoning the notion of dualism in Christian theology altogether. The case he makes may be impressive from the philosophical side, but taken together the qualifications that the word 'integrative' has to cover amount to a persuasive argument that is more in favour of replacing dualism with another term. It is the psychological data, however, rather than the philosophy that shows dualism to be an inappropriate idea.

It is good for the study of theological anthropology that Taliaferro has argued for this distinct form of dualism between the physical and the non-physical, because it shows the strength and the weakness of the tradition that the Church has inherited in this context. In today's materialistic climate of opinion, it is only too easy for the unwary Christian and others to be led into thinking that the case for a plainly physicalist view of human nature has been demonstrated and is compatible with biblical Christianity. That thinking encourages the idea that the Holy Spirit is, as it were, an occasional agent in the world. As he points out 'being labeled a 'dualist' is almost as bad as being branded a 'fundamentalist' (p.231). Perhaps it is largely because Taliaferro is concerned to expound a philosophical anthropology which will counter the views of a variety of atheistic materialists (Daniel Dennett and others) that he feels, as a Christian theist, he should stand close to other Christian dualists (Richard Swinburne and others) and argue that the dualist position simply needs reinforcing with a firmer emphasis on persons being 'integrally related to their bodies so that the person and his or her body function as a singular unit mentally and physically'. Starting from the assertion that '[t]he person and body are not strictly speaking, metaphysically identical' (p.115) his position is that 'persons are themselves nonphysical individuals' (p114), however

> profoundly unified. I hope to … take great care … in developing a version of dualism that underscores the integrative holist character of being an embodied person. It is to emphasise this point and to guard against seeing the person-body relationship in terms of lodging or a *mere* attachment, that I have elected to employ the term 'integrative dualism' … According [to which] the person and body differ metaphysically in the sense that they are separable individuals, and yet they function as a singular reality as an embodied person. The theme of separability will be central … (p.116)

Taliaferro develops the idea that the distinction between the physical body and the person can be satisfactorily envisaged in a way that would allow the body to be separated from the non-physical individual who, in some conceivable circumstances, could live in another body. It is strange, I think, that Taliaferro can pursue this kind of thinking while at the same time appreciating the importance of psychological learning. He writes

> I am very much drawn to the Attachment Theory of John Bowlby and Mary Ainsworth and impressed by aspects of the thought of some of those who have refined Freudian models of consciousness like D.W. Winnicott, Melanie Klein, and Wilfred Bion.... [I]ntegrative dualism can take on board

more specific theories of personal development that bring to
light the intersubjective, shared dimension of personal identity. Winnicott has, I believe, correctly grasped the role of
the caretaker in infancy, noting how the varying degrees of
care, attention, and need-satisfaction create natural stages by
which an infant comes to realize her independent identity.
(pp.302-303)

Through a particular body

Despite this attention, Taliaferro does not seem to grasp how fundamental is the psychodynamic formation process in establishing
not just the inner security of a person but also the social and organic
particularity of each unique member of the race. It is this, I think,
that precludes any *transfer* of one embodied person into another
body without damaging the integrity of the self, for the fundamental
reality of the human condition – and this is a matter that science can
perceive, as well as Christian orthodoxy – is that the process of life
involves bringing into existence a non-physical life (whether recognised in such words as mind, spirit, person, heart or some other)
which is *essentially* formed out of the experience of bodily life. So
radically is this non-physical life mediated within and determined by
its physical conditions, that believer and unbeliever alike are logically obliged to acknowledge that once fused by the process of life the
two elements, physical and non-physical, are inseparable. What is
open to controversy, of course, is whether and in what circumstance
the process of life in the universe leads to resurrection; namely a
further dimension of the process through which the physicality of
the person is not abandoned, but rather transfigured in such a way
that her physical humanity becomes more deeply subordinate to its
spiritual ground in God. It seems to me that all who have died will
take beyond the moment of death the entire entail of having lived
in their earthly bodies, even though they may already enjoy forgiveness of their sins, healing of their emotional wounds and some
release from the burdens they have been carrying. I say this because
both the NT and psychotherapy seem to indicate that God's way of
redemption changes people, not by denying what they have been
through but by a personal reconciliation which reverses the direction
and character of their lives. He then mends, rescues, and conserves
all that can be saved and transformed from its previous disorder and
contamination. God does this from his own personhood in which
he has defeated evil and exposed it for what it is. Thus migration
from the earthly body at death is not total abandonment. It begins

a process that takes place in two stages, leading eventually to the transformation of the whole person. From the time of the body's death the conscious life of the person continues in a non-physical medium equipped, as before, with what we know as memory and the unconscious. This is *not* resurrection, but what has been traditionally and misleadingly spoken of in terms of the 'immortality of the soul'. For the Christian, faith in this first stage of survival, to be with the Lord 'in paradise', is of immense comfort, but even in that secure relationship it will be incomplete. What the Church proclaims as the gospel of resurrection concerns the second stage of transformation, through which what happened in Jesus himself becomes reality for all who are incorporate in him.

Towards a new form of integration
We have to go on stressing that the transformation of human life that is evidently intended will eventually take the non-physical life of the person into a restored and 'spiritual' form of the body. While we have good reason to believe that God is non-physical and in himself changeless, we can be equally confident that the human condition is intentionally created within the physical universe, and that some form of physicality will remain proper to its destiny in a way that will be lasting. Thus the term duality, as I propose it, affirms that body and spirit belong together, but in a way that recognises that the person's life changes its form because of death. The notion of duality also allows for the fact that if spiritual growth is going well there will be an increasing interaction between and sharing of human and divine activity, in forms of joint-agency.

    Dualistic thinking has to be rejected as unhelpful and misleading, but while many contemporary theologians have combined to discard dualism, and with good reason, we have to ask what have they pro-posed in its place? The Christian position has to be that the total human person is as much bodily as spiritual, although the process of human development towards maturity reaches a significant stage with the death of the earthly body. The Christian world-view takes seriously what is happening in the whole historical period through which the spiritual in human nature becomes more prominent and takes centre stage in the evolution of the universe. There is a process leading towards sactification and spiritual maturity for individuals, and the potential for transforming communities accordingly. From beginning to end the physical is needed that through the ascended Jesus there may be a finite form of the divine life gathering up and fulfilling creation as a whole.

D. Being responsible and submissive to God

It will be apparent in what follows that we are not by any means finished with the theme of duality in creation, and that the task now is to see more of its implications with reference to human co-operation with God. I look at the way modern Christian thinking about humanity has developed in the light of Wolfhart Pannenberg's work *Anthropology in Theological Perspective*,[15] but I lead into that by considering other comments on dualism by Richard Norris in *Keeping the Faith*.[16] In the modern era the prevailing Christian atti-tude to the Bible seems to have changed under the secular influence of "the philosophers' obsession with the problem of knowledge" and the "culture's obsession with the need to explain for the purposes of control. If there is a dominant mode in which the modern individual or group envisages its relation to the world, it is that of 'knower'". (p.85)

The human as compulsive valuer

Norris was pointing out that this reduction of the world to the status of an object, over against the knowing subject, led directly to the dualism of mind and body. Strangely but consistently, on this view the object of knowledge becomes 'value-neutral. The human person ... is isolated as a compulsive valuer over against a valueless world' (p.86) and both individualism and consumerism are thereby enthroned. But how can those who believe in the Creator respond appropriately in a world so greatly obsessed by the cults of individualism, where the concept of human 'rights' has acquired an excessively unbalanced bias in favour of those who have, to the disadvantage of those who have not? For it is individualism more than any other outlook that requires dualism, both with regard to God and to the human person. People wish either to deny God's existence or to embrace a theology which keeps him harmlessly at a distance, leaving humankind free to manage the created order as it chooses.

Being answerable to the Creator

It is also true, at the intellectual level, that however strongly humanists of varying persuasions, including Christians, combine to condemn dualistic thinking in favour of holistic answers, they can let dualism in again by the back door because they want to adopt some particular socio-political philosophy, some theology or anti-theology, as a matter of their own 'free' choice. Where private preference is enthroned in this way there is a dualism between the world as it has been created

and the world as we want it and intend to make it. This consideration
leads back to the question raised already in considering the flaw in
Macmurray's account of where and how the life of the human person
begins. It will be in the answer to that question that we shall discover
the key to the mystery of this dual factor in the universe, the bond
between Creator and creation. The "modern 'subject-object' schema"
(p.89) that Norris describes is based on the assumption that real
'knowledge' is of the kind that the physical sciences presuppose, in
which the world can only be known as object. The "desire for human
autonomy ... identifies freedom as strict autonomy and limitation as
strict dependence, and thus constitutes them as contraries" (p.90). In
contrast the biblical understanding not only witnesses to a redefini-
tion of the polarity of subject and object, but also to a different mode
of living in relation to other people and other things. Christianity

> pictures every finite being as ... embodying a divine in-
> tent.... To encounter another creature is always to meet
> something which, because of the creative intent that informs
> it, demands cooperation more than it invites mastery.... Not
> merely in relation to other people but in relation to 'nature'
> itself, the human person is intrinsically social: it appears
> as one focus of a network of engagements and connections
> within which it is at once dependent and active, puzzled
> and knowledgeable.... Adam ... this wholly dependent crea-
> ture ... responds to God in an unique way.... The 'other' is
> something that Adam recognises and answers; at the same
> time it is something that limits Adam precisely because it is
> there to ground and to demand such response. (pp.91-93)

From that last sentence Norris expounds the status of the human
in terms of answerability. Hearing and answering the call of Christ
usually involves subordinating our own natural loyalties to the gospel's demand (cf Luke 14:26,27). Yet in spite of what we know of the
New Testament faith, we continually fail to do justice to what we read
and what we believe. This odd truth, as I take it to be, is exceedingly
significant when seen from the perspective of psychology. We are
prompted to ask why do we find it so difficult to be consistent as
Christians and to believe that God really does confront human beings
so directly in the bare facts of the world's ecological, economic
and social conditions as well as in the immediate circumstances of
individual lives?

Pannenberg's extensive work on the human condition has particular importance for the Church at this time, especially chapter 5 on

'The Problem of Identity'. He takes the eighteenth-century German philosopher J.G. Herder as the 'point of departure' for his philosophical anthropology. This approach is valuable in its reference to the early life of the individual and in its understanding of the imago dei as a gift of personhood which develops within the evolved human organism. Human beings properly ask what is the purpose and meaning of the universe? Does some part or aspect of it contain particularly relevant clues? The Christian tradition has consistently answered that humanity itself constitutes the best evidence of such meaning.

A creature in need of education

Herder emphasised the difference between animals and humans in order to show how the human organism is able to develop its own peculiar and astounding capacities. Herder wrote that

> "man is by far inferior to the animals in the intensity and reliability of his instincts and indeed ... he does not have at all what in many animal species we regard as innate artifactive skills and drives". The life of animals is confined to an ever narrowing "sphere", the more specialized its sense organs become.... Of human beings on the other hand, Herder says that the "distinctive trait of the human species" is "gaps and wants". In comparison ... the newborn human infant is "the most orphaned child of nature. Naked and bare, weak and in need, shy and unarmed" ... Herder regards the 'wants' as ... the necessary counterpart of the highly developed human brain. (pp.43-44)

Moreover, along with this attention to the needy character of the human, which I want to keep in view throughout, Pannenberg observes that Herder pointed to the equally distinctive and yet often unnoticed fact that 'human beings never owe their development first and foremost to their own action'. They have to be educated to their responsive part in the process of their own development; 'no one of us became man of himself'. 'Man is not his own beginning' (Augustine and 1 Cor 4:7).

> In Herder's view, the animal instincts are replaced by a divinely supplied direction for human life.... What human beings possess initially is only "the disposition to reason, humanity, and religion". (p.45)

Herder saw that there was not an original state of human perfection in history. The effect of the fall was not that the image of God was

lost, but that the potentiality for it to develop was radically impaired.
In his account of the traditional conception, Pannenberg writes

> Latin scholasticism distinguished original justice as being
> the actual union of the first human being with God.... [T]he
> additional grace of original justice was lost through original
> sin, whereas the image, being a property of human nature
> as such, continued to exist ... human beings did not cease to
> be human even as a result of the fall. The distinction made
> here goes back to Irenaeus of Lyons toward the end of the
> second century (p.47).... The reformation view ... departs
> from this ... [seeing] the image ... as identical with his actual
> relation to God. Consequently, the fall was regarded as
> bringing the loss not only of the *similitude* but of the *imago*
> itself.
>
> The difference between ... Reformed ... and Catholic views
> ... also explains the dispute ... between Karl Barth and Emil
> Brunner ... whether (as Brunner claimed) a "remnant" was
> left which consists in human rationality and the capacity for
> being addressed by God, for in these Brunner sees summed
> up the distinctive ... characteristic that perdures even after the
> fall.... [T]his disputed question was directly connected with
> another: whether there is "a point of contact" for revelation.
> (p.49)

Over against that dispute I suggest we can now find a convergence
towards an answer which is more accurate both theologically and
psychologically.

Development through dependence
Renaissance/Enlightenment thought saw human development more
and more 'in the sense of a self-perfecting, conceived in moral terms'.
Herder stood within this history but was critical of its prevailing
view.

> Herder ... looked with increasing scepticism on the idea of
> a human moral perfectibility through "self-enhancement" ...
> [and] disputes the idea that "the mere actuation of a capacity
> is able to change something merely possible into something
> real".... The human lack of instinct does not mean as it does
> for Kant, that the individual should "bring everything forth
> out of his own resources"; it means rather, that human beings
> depend on external forces for their formation ...

It is here that Herder's account comes close to the one I shall gradually set out, which involves the possibility of a more precise participation of the human person, under the influence of the Holy Spirit, in the mind and will of God. The influences from beyond the person's human individuality include human culture in all its dimensions but they must also include all that flows from God's personal presence. In this regard Herder has part of the solution in that he recognises the place of faith, but to use that word alone is insufficient.

> Herder was not content to reduce the supernatural elevation of human nature by grace to the natural strivings of nature, as the Enlightenment thinkers before him had been. Rather, he succeeded in removing the restrictions imposed by a purely moral description of the thematic of human life. Precisely in this way he was able to express in a new manner the dependence of human beings on God's gracious action. (pp.50-53)

Herder had set out an approach on which we, over 200 years later, must now build. Those years have been wasted in theological conflicts and confusions, but at the start of the twenty-first century the real issues can be seen much more clearly.

Living through the Creator's Personhood

While Herder could do little more than think in general terms of God's *providence* effecting the decisive work of direction on which the development of humanity in the image of God depends, we need to look for a more specific insight into the way God acts. Theologians like Barth and Bonhoeffer, and many who have followed them, have been convinced that the various questions that arise in pursuing such an anthropology must be answered in christological ways; but the answers given, until very recently, have remained abstract and without psychological clarity. In order to resolve this we have to focus on the origin of individual personhood on the basis of experience and observation, until it becomes evident how the Holy Spirit creates persons in a truly christological way. The belief that 'God was in Christ reconciling the world to himself' (2 Cor. 5.19) is a sustained divine activity in history culminating and continuing in Christ 'the firstborn of all creation' (Col. 1:15). Thus what God does through his incarnation in Jesus and its progression up to the ascension and Pentecost is to enable the life in Jesus to be extended to all humankind. This is possible *because by incarnation God identifies himself with the actual fallen conditions* in which human beings are obliged to live. As Jesus lived within the personhood of God so we are enabled, through him and in him, to do the same, despite the weaknesses of the condition from which we embark on the Christian life.

If we think of a particular baby, we can reflect on the responsive and creative activity of the Trinity being evoked in that child. The human person's being in the image of God must mean that there is something about *the way the human being develops and lives* that not only indicates the divine source and purpose of humanity, but also exposes God's action in making that development occur. I wish to argue that the way a person comes into existence as an individual baby reveals a great deal about God and about his action in creating humanity. Evidently we are called to be active subjects within a world where God also acts. Therefore we need a better starting point for Christian thinking about the image than the stress on rationality which has been traditional for most of the Church's history. My proposal is to go a stage beyond Norris's concept of answerability to express the particular claim that God is making on his human creatures. This will be to say that people are created to be available-for-God, by living deliberately *in his presence* and under his influence. To say this is to affirm that God intends to act with and through people. By the activity of the universe and the closeness of the Creator's presence he inspires and incites people to share in what he does and in what he intends. But for this to happen the creative Trinity must identify himself with every human individual, so making it possible for each to respond as a participator in his agency.

Availability and the individual

The capacity to cooperate freely and willingly with God is what makes availability the best category through which to convey God's purpose in creating humanity as sensed in the Bible and Christian tradition, but fulfilling this capacity to cooperate depends on God's trinitarian gift of himself. The doctrine has to be understood in a christological and trinitarian way, for only the Holy Spirit can stir the latency to conform to Christ which is present in every person. Every creature is by virtue of its creation available for God, but the human creature stands in peculiar ambiguity towards the Creator. People have the capacity to resist being available to God and so through sin to thwart God's intentions, while at the same time through consciousness and sensitivity to the Creator's leading they are able to participate in the endlessly abundant range of the divine purpose.

Not all Christians agree that today's culture undermines the Church's understanding of the gospel. Simon Parke, for example, thinks that individualism "loves you; it affirms that you matter ... your sanctity ... Jesus ... expressed this supremely".[17] But, Colin Gunton took a lead in showing that individualism actually prevents the valuation of individuals and the protection of each person's essential humanity.[18] The word points to an obsession with the individual's 'rights' and independence which in practice undermines the integrity of persons. By treating her rights in isolation from the person's roots in community, individualism has set up a false definition of individuality which fails to recognise that a person's wellbeing does not lie solely in the Creator's self-gift, nor solely in an independent exercise of her own initiative. By infringing an individual's rights we not only offend her but ourselves and all who stand to benefit from being related to that person.

In the biblical perspective, observes Pannenberg, the 'special dignity' of humanity lies in belonging to God. This 'sets human beings apart', and so the notion 'image of God' must connect with the concept that God is *holy*. Accordingly *the* distinctive human capacity is to *become* holy in personal being, by living in dependence on the Trinity and so reflecting the divine being.

> [T]he relation of the person to others is not basically one of conflict, as Sartre maintains, but ... takes its character from the destination of the individual to community, and this from the symbiotic beginnings of individual life onward. (p.241, 242)

The broadening range of Christian mission over the past half century, with its increasing interracial mutuality and interfaith co-operation surely shows that Christianity and the Kingdom are concerned with the unity and complementarity of world communities in submission to God. For the individual to fulfil the potential of being made in the image of God there must be a gradual but real subordination of individual separateness to the corporate character of human nature as fulfilled in Christ, the New Adam. Yet at every stage of this gradual movement towards holiness, which takes place through a process of maturation and sanctification in personal being, the Holy Spirit works to uphold each individual person as a precious enhancement of the corporate whole. This vital aspect of the Christian doctrine of creation was expressed, on the day I write this passage, by Angela Tilby in 'Thought for Today'[19] when she spoke of our common humanity being visible as our eyes meet and we see in each other what we share. Christianity is a sharing in the One we worship. Those might not be Tilby's exact words but that is the substance of what I heard her say. This is of significance for human welfare, and so for theology, and it negates every form of individualism which wants, in one way or another, to assert that the divine spark belongs primarily to the individual human person and only secondarily to what persons are in complementing each other.

To sum up the usefulness of availability-for-God as a phrase to interpret the meaning of *imago dei,* we could say that to encourage holy living and holy thinking, over against pathological religion, there needs to be an emphasis on the primacy of God's action, and on a corresponding level of passivity in human beings. The Spirit's great work is to penetrate human spirit eliciting human consent in order to restore and enable the divine-human partnership which has been brought to its proper fulfilment through the incarnation. God is the chief actor, even when people are most active, because they have been created for a gently hidden joint-agency with their Creator. Thus in each area of the Church's mission, the guiding principle has to be that human beings and cultures exist in God, and that any theology and spirituality which weakens this perception tends to be idolatrous.

E. Subjectivity and the Spirit

Throughout the chapter so far I have been concerned to stress the intimate relation between God and the world, and the theological need for self-criticism in an age of obsessive individualism. The general theme of joint divine-human agency is now to be sharpened into the beginning of an account of human life, which sees 'living through the Creator's Personhood' not so much as a religious aim, but rather as the principle on which the life of all human persons is structured for the creation of loving communities. If this is a correct observation of what underlies the complexities of human psychology, we have the remarkable doctrine that every human person's psychological life is created to be that of sons and daughters related to the Father in God's Spirit. This part of orthodox Christian faith is the foundation on which Christians can encourage others to recognise that God is present within the actual and often extremely faulty ways in which people live in any society. People need to discover that it is in the immediate, bodily setting of their lives that God intends to lead them and make himself real to them. Experience of living *consciously* in relation to God the Father, in Christ Jesus, through the Holy Spirit exposes the trinitarian structure of ordinary human selfhood, illuminating the pathologies as well as the healthy forms of worldly living.

The particular goal of human growth
Following through these considerations with appropriate rigour will involve the Church in rethinking her faith and the way it is presented to the world. As far as possible Christianity needs to be set free from unhealthy habits that go with treating it as a 'religion', in the sense of a range of cultural activities that can be understood apart from the rest of life, rather than a particular way of being human. It is understandable that in earlier periods of the Church's history, theology usually represented the origin of human nature along the lines of the biblical accounts of creation in Genesis. Today however we have a responsibility to do more than just make a commentary on these accounts; the Church has to explain the faith in a way that takes seriously what we know of humanity from a developmental viewpoint. If we expound the biblical testimony to God's 'continuous creation', the question of human origins can be pursued not only in relation to the broad evolutionary programme but also to the way he creates every particular human baby that she may develop as a person in relation to himself. If it is meaningful to express the Church's faith metaphorically as the Creator breathing

into human beings the breath of life, we need an account that goes beyond the metaphor, and shows that God is in action in a continuing way and with reference to each individual. Such an account should also explain the underlying fact that throughout history, and prehistory, people seem to have had a deep-seated awareness of the divine. In the context of the faith of Abraham and his successors particularly, we see how believers can and do live and grow in the faith that God is personal. I shall argue that a satisfactory statement of Christianity must affirm that God reveals himself in universal nature and history as well as in particular historical events. The logic of this view rests on the observation that human beings have an intuitive knowledge of other persons that has usually included the sense of God and of moral goodness in one pervading expectation or hope of goodwill. The capacity for such intuitive knowledge appears to be 'innate' and evident before brain development makes conceptual thinking possible.

Making sense of intuitive knowledge
This can now be verified to a very large extent through the work of developmental psychology, in which Frank Lake was a particularly sig-nificant pioneer. In conjunction with the process of inter-disciplinary research which has brought the human capacity for intuitive aware-ness of persons into reliable focus, we also have a welcome change in academic theology. Following Pannenberg's lead, theologians are now taking more notice of psychodynamic thinking, and in this James Mackey's recent work is of exceptional importance. But before setting out his next contribution I gather up my further observations on Pannenberg's account.

Herder 'was able to express in a new manner the dependence of human beings on God's gracious action'. This was a check on the human-centred outlook of the Enlightenment, but we have seen that the gracious action of God has to be more than the influences constituted by 'tradition, learning, reason and experience' of which Herder wrote. So we need to confront the question afresh, how does God act in the world of people? At this point Herder does not help because he has no concept of God's active presence other than the notion of providence.

Until modern materialism became dominant in Europe most people took the spiritual activity of God for granted, but from a much earlier date a large measure of pagan superstition had infiltrated the Church to the degree that divine grace had come to be treated in an almost pseudo-material way. Therefore it is not surprising that Herder did not get beyond a mainly conceptual position. He is content with the idea that the image of God being present as a disposition-to-be-like-God awaits activation by God's provision of ideas and culture received through religious faith. Pannenberg is aware that the Church today must get beyond this position because it distorts the New Testament gospel and makes the message barely intelligible for thinking people today. He defends Herder's conviction that 'God himself... is influencing us' (p.58), but affirms that his reliance on 'the idea of providence... introduced into the anthropological data from outside' would not do. God's activity in the world is not in the nature of an entirely transcendent intervention as traditional Christian thinking had supposed.

> If there is to be any justification for Herder's procedure, it must be shown that the religious and theological concepts are not extrinsic to the phenomena but correspond to a dimension exhibited by the latter. (p.66)

My account of the individual's origin as person, which follows in this chapter, proposes that God does act within the world's life in a way that fulfils that condition. Pannenberg's attention to the psychological as well as the theological nature of that divine action therefore prepares the ground for my consideration of Lake's work in the next chapter.

The centrality of 'basic trust'
As Lake had done, Pannenberg saw that Erik Erikson's concept of basic trust as the foundation step in the ladder of psychological growth was paramount in understanding human wellbeing. As this truth becomes increasingly verifiable today, the nature of subjectivity and intersubjectivity can be understood more fully. Basic trust is seen to be the centre point from which a reliable anthropology can be built up, so it is especially welcome that Pannenberg wrote this.

> Basic trust is directed to an agency that is capable *without limitation* of protecting and promoting the selfhood.... [This agency] transcends the limits that in every case affect... the capacity and readiness of a mother. Because of its lack of limitation, basic trust is therefore antecedently a religious phenomenon. God is the true object of basic trust even in its beginnings. (p.231)

With these words most of those who stand in the clinical theology movement will agree even though there does need to be a qualification over using the word 'religious'. Here it just means grounded in God. In some cases mothers overwhelmingly, and not just occasionally, fail to deputise for and represent God's love to the child. Following such failure the emotional consequences are catastrophic, and yet there remains a capacity that keeps open the possibility of not being dominated by the damage which misfortune or abuse has caused. Research shows actual trust in ontological goodness is not to be traced in terms of the simple sequence: first via parents, and then through the influence of 'explicit religious faith'. I shall contend that God is present at all stages in a way that babies before birth are able in some degree to recognise and enjoy, albeit unconsciously. That ability, however, may later be all but extinguished by human neglect or abusive treatment. What such unconscious influence on the baby can be is an important question for theological anthropology. To move towards an answer we need now to point out that the way in which basic trust is established is considerably more subtle than most psychology has supposed so far.

Baby realising his identity

The conclusion that 'this comprehensive trust is the permanent basis of all later personality development' (p.226) is the very widely agreed outcome of psychodynamic thinking, and has been well established now over the past half century at least. But Pannenberg points us towards the complexity of the situation when he writes in respect of society's part in the development process on the one hand, and in respect of the individual's own participation on the other.

> Because the identification of individuals is a *self-iden-tification* that is mediated through their perception of their own being as different from or in harmony with the iden-tification made of them by society, it is not reducible to a matter of the influence exerted by society.... While the identity of individuals is not to be conceived as the product of a subject that already exists with its own identity, neither is it to be understood as a simple internalisation of social appraisals and expectations. (p.225)

So Pannenberg poses the important question, 'what is it that makes the individual capable of this achievement, especially at the beginning of ego development?' and goes on to suggest that

> there must evidently already be a familiarity with that with which identification is to be effected. And this familiarity cannot be a familiarity with 'itself', even if the latter is

> thought of as the individual's own body…. This development
> takes place, rather, in a sphere of familiarity that is more inc-
> lusive than the individual and connects the individual with
> its environment so closely….

As he says, developmental psychology speaks of a symbiotic stage
where 'the child's life is not clearly demarcated from the mother's,
even though the child distinguishes the mother from the rest of the
environment'. Here 'we may probably see the autogenetic point
of departure of human exocentricity' (p.226). What Pannenberg is
reporting is important, a common mind in general terms, among
those who specialise in various disciplines concerned with the developing human infant. The intense bonding of the symbiotic stage
in anthropoid apes lasts only to the fourth or fifth months while
in human beings it extends initially to between nine and twelve
months but then continues, in a loosened way, through all the years
of early childhood. It is evident, however, that the situation is more
complex than that, because what we call the symbiotic is not a stage
of undifferentiated union, but a condition of interpersonal oneness
in which the baby 'knows' himself quite distinctly as himself living
in dependence on *her* – the personal environment which is 'mine'.
The baby knows mother, the personal environment, as belonging
to himself; not so much 'I belong to mother', nor 'mother and I
belong together', but *'mother belongs to me'*. This is what we can
reasonably surmise as the symbiotic stage experience; bearing in
mind of course that none of this can be knowledge in the conceptual
sense for the child.

That God is personally present
By keeping in mind this distinction between the baby and his more or
less beneficial environment, and also Pannenberg's perception that
the baby needs to participate in the process of his own identity formation – 'accepting' and being able to 'modify' the identity which
his situation offers – we shall be able to envisage an answer to
that question, 'what is it that makes an individual capable of this
achievement?' The baby's 'situation' is, in Pannenberg's phrase an
'inclusive sphere of familiarity'. We need to explore the nature of
that sphere because he is right in saying: 'there must… already be
a familiarity with that with which identification is to be effected'.
Identity formation, and 'identity problems', are about personal encounter and reassurance in the world as we experience it. This search
looks beyond its objectivity to that second aspect of the cosmic

duality which testifies that notwithstanding the world's strange, unmanageable and threatening features there is a benign personal presence undergirding it.

The logic of the situation, if I have sketched its parameters correctly, requires us to recognise that basic trust is grounded in more than parental love which is 'good-enough'. In view of the clinical and research evidence there can be no doubt that basic trust is the essential psychological foundation of human wellbeing, but what will be the necessary grounding of such a critically important benefit? The argument I shall build up is that God is more directly, deeply and antecedently involved in the roots of all human experience than has yet been made explicit, and that this is most markedly to be perceived in relation to basic trust. God's love is indeed mediated through the baby's mother, father and other carers, but that parental input is not sufficient to provide the assurance on which present and future wellbeing has to be founded. The precarious and variable degree to which in actual fact people find, or conversely fail to find, real happiness and an inner sense of security, indicates another source. The satisfaction we yearn for and may enjoy is grounded in the presence of the mysterious and immanently transcendent Creator. This is where the world fails to believe, and in that failure the Church is called to minister.

As I shall affirm in discussing Frank Lake's work, nothing I write is intended to diminish the reality and necessity of the human mediation of love to babies and children, but what I am pointing to concerns the *origin* of the unborn child and his grounding in personal confidence, which will need to persist or be recoverable whether parental care is good or not. Of course the question of *when* the origin occurs remains highly controversial and my discussion of it will be delayed. But for the sake of the argument the reader is asked to keep an open mind and to entertain the possibility that it is not unreasonable to suppose that the beginning of individual subjectivity and thus of some very simple self-awareness will be around the time of conception. Even if, however, the origin of self-awareness is not as early as it seems to be, the psychological and theological case for God's immediate presence to the human foetus being *even closer* than is the mother's presence is immensely strong. The good reasons for this case are complex and arise from three areas of consideration, from each of which a particular conclusion can be drawn. The first is about the kind of trust that is needed; the second, where such trust can be placed; and the third, concerns the way basic trust can be renewed, even when it has been shattered.

Sensitivity and the 'room' of consciousness

At the heart of the view of human nature that I am presenting is a very strong emphasis on the condition of neediness, which is likely to provoke at least the reaction that this must be exaggerated. Yet the emphasis can and must be sustained, I suggest, the more we realise how extreme is the sensitivity and vulnerability of the human subject. Only the discipline of psychology and the practice of psychotherapy can show just how great this is, although history, literature and the media coverage of every day provide constant material for insight. Despite all that, the common structure of our consciousness is such that most of us have built up patterns of self-justification or 'defence' in order to pretend that psychological problems belong to others and not to us. Westernised society has made the analyst, psychiatrist or counsellor a familiar wise man, at least for the well-to-do, but very often the therapy we want is aimed at repairing broken defences and enabling us to cope by disguising the depth and nature of our need, and to maintain our chosen distance from others in a way that satisfies the desire to control.

For the Christian however the aim should be very different. If the thesis of this book is correct, *the subjectivity of the self provides the setting from which personhood develops*. There are on this view two 'areas' of the self, the centre of focused consciousness, and the extended personal reality which is not confined to consciousness. What I call the subject-self is a door of consciousness which is acutely sensitive. Lake suggested the image of the door giving access to a room-with-a-view from which, and in which, we can explore and discover the world's life; an expanding and contracting room which is continually open to invasion from beyond. This room is where the subject-self *both desires to be penetrated and resists being penetrated*. This is the created spiritual place God has designed where every human creature is given some opportunity to discern reality or to mask it with various degrees of pretence and fantasy. In this metaphor the door is the consciousness of the subject-self, giving access to the room in which she develops her full personhood in interaction with many personal and impersonal influences from beyond her. The issue of truth and falsehood is central, because of the extreme sensitivity and liability to emotional and physical hurt in the human condition. Each individual's room-with-a-view is inclined to be closed off, with an arbitrarily censored outlook and a narrowly selective immigration policy. The kind of basic trust that is needed has to be confident enough to make change possible, so that gradually we may allow our real condition to be exposed and our true needs to be met. On this understanding basic trust is not just the necessary foundation step from which the infant can move with confidence towards independence and growth into other relationships. It is seen to be also necessary for developing adult *maturity*, through which people learn to face the uncomfortable facts of their sensitivity and vulnerability, because only by recognising weaknesses is it possible to live creatively and realistically – and eventually share in God's holiness.

Mental pain and discouragement

Against the background of *universal* human need and liability to mental suffering with all its complicated consequences of conflict and tragedy, the second area of consideration addresses the question: if basic trust is so essential for well-being where can trust be placed in order to meet the demands raised by mental pain and emotional distress of the magnitude that people so obviously experience? Evidently the person's 'room' is, on the Christian view, the place where every human creature can adjust his relationship with the Creator, and can do so because God, in being triune Love, is Revealer and Enabler as well as Creator. This trinitarian view means that people are not made for the kind of solitary experience of contact with the 'higher' part of the universe that William James had in mind. The whole context of the person's being is *earthly* and *communal,* and in that community setting of personal relationships, the issue of truth and falsehood is central, as is the question of value, of good and evil. In this context, of individuals, families and communities as they are, we have to ask: how do people assess personal and moral value in the assured way they usually do or expect they should do?

For orthodox Christianity, and I suggest for any viable philosophical anthropology, part of the answer lies in persons being structured in the personal being of the Creator. That people frequently deny this is understandable because the subject's guarded 'door' to consciousness supports the pretended claim to self-sufficiency, and so helps to misrepresent the truth both of himself and of other people. Human beings can be admirably strong, able to endure extraordinary hardships and privations, yet capable of perverse blindness and the most atrocious cruelty. In each case the individual's character, by degrees benign or malignant, will have developed from the intensely sensitive subjectivity of that newly conceived person, that will have been refined or blunted through his experiences in infancy, childhood, adolescence, and ongoing adult life.

The highly adaptable capacity for feeling and emotion, to which is added the brain's amazing ability to remember, makes the human subject an extraordinary receptor, having the most remarkable ability to participate with others or to withdraw from all that is involved in personal relationship and community. Yet for the person to grow up into stable wellbeing, as outlined in the introduction, there needs to be a reliability of supportive presence and an ethical quality of character about that presence commensurate with the person's expectation and need. When we reflect on the combination of human behaviour, evidenced in society, with the reactive inward suffering that becomes apparent through psychological observation of the same people, an answer to the question about knowing good and evil becomes clearer. The answer is the same as to the earlier question about basic trust. A critical part of the reason for this is that moral value does not have its distinctive character apart from personhood grounded in God. Basic trust then is founded in the individual's origin, which establishes a relationship directing creature to creator. That link is what shapes the person so that his nature consists in being the object of divine goodwill. Thus within this primitive situation *there is already an expectation of caring.* The baby has a meaningful awareness, but not conceptual knowledge, of personal goodness, yet it will not be without shadows for this creature has been made a person within a corporate, generational history. Nevertheless here is the bedrock of all our ethical awareness, at the point where we are being welcomed into life.

Not religion but God
Many will argue that human mothering provides the child with sufficient grounding in personal love so that he is able to internalise memories of actual human parenting which establish an inner resource for the rest of his life. But I contend that this cannot be enough. Taking account of all the disorder in society we must not attribute too much to the agency of human support. There is no substitute for God's personal presence, either in the origin of the human subject or in subsequent adult life. This is not to deny internalisation, which refers to the psychological process, largely unconscious, of relying on deep 'memories' of previous good experiences. But all that is grounded in the divine presence, the Spirit of God, who provides a creative resource which is deeper than the native environment of the self's social support.

I have now reached the point at which I have to move beyond Pannenberg's thesis. I have welcomed his statement that 'this trust is, by reason of its lack of limits, *implicitly* directed beyond mother and parents to an agency that can justify the unlimited character of the trust' (p.233). However religious formation and 'implicit references' to God may remain a matter of ideas and inferences. Ideas about God do not provide adequate channels to link us with God, and satisfy the extremely sensitive and vulnerable human person of any age. Basic trust can only be real because it is founded on actual contact with God, even though the great majority of humankind, who enjoy the security of a more or less confident level of basic trust, do not consciously realise in whom their trust is actually placed.

The tendency to social deterioration

We come then to the third area of consideration that concerns the enduring quality of basic trust. Because the human situation is so severe in being subject to suffering and discouragement, the original gift of trust must be renewable throughout life. This is just as essential a conclusion as was the recognition that God himself is the source of love which elicits trust in the first place. The sense of God's loving presence, which enables the primitive self to respond at the very start of the organism's life but it is likely to be quickly obscured. As personal life develops it will always be under some degree of threat. For many this results in the original gift being split off into the deep unconscious. Although human beings so frequently reject the very idea of God, and live on the assumption that they do not need to trust in anyone stronger than themselves, those who stand in this position will eventually have to wake up to their real situation. In 'this world' or 'the next' the personal source of their identity and the fallacies of their previous suppositions about themselves will be exposed.

Because of people's acute sensitivity and liability to mental suffering, history tends to be marked as much by periods of general social decline as by constructive times in which there are improvements in the human condition. The tendency to decline is not so much a falling away from religion, which may remain defiantly buoyant, but rather a moral and psychological deterioration that may continue despite great human achievements. It is arguable therefore that the outcome of history would be progressive decline if it were not for an inbuilt restorative influence which is always there, and which, I suggest, can only be accounted for by God's constant presence. It would seem that human societies would collapse into greater and greater disorder without this prospect of continual refurbishment towards wellbeing. Even so, the evil which leads to the world's endless problems obviously does not abate. The moves that counter deterioration evidently emerge through individuals, who in company with others can draw on their sense of underlying human value, first given to them by the Creator in their origin as people. Potentially, the community of those who acknowledge that their lives are rooted in God is universal, but in practice it is hardly recognised to be international and interracial. Instead the awareness of God is associated possessively with the particular religious culture in which its meaning has been discerned.

The implications of this section

If the argument has been correct the capacity to live in basic trust is not to be defined as religious, for the sense of God being present to uphold all people as persons is grounded in foetal experience. Although all religions strengthen the sense of God's reality, the divine self-revelation in the origin of each individual's life puts into question all religious propositions which limit his reality by defining it in sectarian and possessive ways. This psychological and Christian critique of human religion can sharpen the perception that subjectivity, the seat of experience, with its expanding capacity for feeling and emotion as well as thought, is the place where neediness rather than self-sufficiency can and should be welcomed. Since the presence of God with the growing person provides assurance of his unchanging goodness, the most deep-seated and hidden mental suffering can eventually be faced and its effects healed. Through continuous meeting with the infinite God, people can gradually bear the full exposure of their defences and fantasies, and so find their fulfilment in conscious relation to God as Creator and Redeemer.

F. Within a divine matrix

I wrote at the beginning of the previous section that the idea of everyone 'living through the Creator's Personhood' implied 'the remarkable
doctrine that every person's psychological life is in truth related to
the Father, in God's Spirit, whether that person is living sinfully or
faithfully'. The description I now give of human constitution begins
to show how such a doctrine can make sense. It shows also that what
God is doing in creation prepares the way for what he goes on to do
in redemption; and that these divine activities are in continuity. God's
action brings the influence of his presence to inspire, encourage and
develop people in whatever state they may be in. But the progress
he can make in this depends on many variable factors, most of all on
the willingness of other people to be kindly supporters of those who
most need his touch in some way or another. The gracious acts of his
initiative come through all the circumstances of life but particularly
through people who are themselves responsive to God, and are looking away from themselves to those in need. The significance of God
working through people is central to understanding Christianity and
to the way the Church's mission operates through congregations and
through other communal organisations. God's touch through pastoral care is needed at so many levels, in every home and in every
community group, but its effectiveness depends on the recognition
that everyone has a role in this divine activity and can contribute to it
if each is willing to allow the Spirit to lead.

To some extent as adults we can be assured, from our own experience, that this is a matter of divine initiative. In understanding
myself, and I encourage other believers to check whether this applies
to them as well, I did not, do not, first respond to God (or just to the
world) by initiating a relationship with him (it). Nor is it correct to
say, 'but you did become personal by responding to your mother in
infancy'. The observations of recent developmental psychology do
not bear this out at all. Rather it would be true to say that mothers are
(almost) surprised to discover that their babies are relational persons
already. We do not have to act or respond in any way to realise our
personhood; we simply discover ourselves to be persons. And of
course, we make this discovery usually without any concept that it
has anything directly to do with God.

Created to experience love
How has this personhood secretly emerged? The hypothesis I offer is
that God is present to provide spiritual support for interpersonal life

wherever babies are conceived. So he embraces every instance of the psycho-physical matrix that unites mother and baby in the symbiotic union of infancy. That divine embrace is the permanent environment of human life constantly enabling loving community life to grow in so far as the people involved are responsive. The divine matrix has two functions. The first is to draw into existence the incipient organism – latent in the sperm of the father and the ovum of the mother – thus creating each individual as a personal self. And the second function is to go on sustaining each one, within a complex of community relationships. This complex becomes the setting in which a person's basic trust can be developed, and when necessary repaired. The divine matrix is fully effective where the Spirit has drawn believers to live and mature as members of Christ, but already it undergirds the life of all humankind in a way that makes it possible for people in any community to grow towards the awareness of God. It will be seen that this way of describing the spiritual condition of people is radically different from the notion of a soul implanted in the organism. Human personhood is seriously misrepresented by that theory, although we must acknowledge that what the European tradition of the soul intended to describe is the same reality for which we are now seeking a more accurate conceptual account. What I mean by subjectivity and personhood making up the self is the wholeness of the person.

God identifies with each in particular
To create a person in direct dependence on his triune life, God identifies himself with both parents within the whole of their social existence. The new human being coming into life is being given a finite grounding in the divine nature which will remain throughout her existence. This grounding I have suggested is the root of the human capacity to know moral, that is personal, goodness and is thus a mere taste of God's limitless, infinite beneficence. Almost as soon as this grounding in God's love occurs it may be violently threatened, and even in better circumstances the memory of it is likely to be fleeting and precarious. The inter-generational context into which babies are conceived will often be at odds with God's loving intention. It would seem that for too many the good experience had at conception is quickly submerged by a flood of increasingly ambiguous ones. Although unconscious within the infant, however, the memory of this primitive encounter with God will not be without a continuing influence on the person's later life. It will be either sustained and reinforced, or diminished and distorted, by the value-system and style

of life that prevails in the parents' behaviour, and in other aspects of the culture in which the child is brought up. Good parental relations provide a stable environment so that children, in the early stages of babyhood at least, can enjoy something of divine love mediated afresh by the sheer warmth of fleshly contact, shared pleasure and tender caring that is naturally provided over the extended period through which the infant is growing. Ideally that period, of which most adults have little or no conscious memory, will be followed by the stages of childhood in which, with increasingly conscious participation, the child's engagement with parents, peers and others will be laying down a bank of good memories to which people in later life often desire to be restored.

None of this, however, would have its distinctive character if the capacity to recognise goodness were not to have had its constitutional root at the moment of conception and in the short period of some ten days between fertilisation of the ovum and implantation of the blastocyst in the womb. On this view that original touch of God's presence is given to the new creature as *a primitive spiritual awareness of the Creator's beneficence towards her* (and fellow creatures) *as part of the whole created order.* Without that gift at the outset of the individual's life, the characteristically human ability to acknowledge the transcendent character of the difference between moral good and evil would be impossible. To that fundamental proposition we must add this rider to explain why, in my view, the human person must be constituted at this point and no later. It is the loving identification of God with the particular fertilised ovum before its implantation that constitutes the human individual as an authentically unique person who is *other* than either parent, and who somehow knows she is other than they. This sense of God's love for every self will be evident to each if there are twins or more than two foetal lives in formation. The 'identification with' the creature is in effect saying, 'you are my child, and have a specific, personal place in what I am doing', although this can only be perceived in spirit and not conceptually.

The fact that many fertilised ova fail to implant does not seem to me to constitute a serious objection to regarding conception as the start of personal formation. I take this view because the way God's love is fulfilled for his creatures will be appropriate to each one's situation. It is the corporate and communitarian destiny of humankind which is central, and within that the participation of individual persons will be comprehensively varied. What gives life its ultimate integrity and joy is the gift of being taken into the activity of the Holy Trinity.

Personal otherness a problem

While the otherness and particularity of the subject-self and person
is integral to the Creator's purpose, the vulnerability of the human
condition in a dangerous world ensures that each one's development,
and consequently every relational feature of it, will be prone to disorder and hurt. Apart from the many problems involved in guarding
against evil there are developmental difficulties of 'personal identity'
already referred to. These are critical because in our otherness we
can feel isolated, unsupported, and lacking in love, obliged therefore
to rely on neurotic defence mechanisms. So much is this the case
that the assumption that loneliness is the necessary, constitutional
condition of people's lives is a commonplace of our culture. Varying
degrees of anxiety and negativity over personal otherness characterise individuals and communities and cause multiple damage in every
area of social life. It would seem that for most of humankind the
experience of love through fellow human beings has been felt to be
more or less conditional. Thus the problems of depression, of low
self-esteem and an insecure sense of identity (as well as those which
originate in more severely damaging experiences) although variable
in degree have one thing in common. The real healing needed to
meet these conditions is always, in one way or another, through a
recovery of God's *unconditional* love, the love that belongs to the
personal Source of life. A very striking witness to its reality is the
apparently universal phenomenon that, when in a state of extreme
emergency, nearly every human being will spontaneously pray. When
that happens the manner and direction of the prayer suggests that this
is not an instance of regression to infant dependence on parents, but
of recourse to the One who is beyond every human resource.

Because both secular and religious people often feel they have to
be content to live in denial of their uncertainties and in degrees of separation from other persons, there is little incentive to seek more than
a superficial easing of the inner condition. For many the vulnerable
self is kept hidden from themselves as well as from others. Their
long-standing defensive patterns of behaviour perpetuate substantial
resistance to self-examination and the prospect of healing. For both
extroverts and introverts their chosen forms of social interaction certainly give greater self-confidence, but without any real decrease in
the underlying fears which arise from the experience of conditional
love and feelings of isolation. If that is so it can be seen how essential
it is to recognise that social and individual wellbeing is ultimately
grounded in the resource of God's presence. The exploration of this
proposition in the setting of ordinary psychological practice and

research is something to be encouraged in the work of all mental health agencies, and the more Christians support that scientific approach the better. Yet the Church herself bears primary responsibility to deepen the public's awareness that God is indeed present.

G. Intersubjective First

Under the heading of 'a scientific approach from the side of (embodied) psyche' James Mackey introduces this part of his *Critique* in the words printed below. For anyone already involved in the broader social aspects of psychotherapy, it is immensely encouraging to find an academic theologian giving the subject such an appreciative and thorough welcome. In doing so he is aware how strong vested interests and prejudice still resist this kind of discovery, despite its thorough scientific base.

> In actual fact, the leading lights in the rather new movement in developmental psychology ... are professional exponents of a number of different specialist approaches to the overall subject; ranging as they do from those who could be called psychologists simply, or social psychologists, to those like Colwyn Trevarthen who profess psychobiology, and to others whose disciplines fall within neuroscience – neuropsychology, neurobiology, neurophysiology. The sheer fact that such a range of disciplines or subdisciplines is so evenly represented within the cooperative group at the heart of the new movement ... is ... sufficient guarantee that not even the mildest and most insidious presence of dichotomous dualism can hold sway here.... [T]his movement in developmental psychology analyses and describes the elements and processes of its subject matter as clearly, and often simultaneously, in neurological as in psychological terms. (pp.150-151)

Mackey outlines the view of infants' mental development that prevailed for most of the twentieth century, the view which stems from Piaget, and is now seen to be inadequate.

> Briefly, human minds, separate from their bodies, and from other minds, seek rational clarity. In infancy they take in information ... through early stimuli, at a stage when ... governed by biological instinct and self-serving emotions,... they are aware of other persons more or less as objects.... On being taught a language, their acquisition of knowledge increases exponentially, both knowledge of the nature and structures of reality and perhaps even more crucially, of the conventional rules of socially acceptable behaviour.(p.152)

Knowing other persons

There needs to be a more accurate account of developing human awareness which the new research now supplies, one that is already familiar to those involved in the later work of Frank Lake.

> It is not that this account of how the Piagetian child privately and logically solves its epistemological problems is simply wrong. The processes it describes do also occur. The problem, rather, is that in its bias ... towards an individualist, rationalist cognitivism, it fails to explain ... the very elements and processes it so confidently evokes; and that is very poor science. First ... it fails to explain how any individual person actually comes to know another person.... But second, how language, so pivotal for this whole theory of development, is acquired, or indeed how it functions. (p.152)

Of the specialists to whom Mackey is referring, the writer whose work is most helpful for our purpose is Colwyn Trevarthen, whose chapter in *Intersubjective Communication and Emotion in Early Ontogeny* provides an introduction and short history of this new movement in developmental psychology.[20] What this new range of studies in the psychology of infants is uncovering is a very different, and more accurate, understanding of our human capacity to know other persons and how that knowledge arises. In fact we are back on the theme that I called *intuitive* knowledge.

In order to make clear how thorough are the implications of this research for the understanding of personal existence Trevarthen uses the phrase *intersubjectivity first* to speak of the explanatory model involved. Mackey points out that this is

> in clear contrast to the 'Subjective First' position that seems to be entailed in 'Cartesian' dualism.... And it is relevant ... to mention the consistent experimental finding that infants demonstrate that they perceive persons as essentially different 'objects' from anything non-living and non-human; they exhibit such different patterns of behaviour to persons than they do to objects that there simply is no evidence to suggest that they even have to learn what another person is, to infer the existence of other persons by some possibly difficult rational process.

The striking and revolutionary change of thinking that these observations call for is easily missed because in the world of actual living, of 'common sense', everyone takes for granted that the reality of persons and their distinction from things is obvious. So we all have to acknowledge that what the intellect has to struggle with conceptually, the pre-intellectual 'mind' of the infant knows immediately. This is a great discovery. For centuries an intellectual grasp of this phenomenon has eluded the world's philosophers. However the research Mackey is reporting *mainly* concerns development after birth, not human receptivity while a child is still in the womb. That dimension of the subject has been opened up by others, among whom Frank Lake was the leading pioneer. It deepens what Mackey was discussing, and shows in a remarkably detailed way his central conclusion: that emotion and motive play a far greater part in knowledge than has been recognised. His observations place what Lake had been teaching in broader perspectives.

The 'primacy of emotion'

The theological implications of this research, in respect of knowing and believing in God, will be examined in the following chapters but here we note that Mackey mentions philosophers who as far back as the Stoics have held that knowledge is not simply a matter of observation and reasoning.

> The Stoic philosophers were exceptional in giving 'judgement' a central role in their treatment of the emotions. Descartes, for those who take the trouble to read him without 'Cartesian' blinkers, had much that was positive to say about the emotions in his quest for an explanation of the mind-body unity, and even … a little on infant emotions that could with generosity be deemed to anticipate the current theory. But it is rare indeed to encounter an acceptably adequate account of emotions in any philosopher up to the present day, and in particular of their fundamental role in the conjoint processes of interpersonal relationships and the concomitant communal knowledgeable dealings with the fabric of reality. (p.154)

In the next chapter, when I consider the value of clinical theology as a psychological discipline, this complex area of emotion-led experience and thought will be the focus of attention. What Mackey is presenting in respect of 'emotion in active embodied intersubjectivity' and 'the emergence of personhood' sets the scene for that discussion, referring particularly to motivation in this quotation from Colwyn Trevarthen and K.J. Aitken.

Motives can be conceived as patterned states of inter-
neuronal systems in the brain that initiate movements or
behaviour, and that interact with perception in the generation of experiences.... Motives also change the sensitivity,
coordination and discriminative biases of sensory systems;
orienting, opening and closing avenues of awareness. Acting between neural systems in the brain in the forms of
neurochemical transmissions, motives also determine the
accumulation, accessing and combining of memories....
In all these activities motives have the additional power to
produce emotional expressions that have emotive effects in
sympathetic subjects.[21]

One result of this efficacy is that the human infant is more than 'ready
at birth to engage with the expressed emotions of adult companions
in a mutual guidance of infant brain development and sociocultural
learning'.[22]

The newborn infant is conspicuously adapted to seek
intersubjective or interpersonal support through transfer of
feelings, not only in consistent, tender *attachment* with nurturing and protective care, but also starting to build human
companionship with a wider circle of partners who are happy
to be both playmates and teachers.... Humans, whether
young or old, can get into one another's minds in an unique
way, and this gives critical advantages for communication
of ideas and learning.[23]

Faces and gestures
These perceptions endorse the Christian experience of prayer, since
personal attachment and the 'transfer of feelings' are at the core of
human response to and participation in God who is Spirit. Anyone who
had the opportunity to hear Frank Lake teach with some regularity
would remember his emphasis on the life-enhancing benefit of eye-
to-eye contact between a baby and his mother's or other carer's face.
This sharing of mutual delight in being in each other's presence,
Mackey continues, is particularly important for infants, as it is for
intimate adult relationships.

The intrinsic motivating system is connected with the most
complex expressive organs to be found anywhere amongst
the primates – facial organs, the vocal organs and the gestur-
ing organs, especially the hands.... Long before the use of

> language in the normal sense of the spoken (or, later, written)
> words is mastered, the neonate is already communicating
> intention and inquiry, and hence sense and meaning, through
> highly coordinated facial expression, gesture and prelin-
> guistic vocalisation, which are coordinated with similar
> expressions from attendant significant others ... on the ana-
> logy of a sign language used by mutes... it is a true language.
> (pp.157-8)

Trevarthen draws out what is most significant in the perspective of
this psychology when he writes that

> human minds ... sense one another's impulses and prefer-
> ences *directly*.... What is peculiarly human about infants
> and about us is the need to become involved ... in the con-
> tinuous emergence of the thoughts of others.[24]

One important lesson for the Church and for society to learn from
this research is that it highlights the human capacity for empathy.
It confirms the faith that we are creatures whose needy condition is
intentional in directing us to grow spiritually through interpersonal
relations. In this way we become participants with and in God for
creating communities of love. The intersubjective character of God's
plan requires every believer to turn his expectation away from any
form of fulfilment that ignores the corporate destiny of humanity as a
whole. This is the proper eschatological emphasis in Christian faith,
one that does not focus as much on eventual eternity as on the present
reality of the Kingdom which is always imminent within the world
of now.

Conversation the key
Mackey comments on the passage quoted above that 'conversation
is the key simultaneously to the difference in kind between human
and other primates, the key to the definition of personhood, and
to the fleshing out of our understanding of human consciousness,
intelligence, knowledge'. In Trevarthen's words again, but now with
a dog for comparison.

> A dog, while a rewarding companion, quick to follow our
> interest and actions and capable of devoted loyalty, makes a
> puzzled conversation partner.... Being part of that dynamic
> intensity of psychological exchange is what makes a baby
> a person.[25]

Mackey affirms that 'the human neonate is always already a person.
For the very idea of conversation entails not just the ability to sign
and to be directed by signs, but the awareness that what one is doing
is signing'.

> This exchange of signs … entails … a certain reflectivity of
> consciousness…. [T]his reflectivity … can be called self-
> consciousness. This is the most obvious reason for calling
> this level of conscious being a self, subject or person; yet it
> is a deeply mysterious feature of our commonest experience
> of what we are. (pp.161-162)

H. Proposals

This chapter has focused on God's immediate presence effecting the personal or spiritual formation and development of humankind. In drawing it to a close I shall sum up the gist of the discussion in five inter-related proposals, which at this stage are tentative at least in part and yet are deeply rooted in the Christian tradition.

(1) The origin of persons through God's presence

The capacity for intuitive knowledge of other persons that all people have, and which will grow in depth and sensitivity if they are free to develop towards psychological maturity, exists long before birth. Throughout the pregnancy the baby is already a 'self', ready to engage in highly distinctive exchanges of emotional expression and also to grasp some of the meaning of her experiences, through person-with-person togetherness. The newborn has a hunger for conscious and satisfying companionship, unless severe psychological damage has already occurred; and this fundamental need will be met in large degree through the being together of child and parent or parent surrogate. Up to now psychodynamic thinking has made the assumption that in the relation with parents we have the root in which all awareness of 'personal' reality is based. However despite the importance of that relationship, the proposal I am making is that the presence of people with the incipient child before and after birth cannot adequately account for the origin of the newborn's personhood. What constitutes personhood is that God is personally present to her, most critically at her conception. In view of the fact that the circumstances of conception must vary enormously in regard to the parents' awareness of what is happening in the union of sperm and ovum, it seems clear that if the sense of being personal does in truth occur so early the mother's presence to the newly conceived person can hardly be the chief factor in creating personhood; although the whole family complex of ancestors living and departed must certainly be seen as a significant background.

To use traditional language, it is the prevenient grace of God's fatherly and motherly presence which establishes the beginnings, the necessary foundation experience, from which a child's personhood develops. The mere presence of human carers is far too changeable and unreliable to mediate what is needed. Good parenting is clearly needed and the lack of good-enough parenting leaves grievous wounds of mental pain and dysfunctionally directed energies. But psychotherapy in itself does not at all show why, in instances of severe emotional deprivation in infancy, people are still capable of redemption and transformation. It seems that after human beings have fallen into extreme conditions of depravity, there remains, underneath the layers of disorder, something which can be touched by personal goodness. That something, I contend, is a memory of acute original sensitivity being satisfied by a presence that could only be God's own personal presence. The hypothesis is that this primitive 'experience' of satisfaction constitutes the personal being of the incipient organism, and so provides the ground for continuity of selfhood or identity. This is where the thesis about motivation in Trevarthen and his colleagues is relevant to the person's origin. In the Person to person encounter the newly formed individual is given a will to live by participation in a certain kind of interpersonal dependence. It establishes within her a desire for the kind of companionship which the Trinity gives, although severely negative experiences can greatly change the character of that desire. Even so, something of that memory of love given and received will remain as a fundamental need for it to be restored, for its promise somehow to be fulfilled. This original state of desiring, on the evidence already summarised in the last section but also on much psychodynamic evidence to be reviewed in the next chapter, is not just for physical comfort and sustenance. It is pre-eminently desire for the distinctive form of companionship that is able to uphold self-esteem and wellbeing in the infant person who is being drawn into (spiritual) life. Such a state of desire even if only very briefly satisfied characterises the individual's participation in interpersonal or intersubjective life. A capacity for spontaneous response to love has been impressed on this creature who has been made *personal* by that action. That word therefore must not be used lightly, but with careful regard to the psychological features it implies. As the last section showed the human being is not first aware of the world of things, and then, by a process of reasoning and observation, becomes aware of persons who have different attributes from those that are characteristic of objects. The human infant is brought into personal life directly within the context of intersubjectivity.

Thus we can say: the human being has an intuitive awareness of persons, with an overriding need for companionship and emotional support, and for active creative participation with others. Because of each person's creation through God's presence, that need can be gradually satisfied, giving rise eventually to a steady assurance of being valued within the community of those who belong to the Person with whom she is related. It means that the 'disposition', or capacity for personhood, consists in two complementary but very

different realities. First the potentiality in the physical organism, by
way of genes and all other natural conditions for people to grow in
community; and second the Triune presence of God in relationship
with that particular creature and her forbears. The coincidence of
these two active factors, the natural and the divine Personal, at the
very outset (at or around conception) establishes the status we call
'made in the image of God' and brings that individual into rudimentary personhood.

(2) The intersubjectivity that God intends

It is obvious that human beings have enough freedom to be capable
of accepting or resisting the Creator's purpose, which can only be
fulfilled by the co-operation of his personal creatures in union with
himself. The inclination to resist, so manifest in the life of individuals
and in all societies, but notably so in the culture of modernity and
postmodernity, is the chief obstacle to God's purpose being fulfilled.
It leads in the political-cultural field to individualism and to collectiv-
ism, both of which exclude the distinctive communitarian character
of the Kingdom, as Gunton showed.[26] The Church's mission, in the
context of such resistance, involves understanding and fostering
people's spiritual receptivity much more competently than happens
at present. The Christian task of responding to the leading and discipline of the Spirit has to be clarified in exactly this direction. It
will be the agenda for the rest of the book, where stress will be put
on the delicate way in which human creatures are even more markedly dependent on the Creator and on each other than the rest of the
universe. As Norris emphasised we must take into account the conditioning imposed on us by the 'claims' of other human beings and
the world at large. With this in mind I have stressed the particular
embodiment and family membership of each individual and rejected
'integrative dualism' in favour of duality. The corporate character
of humanity is such that in contrast to all forms of individualism
the Christian worldview gives priority to the person's receptivity
and attentiveness to other creatures, as well as in relation to God, a
position which calls for a deliberate discipline against self-seeking
and the desire to control.

Recalling Lash's remark we can say that the human response to
the Creator of which the NT speaks is better expressed in today's
climate of thought by the word 'discipleship' than by the word faith.
The human vocation is to be a partner with God, and one who is led.
The 'thoroughly embodied' subjectivity of the human individual
is the place of access to community membership for which human

selves are created. The essence of bearing the divine image lies in the capacity to share empathetically with other persons in creative projects which have their origin in the Creator rather than the creature. The heart of fulfilled and mature humanity lies in the Creator's intention to act with and through his creatures. Therefore *in being available-for-God people reach their maturity in turning away from themselves to face each other and to see in each other the face of God in Christ Jesus.* In this way they are destined to be a holy community of individuals to celebrate, display and engage in the activities of God's Spirit.

(3) Humanity as created spirit to be embodied in Christ

Our attention to the theme of experience may have enabled us to move towards a fresh perspective on spirit and the human person so that the Christian doctrines of creation and of life in the Spirit can be related explicitly to the concept of created spirit within evolution and the world's life in general. Traditionally the Spirit has been treated too narrowly in churchly terms. Following the biblical use of the word spirit Christians hold that creation is not just initiated by, but is wholly dependent on God's Spirit. The triune Creator upholds and enables both that which is physical and that which is spiritual and personal. Human intersubjectivity therefore cannot but be the arena within which our understanding of spirit develops. In that arena individuals and communities are both privileged, but in their God-given integration. People could not become the communal creatures they are without some autonomy and integrity as individuals. Strangely, however, for all their individualism postmodernists ignore the role of subjectivity and thus intersubjectivity as well, so that the interpersonal is not recognised as the place within which personal life is lived, enjoyed and developed. Christianity puts high value on every person's dignity and freedom but it also affirms each individual's status and responsibility in relation to the wellbeing of every other person, because all are called to a communal destiny in God's Kingdom. The Christian balance between individual and community therefore is distinctive in being neither individualistic nor collective. Instead the trinitarian view of human nature sees that people's response to and participation in, God's creativity and self-giving makes possible their own fulfilment as individuals and as communities. The way the Church uses the word Spirit (and spirit) has to be consistent with this perception. I have sought to show that in Christian usage the lower-case use of the word spirit refers to interpersonal life as structured in dependence on God's Trinity.

Experience in the Holy Spirit liberates believers to appreciate that their subjectivity is facilitated in the Trinity for relationship with other people as with God. Subjectivity is not a concept like 'mind' or 'soul', abstracted from the total human person, but is essentially a psychosomatic wholeness. In intersubjectivity each self is actively and passively engaged in community with others and with God, but it is the Spirit who makes the community to become fully passionate in Christ. In enabling individuals to interact with each other in open and reconciling ways, the Spirit is eager to affect communities, not only in the Church but more widely, in order to change ideas, and to extend humane attitudes in place of fear, conflict and idolatry. Very strong resistance to the recognition of God's Spirit, however, locks society in unbelief, driving people of many cultures to keep only to what is intellectually familiar and institutionally manageable. *This possessive spirit is prone to keep subjective experience so enclosed that its intersubjective capacity is not fully appreciated, with the result that openness to God cannot be enjoyed.* This is where we shall later have to distinguish what the NT means by the gift of the Spirit. For where there is a response in faith to the risen Christ the Holy Spirit is giving believers greater freedom to empathise and co-operate as members of the corporate Christ. We shall see in the following chapters that the duality of creature and Creator makes possible this extraordinary but tangible reality.

(4) God active in the world

The world's human culture and history in all its diversity is the context in which God deals with us. But if our conceptual awareness recognises the intersubjective realm of spirit as *only* human, we will be blind to God's activity. When I wrote of human life within a divine matrix, it was to emphasise the closeness of Creator and creature at the present stage of evolution. Postmodern thinking has led the world into a yet narrower intellectual culture dominated by epistemological anxiety or despair. James Mackey's work, with that of others, can enable the Church and the public more widely to realise the damaging effects of such thinking. In his words it is not relativism that is the more serious weakness of postmodernism but 'the loss of the subject'.

In this situation the Church's responsibility will be to uncover the worldly character of God's presence and activity and to expound the rationality of her theological anthropology and its verifiable grounding in interpersonal life. In this chapter I have begun to outline the ground, and in the next two chapters I draw out further reasons for the view of personhood I have outlined. Then in the last chapter I look at some specific implications of the thesis, including the way the Church's eucharistic life and teaching have a critical role in supporting what God is doing. Of course the very notion of 'what God is doing' is far from being a matter of agreement among Christians – most will acknowledge that their theology allows the phrase to fit into certain areas of their faith but these are commonly perceived in narrowly ecclesial terms of prayer, sacraments and so on. The NT encourages Christians to reclaim the belief that God precedes as well as accompanies people in all situations in order to effect his good purposes. But whether committed Christians or not, people can be led by the Holy Spirit in acting conscientiously. This will be happening much of the time without people being consciously aware that God can be so closely involved in what they do. From the same perspective, however, we are not surprised to see that where people resist the unseen but persistent presence of God, who is goodness and love, the human condition deteriorates. For long periods there are appalling achievements in selfishness, because the desire to be one's own master and so live at a distance from intersubjective community life leads steadily to self-destruction. Open community is the milieu for which the subject-self was created, and even though so much in individual lives is shallow and self-concerned, there is a prevailing tendency to imitate and to absorb other people's experiences, whether willingly or unwillingly. If, however, interest and concern are not genuinely directed to the welfare of others and to the cultivation of the intersubjective whole for which humanity has been created, there is no lasting fulfilment. It is as if the more people absorb with a view to individual possession, the less they are able to be happy. The characteristic emptiness of the *isolated* subject-self sucks up the contents of what is desired for individual possession into an insatiable black hole. It thus appears from the standpoint of Christian faith that *only when the subject-self wills to participate within an intersubjective community which is submitted to the divine Spirit and his activity, is she able to find peace and to enjoy in holiness what the Holy Spirit enables and offers.* This is where human freedom really lies. On the basis of this observation I proceed in the next chapter to explore emotional and spiritual healing and growth, emphasising that God is the agent.

(5) Experience and God

The emphasis I have put on subjectivity and intersubjectivity requires me to clarify what it means, on this view, to say that God is known.

To begin with the broadest view of popular Christian thinking at the present time, there seem to be two primary threads apart from various forms of straightforward conservatism running throughout, and both are negative reactions against the state into which the Church's thinking and practice had hardened. They have much in common while sometimes being in tension with each other. On the one hand there is the burgeoning emphasis on human freedom and creativity, which gives rise to increasing interest in private believing, in spirituality of all kinds, and to some extent in its theological significance. And on the other hand there is a different kind of attention given to the ever-present anxiety of the human condition, which now comes out most markedly in steadily greater doubt that God can be known either in experience or by thought. In more intellectual circles this latter tendency may issue in the kind of theology that seems to favour a broadly sociological approach to the faith and may view psychology with almost as much suspicion as traditional Christians have done. This is not surprising because doubt, if not just methodological, may be sustained by all those fears that constitute the condition of existential anxiety. Instead of being used positively to provoke more careful study and wider questioning, doubt can result in the narrowing of observation and a greater concentration on those methods of enquiry over which human beings can exercise most control, namely those characteristic of the physical sciences.

In this general state, the psychological nature of the predicament in which we stand needs to be understood. Schleiermacher's idea of the 'feeling of absolute dependence' is central to the enquiry about experience in relation to the personal presence of God. Feeling as 'related to the entire area of the individual's symbiotic familiarity with its world' (Pannenberg's words) has now been perceived in scientific perspective through the research on child development. When Nicholas Lash discussed this in *Easter in Ordinary* he pointed out that Schleiermacher's

> father had experienced, in an intensely personal way, the tensions between the rationalism of Enlightenment theology – Christianity-in-the-head, and the anti-intellectualist pietism, a Christianity of the heart, of the Moravians. Schleiermacher's account of feeling was the fruit of his attempts to achieve, not a compromise between these two traditions, but their reconciliation.... [There was] in Schleiermacher's world, no place for the Cartesian 'little person', no 'nucleus of the self shut up in inviolable privacy'.... We are *recipients* of

> our identity, our world, our circumstances, our relationships,
> before we are agents in, or transformers of, that world.…
> Dependence is, in this sense, prior to freedom. (p.121)

This leads to the point where I put a slightly different emphasis
on the matter than Lash. He prefers, with Richard Niebuhr, to see
the significance of the feeling of absolute dependence as in effect
expressing 'the *unity of the self* for which not even the sum of the
world's influences upon the individual can account' (Niebuhr's
words). Accepting this argument, Lash thinks that the sense of absolute dependence simply refers to the self's experience of its own
comprehensive reality; as he puts it, the ability 'to produce an auto-
biography' (p.124).

Lash asked 'what is Schleiermacher's *justification* for identifying
this non-objectifiable "whence" of the feeling of absolute dependence with God?', quoting Schleiermacher's revised edition
that 'any possibility of God being in any way *given* is entirely
excluded, because anything that is outwardly given must be given
as an object exposed to our counter-influence, however slight this
might be' (*Christian Faith*) So Lash comments 'precisely this element
of *reciprocity* of influence … the notion of *absolute* dependence is
intended to exclude'. It is clearly because Schleiermacher was so
firm about this that Lash had been keen to press him 'into service
on my side of the issue' (pp.126, 129). I agree with him when he
writes

> the point that I want to emphasize as strongly as possible is
> that, if we *do* attempt to name – to give an account of, to say
> something about – the "whence" of the feeling of absolute
> dependence, then the name that we give, the content of the
> account that we offer, must be *derived from elsewhere*: it is
> not, and it can never be, given in or furnished by the feeling
> itself. (p.127)

From where, then? But Lash's position may be as it was when he
wrote in *Theology on the Way to Emmaus* that we 'do not know
God by acquaintance, but only by description' (p.163). He takes this
position in contrast to 'theologians and philosophers schooled in
the empiricist tradition', affirming that we use the word 'God' as
inherited in our culture and history and that 'by reflectively and critically appropriating and interpreting' this tradition are able 'to give
an account' of Christian faith (pp.127-128). Instead my position is
that we stand alongside earlier Christians because we see that they

recognised God's presence as we do, both in personal encounter with the risen Jesus and in being ourselves. In this experience we share the trinitarian faith with them. But I do agree with Lash that the sense of dependence is not grounded in the individual's feeling. Our feelings should not be used to make 'an empirical claim of any kind' (p.127). I contend, however, that we are confronted in an immediate personal encounter with God.

I have tried to show, as Lash does, that Christian should reject the notion of a distinct form of experience that is religious. The idea is not philosophically sustainable for in following it one is obliged to use the word God as if it referred to a particular object (p.128). By not giving way to that kind of thinking Christians will make it clear that their faith and witness are based within the totality of human experience where God, who is Spirit, is making himself known. I suggest the issue here is not just about experience because it concerns the extent to which communities may rely on conceptual thinking rather than being more fully engaged with people. If then we refrain from giving language the priority, as theology often tends to do, we shall be in a better position to identify the universal presence of the one who creates and redeems, the triune Person in whom we exist, and through whom we relate to other persons.

Thus the question here is not about interpreting Schleiermacher, but how the Church's theology is to be understood. Lash makes it abundantly clear how critical he sees this issue to be. I share his sense of its 'fundamental importance', but come to a different conclusion. The essence of my position is that the *experiential* base, from which any and all communities come to speak of 'God' and live within a culture of meaning associated with the word, is primary, and the *theological tradition* by which the word's use is defined and regulated is *secondary*. I say this because if the argument of this chapter about the nature of spirit and about people's awareness of other persons is correct the sense of absolute dependence, must be an experience of the Creator's personal Presence. This proposal then is that as human persons, constituted through and in God's personal being, we are enabled to know him as *supreme Presence*. Only in this way, I suggest, can a viable doctrine of God's self-revelation be maintained, at the heart of which is the belief that *spirit is the medium* in which the knowledge of persons is recognised before people put their understanding of it into conceptual terms. This remarkable capacity to recognise persons enables us to have assured awareness of the One we call 'God'. That sense of being absolutely dependent within our receptive existence must involve being related to the personal presence of God, whether his presence is intellectually understood or not. Certainly the sense of absolute dependence does not constitute empirical knowledge which is subject to scientific verification, nor is it to be classed as a 'sensation' as of a thing. But since it is basic to our embodied existence it needs to be acknowledged as a matter of 'experience'. We do not come to believe in God through any process of reasoning, although we do need to use reason in reflecting on the fact and significance of our believing. By making this claim I am affirming that this actual and immediate 'knowing' of *God* refers to the One who reveals himself *through our own realisation of being a person in community,* that is, in the *receptivity* of being involved in intersubjectivity. This view would explain the widespread belief, in ancient and modern times, that God is to be discovered in the depth of each human being. However there is a mistakenly spatial aspect to this belief because God is not "in us"; rather, we are in him.

Chapter Two
Need, defence and
the stages of life-change

A. The inner dynamic for emotional healing
and growth

Healing damaged sensitivity
Building on the understanding of personal being that I have set out
so far, I consider in this chapter the contribution of psychology to
Christian thinking from a psychodynamic perspective, exploring
Frank Lake's work with particular reference to mental suffering and
also the kind of spirituality that is relevant for the full range of healing
that the New Testament gospel declares is God's intention. By the end
of the chapter I hope to have shown how radical and extensive is the
personal change that is involved in the transformation that God plans
for humankind, and then in the remaining two chapters I discuss the
way in which the Church takes part in that mission.

Lake chose the expression *clinical theology* to identify the discipline of pastoral care and counselling as he taught and practised
it. He used the word 'clinical' to mean giving attention to the actual,
concrete instances involved and the 'bedside' manner of the one who
listens to the person who is suffering. In the clinical theology training
syllabus that Lake established the first step is to learn the practice
of reflecting back the sufferer's words and feelings with sufficient
accuracy to ensure that the listener has really heard her meaning
and so encourages her to stay with the pain of the experience she
is recounting. In perceiving the relevance of psychotherapy to the
Church's work we could use the expression 'heart healing' in the
Hebrew sense of the heart encompassing the combined faculties
of emotion, intellect and will which identify what is spiritual and
personal. As we shall see the ministry of emotional healing is an
inescapable commitment of the believing community because it is
integral to God's work of reconciliation and healing that leads to
redemption.

The Christian motive for mission
'Come, follow me, and I will make you fishers of men' (Mark 1:17).
To what extent have Christians understood the mission to which they
have been called, the work for which they have been recruited? Zealous Christians may respond positively to the summons to mission
that Jesus presented to his first disciples, and gradually unfolded
in training them. But the tragedy of the Church's history might be
summed up as her failure to make the call to discipleship sufficiently
relevant to all her members. Certainly the message of the Kingdom
which Mark had recorded two verses earlier has been preached but
so often in uneasy relationship to the call to discipleship and mission.
Repentance and faith have been understood almost invariably as if
God's chief concern is the moral correction of individual lives –
with an understanding of morality which often declares or implies
implausibly that human destiny is to a state of individual purity, to
be reached immediately after death if the necessary conditions on the
believer's part have been met on earth.

Although the long story of Christian practice has habituated
many to assume that broadly speaking this was the Lord's intention,
the actual texts of the New Testament require us to correct that
assumption and to revise our understanding of sanctity and God's
purpose. As scholars have always stated, Jesus' priority throughout
was the Kingdom, but understanding that mysterious reality has not
been easy in any period of the Church's life. What has made it difficult
from an early date has been an increasing misunderstanding about the
nature of repentance and faith (the two being inseparable); and their
relation to discipleship and mission. Today we are learning afresh that
we must understand the mission within the perspective of Jesus' own
vision and teaching, gaining a more accurate grasp of his place in
Judaism and the function that he believed he was fulfilling in God's
long range purpose, a purpose which required a radical revision of
Israel's world-view and of her vocation.

God the hidden heart of the universe
If, as I have argued, human nature shows itself to be essentially
communitarian it becomes clear that God's ultimate purpose in the
universe is to create a community of communities. But even that
recognition would miss the point if community is thought of simply
as a collective of individuals. The tradition that stems from Abraham
reveals that the harmony and wholeness of a human community as God
intends it to be lies in its focus on the One who enables community
to flourish. Keeping that intention in mind this chapter will explore

the psychological obstacles that stand in the way of the divine purpose being achieved, and also the therapeutic and pastoral methods
through which the Spirit facilitates that purpose. To support God's
work in and beyond the Church it is vital for Christians to commend
the view that *all ministry* towards human wellbeing, whether carried
out by religious organisations or not, is grounded in the mind and
heart of the triune Creator. We have to identify the Creator as himself
involved secretly in the world process, initiating and empowering the
work of caring and curing. Hence the significance of the notions of
duality and joint-agency of human and divine discussed in chapter
1. This presence and activity of God in the day to day life of people
needs to become the focus of the Church's witness, for as we learn
to be more accurate about our own personhood, we discover the true
meaning of the gospel.

Learning and growth through pain

The evangelists make it plain how obtuse the disciples were at times
and how slowly they progressed under Jesus' teaching, in exactly the
same way that we find Christians developing or not developing today.
That they became sufficiently able to lead the young Church after
Easter and Pentecost was, we may conclude, very much because they
were growing in sensitivity to the Holy Spirit through the crisis and
suffering that was focused at Gethsemane, on Good Friday and in
the months and years that followed. There is an abundance of world-
wide testimony in today's Church and in history that the Church may
grow best through persecution, martyrdom, accidents of personal
suffering and under the duress of secular contempt. The same principle is at work in the lives of believers and potential believers as in
the corporate growth of the Church. We do not mature without the
experience of substantial pain, and it is the dimension of mental pain
that is of most significance. The place of emotional suffering in the
creative and redemptive process appears constantly in the scriptures,
one instance being Paul's recognition of its significance through the
events of his ministry, as in 2 Corinthians 7: 4-11. Frank Lake was
deeply observant of the way suffering and the fear of suffering affect
people's lives. He was able to show that in realising that Christ is
suffering with them people can find reconciliation and healing as the
Spirit turns their negative experiences into opportunity for growth
towards personal maturity and openness to others.[1] In applying
these insights the Church has an immensely promising prospect for
renewal in Christ and for witness to God's holiness in the twenty-
first century, particularly in the sometimes tired, discouraged and

confused denominational churches of the present 'developed' world.
The urgent need for this move towards Christian maturity is now
freshly obvious, if we reflect on the bitter divisions and intellectual
insufficiency which shame the Church's life at present. That dire state
of the Church is especially evident over the major dilemmas concerning women's ministry, homosexuality and abortion, alongside the
broader international issues of ecology and unregulated capitalism.

The subject-self's tenderness and need

In the context of Church and society grappling with these matters I
take up the distinction introduced briefly in the first chapter (section
E, under "Sensitivity and the 'room' of consciousness"). The hypothesis sees the self under two aspects and points on the one hand to
the immediate subjective centre of consciousness where the individual lives within his body. On the other hand it draws attention to the
extended area of the self who relates actively and passively with
other persons and engages with the physical environment. Although
the two aspects are inseparable we can point beyond the subject's
consciousness to the whole range of behaviours, attitudes, habits,
opinions, memories and knowledge that have been accumulated
through the life of the person. The focus of consciousness which I
call the subject-self, is marked by activity and passivity because it
is the place of decision making and action and also of receiving and
suffering. What I call the personhood is the much broader spiritual
or non-physical continuum that makes up the person's being as a
whole. It is recognised by other persons as constituting the particular
character, style and personality of the self.

The importance of making the distinction between the two aspects,
as I hope to show, is that it enables us to identify something of how
people change, and for this reason it is relevant in understanding the
nature of personhood in its totality and particularly its significance as
perceived in the Christian doctrine of redemption. Initially I described
the subject-self as a highly sensitive door of consciousness that leads
to the interior sense which could be thought of as a room from
which the world is observed and in which that individual develops
his personhood. From the beginning of life in the womb a person's
'room' of consciousness starts to be defended, yet in essence it is a
permeable habitation, made to be open for relationships. The walls
seem to be porous, however determined the occupant *may* become
to be self-contained, exclusive and reclusive. This imagery helps
to indicate something of the embodied setting in which we should
think about the way everyone is related to others and to God. As

we ponder the status of the subject-self observable in the new-born infant (before her development into a frustrated and wilful toddler is even on the horizon), it is evident that the experiencing subject is dependent, sensitive and needy – even though she has from the start a remarkable measure of coherence and autonomy that qualifies her dependence on other human beings. Because at this stage her coherence is qualified by neediness, the newly created person is being constituted with an inherent capacity for empathy, for sensitivity in personal relationship, for participation in communitarian life, for disinterested love. All these, however, will wither unless repeatedly sustained by the presence of God who is their source. Although the individual's will-power becomes dominant all through childhood and most of adult life, the outward direction of personhood remains its intended character. Unless that underlying direction of personal energy can be restored through God's initiatives there will be, I suggest, no prospect at all of godliness ever developing. Since God personally involves himself in the process of the universe, he makes the subject-self to be a suitable receptor of his initiatives and the spiritual place from which a reformed personhood can develop eventually, in union with Christ. Need and vulnerability are the conditions in which God's offer of love can be freely accepted or freely denied. He wants to share with us his holy joy. But as the child develops, the emotional pressures are such that the satisfaction and the tenderness of being created by the Father are likely to wane, although we can in some measure recognise and share in them again as we first take delight in our own children, and then gradually come to give ourselves more non-possessively by growing in God's holiness. Although the subject-self is rooted in the body and is a function of the organism's development into consciousness, it is not an end in itself but is the place of consciousness and experience, the place to think and to make decisions that lead to action in the personal world as a whole. Its role is to give the individual access both to God and to the intersubjective life of community in its full corporate dimensions.

Subjectivity the gateway to change
In her subjectivity a person has the capacity to withdraw in some degree from her extended and established personhood, and to move in self-criticism. To do so is often immensely hard, but this is why it only happens under the influence of divine grace. Consequently the subject-self *as place of experience* is offered *the sense of being acceptable*, even when objectively (in personhood) she is not. In the apostle Paul's terms she is freely justified in Christ, being offered

forgiveness and love before her own free response to God's initiatives becomes possible. Whether she perceives it conceptually or not, the subject-self has an underlying capacity to dissociate herself from anything her consciousness sees to be wrong or contrary to her deepest desire. And that is also a matter of grace since it arises not from her own self-established efforts but from God's self-gift of insight.

It follows that everyone needs to be understood by reference to that broad social setting in which his life is constituted; and in considering that person's evangelisation a similarly wide-angled lens is needed. To gain the full benefit of the gospel everyone's personal changing will involve emotional healing as well as forgiveness and release from sin, for without a radical reordering of personhood the new believer will be unable to share the world's redeemed life as God intends it. Whereas for some in recent years this healing has been approached in ways opened up through charismatic renewal and prayer ministry or in a more deliberately psychodynamic way, attention to disordered emotions and relationships has always been at the centre of pastoral care. It requires access to buried memories of hurt whether they lie in the comparatively recent past or in very early infancy. Usually it is in both because disturbed memories characteristically interlock in a multi-layered complex. Recovering buried memories of past situations makes it possible for them to be re-experienced when a person is motivated towards change. However, what is needed for emotional healing is something more than the exposure of what went wrong. Two other inter-related factors have to come into play. One is the personal touch of the Holy Spirit, not necessarily consciously recognised; and the other is a change of attitude on the part of the person who seeks healing, and responds to the Spirit's presence. It is the latter that can be discerned in terms of the distinction I am discussing. The change of attitude is a conversion combining faith and repentance, because it involves, in some measure, the person's deliberate disassociation from her original reaction to being hurt or thwarted. In that change of attitude she is acknowledging a need and a desire to abandon something of the defensive personhood that was formed by her original reaction to the pain. Moving from that position and modifying the behaviours that go with it, the person starts to return to the openness, simplicity and receptivity of the subject-self as created.

God identifies himself with the sinful
This model does not pretend that the person's subjectivity is free of sin since, being the place of thinking and decision-making, subjectivity is where sin as well as obedience is conceived. However the subject-

self, like the dimension of time in which consciousness normally finds itself, is constantly in transition, making its contribution to the personhood either positively or negatively. So I am arguing that God could not reconcile and heal his personal creatures unless he had made them with the dual features of subjectivity and personhood, making it possible for changes in attitude towards him. We say God hates the sin but loves the sinner because he abides close to all whom he has made to be his children even when in active personhood and behaviour they try to move away from God, and in their fantasy succeed in doing so. The continual presence of God is fundamental to his purpose, and unless we keep it in mind Christianity becomes unintelligible. In being beside us God is mercifully identifying himself with us *in our sin*, while at the same time what we have made of ourselves in personhood, culture and behaviour is under his judgement. This truth Jesus expressed for all time in his parable of the two sons. Thus we can say that the situation of the individual's subject-self has two sides in relation to the way the Trinity is with us, one being his surrounding presence with us, and the other his inward support enabling us to respond. On the one side God gives the person unconditional acceptance in loving-kindness and warmth and on the other side the outcome of that acceptance can be enabling that person to repent. However long he has been committed to sin the subject-self still has some latency as a child of God to reject the person he has become. So he can, by God's grace choose to assert a contrary will in order to begin dismantling those psychological defences that have stabilised his personhood previously. Moving in this direction he may confess his claims to self-importance and self-sufficiency and start the process of dispossession. Here then the 'new creation in Christ' can appear, as personhood is rebuilt on its original foundation, of God's triune presence rather than the false foundation of self-constructed denial. However tentative and subject to error that process of rebuilding is, God is present and his resources remain with the person to give him what he needs, if he is willing to go on receiving. As we shall see, the dismantling of such defences is not possible unless the mental pain or fear that created them begins to come back into consciousness.

Self-awareness and God's centrality
As the chapter proceeds I attend to those psychological defences that are damaging and to the slow healing process through which they can be diminished. The process as a whole, however, is more than psychological change in that the intersubjective life for which

humanity has been created is centred on God the Trinity himself. This focus on God is very different from what people might expect, for God is the One whose own attention is not only comprehensive but also disparate. He is set on giving himself to his creatures. It is because of this unexpected character of the divine that Christianity proves to be so remarkable, and difficult for human beings to fathom. For the same reason theological psychology becomes a necessary tool for the Church's work – because it provides the key to real spiritual gifts, and of these the one that matters most is self-awareness. Unless we become increasingly more conscious of the kind of personhood we have grown into, and in contrast come to recognise something of what we are intended to be, we may continue to disrupt what God is seeking to do in our lives. Thus Christians, who already have the privilege of knowing something of the gospel, need to understand the psychological obstacles that are set up in themselves and in their neighbours. We have to be saved from ourselves if we are to play our part in Christ's ministry to others and in God's creativity as a whole.

Understanding the effects of mental pain and the consequent defences to protect against its recurrence is particularly important for Christian ministry. The gospel of God's forgiveness enables us to uncover feelings which were originally too painful to keep in consciousness. Defences against those feelings may have led to sin and disorder in some way or other, and sanctification always depends on recovering something of the original defenceless position of the newly created subject. In this way some of the effects on us of the world's ungodly cultures can be overcome. This perception underlines the Church's faith that God is the healer whose unchangeable love offers the resource of his own presence. The process begins in enabling the pain of past situations to be brought to mind that in the light of his love it may be experienced with adult consciousness and changing will. In that context there is the prospect of forgiveness being appreciated and accepted at the deepest levels of human wilfulness. Because God is incarnate in the world, people find that their capacity to respond to him increases when they recognise that he continues to identify himself with all who suffer. This insight leads also to the perception that many people act partly under God's initiatives without realising it and while intellectually doubting his existence. Christians should be affirming that God relates himself in love to both the redeemed and the not yet redeemed, for he is not differently disposed towards members of the two groups. On the contrary, part of the significance of the distinction I have been making is that God stands towards all subject-selves in the same benign and non-judgemental way.

The alternating movement

I have developed the distinction between subject-self and person because it brings into more accurate perspective the basic character of Christianity as faith in God's grace, a grace which is inherent in his revealed nature as holy Trinity. This perspective shows the healing and sanctifying process to be one of restoration and reformation. Even in their fallen condition human beings have the potential to receive help from beyond themselves. It is in this area of subjectivity, as distinct from the established shape of their personhood, that an individual has some freedom to receive the personal help that is traditionally called *grace*. So I am pointing to an alternation between these two aspects of the self, the one more static condition is personhood but within the life of subjectivity there is always scope for some change. God's self-offering is always there but he is likely to be ignored or treated impersonally. My contention is that the Spirit leads us towards healing and holiness through the alternating movement, between the subject-self open to God and the subject-self turned back on its settled personhood. The idea of such a movement is based on the observation that as moderately free people we have and do exercise the capacity to reflect, to some degree critically, on our own performance. If we seriously question what we have done, and what we have become, we can withdraw a little from the settled position of being a certain personality with a particular repertoire of behaviours in which we put our confidence and that may include religious elements. That withdrawal, however slight, is a move back towards the original sensitivity of the subject-self and is one of the two parts of the alternating movement. By standing back in this way we give ourselves the chance to pause in a self-questioning state, and to open ourselves to a different viewpoint. In doing that we may be willing to listen to God, to allow ourselves to be influenced by the Spirit, to repent and to amend what we have been. This challenging of our personhood exercises the most precious of our human capacities in having a tender subjectivity. It makes it possible to change, towards holiness, learning to live as God's children by his grace. The subject-self, just because it is essentially empty, as emphasised in the previous chapter, is the more easily wiped clean, so that to some extent, the personhood we have settled into may be de-contaminated step by step. Thus the Spirit works in the extended self through the readiness of the subject to think again.

But of course our engagement in the world requires us to leave that open position and to act again as persons in the intersubjective world. The movement back and forth between these two positions of the self enables the reformation of personhood and behaviour, provided the worldly engaged activity of the person is followed by further self-examination. That movement also points to the 'gently hidden joint-agency' of God with human persons which I began to discuss in chapter one, section D.

Needed also for the Church's change

Obviously however the building up of personhood and culture is not often in practice a steady advance towards well being and maturity; the alternating movement may operate negatively as well as positively. In that case we abuse our capacity for openness, empathy and sensitivity for community life, by making it a base for privacy and for further intrigues towards the manipulation of others, as novelists and scriptwriters constantly portray. The human propensity for idolatry and self-aggrandizement strongly resists God's healing and sanctifying intentions. By nature we withdraw into ourselves, to rest, recuperate, nurse our wounds, and often to ponder our next move before returning to the competitive business of self-assertion and self-advancement. The rhythm of standing back and going forward again, which could lead to greater self-awareness, more caring relationships with other people and a better grasp of reality, is then subverted to aid the neurotic life styles that I discuss in section D of this chapter. Nevertheless the alternating movement in its positive intention to be a dynamic of restoration leading to reformation, in continual development, constitutes a feature of huge importance for the transformation of human life. It is the possibility of this alternation being used positively in response to God's presence which ensures the truth that persons are free to choose the good and turn from evil.

Yet because our disinclination to rely on divine leading is great, the most severe resistance is only overcome in Christ. Ultimately it is the presence of the Creator mediating his grace by way of the crucified and risen Jesus that is able to keep the alternating movement of our lives advancing in its intended direction. Even converted believers can prefer to live by the 'law' of a humanly chosen standard and not by divine grace. Individually and in churches Christians find it most difficult to let the Spirit lead them in this self-critical direction especially because they are prone to be anxious about the coherence and integrity of their faith. So it is critically important that this reluctance be faced and overcome in the only way it can be: by responding to the gospel, when it comes to us in a way we can absorb. As believers we are repeatedly called back to begin our discipleship again.

Intellectually it has been a puzzle: how can we be responsible for our own actions and responses, and at the same time be utterly dependent on the salvation that only God can achieve? The solution I am proposing to this long-lasting quandary lies in the dynamic movement I have described, whereby God constantly upholds us as subject-selves that our personhood may eventually become both free and godly. It is people's capacity for this dynamic, of subjectivity and personhood in movement, which makes it possible for God to ensure that in the end his grace prevails.

B. Models of the self compared

I turn now to the psychology of Frank Lake and others, and in that context to further aspects of the way human nature is made to be dependent on God. Lake did not specify the origin of the human being's personal relationship with God in exactly the way I have proposed in the first chapter nor did he suggest the form of selfhood with alternating movement I have just described. His main focus of attention was on the biological and psychological interaction of mother and child before and after birth, but his teaching also gave attention to the wider social dimensions of developing personhood. He expounded the multiple scope of personal life using a model of concentric circles which shows why personhood has such a broad constitution. This appears in an article (1971), later published as 'The emotional health of the clergy'.[2]

> Let the innermost area represent the central selfhood. Its immediate environment is his own inter-psychic world, the world of his own needs, his fantasies, his experiences … these … may be so overwhelming as to occupy most of his attention. On the other hand, he may have 'a heart at leisure from itself', so as to be free to interact generously and openly with all the outer circles.… For some unmarried clergymen [the] second circle is almost empty. Nothing happens in it … because he conceives himself only as a person relating to the third concentric area, which is the parson in relation to his congregation and their expectations, the Bishop and his fellow clergy and their expectations. The fourth … representing his relationship to society and the community outside his professional life.… Some clergymen would deny that this area has any validity for them at all. Others have become so disenchanted with … parochial life, that all their emotional investment is in some form of activity outside the parish.

The individual's personhood is being shaped by relationships and activities shared or avoided at the various levels in which he exists. The ones in which he invests most emotional energy and intellectual imagination will do much to constitute his character, even though there will be strong influences from the past helpfully or unhelpfully restraining the way he develops. Lake's model indicates how conflicts develop within the self and how easily a person's life becomes unbalanced, obsessive and self-centred. It draws attention to the tension between competing moral claims, and it indicates that emotional healing will enable the person to be whole or united, in being ethically directed towards all other persons and towards the One who created her. I also cite a similar pattern adopted a few years earlier by an Anglican priest, Canon Eric N. Ducker, whom Lake knew and had commended for his remarkable skill as a psychotherapist in parish ministry. To describe the psychodynamic situation of people whom he had helped, Ducker

> presented our life as contained within three bodies, the inner-body, the outer-body, and the spiritual body. Between these three bodies a due proportion must be kept, and troubles descend upon us whenever we try to live in fewer than these three (p.78).... For example if the outer-body (our environment, material and personal) appears to be too threatening or demanding, too frightful or painful, then the door may be closed on that outer-body and the person shuts himself up within the inner-body, which now becomes a fortress with lowered portcullis.... The outer-body is interpreted as being hostile.... But the inner-body... can never sustain life fully ... and becomes poverty stricken.[3]

As with Lake's, this model of the self provides a structure that expresses psychodynamic insights, and points to the need to explore the nature of the intersubjective life of individuals in its dependence on the Trinity, since Ducker stressed that personhood would be

> inadequate to satisfy all the requirements of the Self.... It is here where we see the third spiritual-body to be the key to the whole. (pp.199, 201)

A more dynamic model
In contrast to those models, the one I am proposing, of subject-self and personhood in alternating movement, looks beyond the individual's task, of balancing and integrating a variety of responsibilities, to focus on where the Spirit facilitates personal change. Like the other two this model implies the subjective and intersubjective interacting, but it adds the dimension in which psychological and spiritual change takes place and so indicates something of what the Creator is doing among people. Through such change the tension between competing demands can be eased when the individual understands and *accepts* that her capacities as subject-self exist to serve the intersubjective life of persons in community. That acceptance is a critical matter of

will which only occurs fully through psychological healing and the process Christians speak of as conversion and sanctification effected in dependence on God's Spirit. In this the individual responds to the initiative of the Spirit, allowing herself to be led and to act in partnership with the Spirit. Her life of personhood is redeveloped more readily because she accepts the joint-agency of divine and human.

Unconscious personhood

But what about the unconscious? At first sight it might seem that what I claimed about the subject-self being essentially empty (initially in discussing Sartre's opinion) could hardly be the case. It seems to be contradicted in two respects. On the one hand we know that empowered by the brain, the mind, in so many cases, has abilities of prodigious memory as well as other remarkable capacities of intellect, and of aesthetic sensitivity and creativity. Accordingly I take the view that these great mental feats performed in the subject's brain are building up the personhood of the individual, and so contribute to her part of the intersubjective realm. The individual's subject-self is 'empty' simply because the subjectivity we experience is a kind of terminal, a centre of communication through which our experience of living is continually passing. We pass, as it were, via immediate consciousness into the inter-personal theatre of people in community.

On the other hand Sartre's perception seems contradicted when we think of the wide agreement in psychology that the bulk of the individual's self is held in a mysterious system called the unconscious. In part the system is conceived as being the outcome of the individual's experiences from early life onwards, some of these memories being cut off from the individual's consciousness. But the system is seen also as having a universal dimension, whereby the individual's unconscious is penetrated by collective memories and ideas issuing from earlier generations of humankind.

> The unconscious part of the mind has its own thought-life in which are many themes, and upon them a vast number of variations are played. It is a realm with its own laws and patterns of behaviour, and it is by no means the formless chaos we might expect. In this hidden realm there is a reasoning, a vivid imagination, a fantastic memory in which nothing is really lost, a powerhouse of emotion of colossal magnitude, even its own sense of humour ... is a prominent feature of certain dreams. (p.95)

I take this useful sketch from Ducker because it can help us to realise how the unconscious elements of the individual's life belong to her personhood as a whole. Since the subject-self is the point of receptivity and of access, and also where we take executive action, we have to go on reminding ourselves that it is not to be understood as a container – other than the brain as the physical receptor and recorder through which the subject-self has its life of normal consciousness. (I say 'normal' to distinguish brain-dependent consciousness from the purely spirit-dependent consciousness of which Christians and others may have some occasional awareness.) What we receive in the subject-self will pass in some form into our personhood, existing as one complex of personal life within the intersubjective realm. Paradoxically therefore the individual's personhood, the supposed interior 'room' he defends is not contained within him as we usually imagine it is. That sense of interiority belongs simply to the experience of being a subject-self, who can engage in intersubjective life. Thus our status as persons is always facing outwards in that intersubjective realm even when we are reflecting and suffering or enjoying ourselves, as we say, 'inwardly'.

It follows that the individual's unconscious, with all its strange features, is to be understood as a live data bank which belongs to the personhood that is being brought into existence through the focusing agency of the subject-self. Indeed as 'focus' our subjectivity could well be likened to a self-adjusting camera lens by means of which an individual as person is injected via the body with the effects of the world of persons and things, while at the same time she is able to project through it her own reaction to those persons and things. The self-adjusting character of this lens, because of its sensitivity (having reactive and creative powers), ensures that the personhood which is always coming into further existence via the subject-self is a complex of personal being in which memories of suffering as well as satisfaction, a mingling of her own and others are stored in varying degrees of consciousness or unconsciousness. However these memories, especially the ones of suffering repressed into the unconscious, may constitute a source of powerful feedback of a damaging kind. Because they relate in varied respects to the one individual's existence, including her suffering, this can have the effect of distorting the 'lens', thus preventing the subject-self from being able to experience and focus the world as accurately as she should. Since subject-self and personhood are inter-dependent, both will be in need of healing. Being constricted and out of order in the way I have just indicated the two elements of the self need the life-giving

and life-restoring influence of God's presence. But the subject-self is
the point of access. In this way the alternating movement can make
possible a softening of the defensive resistance that has been built
into the person's extended life. This softening by the Spirit with the
subject-self's consent is the beginning of healing.

Heart-healing of individuals and community

On the basis of this argument the critical place of human will in relation to neurosis has come into view. Tensions between the various
moral demands of personal living cannot be reliably overcome by an
individual's independent determination only because the agency of
such determination, the person's will, is itself part of the problem. The
will is at every point in the individual's history already contaminated
by imitating others and shaped by previous experience, some of
which will have been more disruptive than the individual can bear
without being distorted by it, and developing a neurotic life-style
to some degree or other. Healing will only happen *provided* the
alternating movement is operating in positive mode. For there are
those two underlying factors mentioned earlier: *the dependency* on
God's trinitarian being that all personhood involves and *the attitude
of will* (conscious and unconscious) that individuals adopt towards
their Creator and towards the world as they experience it. Thus the
dynamic between subjectivity and total personhood will be operating
in positive mode when the sensitivity of the subject-self is receptive
to the presence of the divine Other.

This means that when God's goodwill is apparent *in some degree*
to the subject-self, she is in a position to *move towards self-critical
reflection* and in that measure she may be able to amend or find herself
amending the attitudes of will previously adopted. It is the will as
well as the mind-set and emotions that are being healed, as movement towards a healthier and more mature personhood is taking
place. Although the work of healing may be primarily directed to
the emotions, the will and thinking mind must be involved as well.
For this reason the comprehensive Hebrew meaning of 'heart' as the
seat of the person's life in emotion, intellect and will is appropriate
because it indicates the entire field of created spirit. This field is
open to the influence of God's Spirit and also to a multitude of finite
worldly influences of a spiritual kind, malign as well as good. When
the alternating dynamic is functioning in negative mode it will still
be constructive, but counterproductively – that is in the building up
of protective barriers and tactics of avoidance and pretence which
tend to blur a person's perception of reality, especially in matters that

touch on the person's sense of confidence in himself. That will prevent healing and reduce his capacity to empathise with others, just because he does not see the truth about himself.

The nature of neurosis

Lake defined the occurrence of neurosis in relation to the phases of the dynamic cycle model. He asked why it is possible for people to

> react to minor losses of personal security, which do not really threaten their personal or social status at all, in a disproportionate manner ... as if they were final and devastating? Why, in other words do people behave neurotically?

Most critical for human beings, but also for animals is the deprivation of necessary social contact. Referring to research published in the United States,[4] Lake wrote that

> when a kid or lamb was subjected to stressful and painful stimuli in the presence of its other, the reaction was entirely different from that of its twin, tested under exactly the same circumstances, except for the absence of the mother. Whereas the lamb tested in its mother's presence reacted actively and adjustively, as if to do something about the frustrating situation, with continued urgency of effort, its twin, tested under conditions of aloneness, became immobile, trembling, attempting nothing by way of adjustment, and lapsing into lethargy and passivity.

When after two years or more the same animals 'were brought back into the same stress-producing situation, with no mother for either of them, their reactions were by no means the same as each other'. The one who previously suffered in the presence of the mother 'reacted again courageously'.

> Though now adult, the sheep which had originally been stressed in isolation, deprived of the mother, again reacted passively, un-adjustively, anxiously, and finally apathetically. It became a picture of confused agitation and then of despair. (CT, p.142)

What transpires from these observations is, firstly, that neurosis reveals itself in *persistent* behaviour which is inappropriate because it does not correspond to the real facts of a person's situation. Reality is being consistently obscured in some area of life; and that area is one in which the person suffered in the past, usually in very early infancy, under similar stress. This phenomenon shows itself continually in international and religious divisions, as well as between individuals. Secondly, the suffering that produces the irrational, wrongly perceived response to crisis in a persistent, inflexible way is at its root the deprivation of another person who is needed for support. The difference between animals and humans in this respect is that the human being has a deeper sensitivity than the animal, and a greater and more subtle range of defensive manoeuvres with which to ward off and compensate for his suffering.

The analysis that I have just described explains why I affirm throughout this study that neurosis is the common condition of humanity in its unredeemed and unhealed state. The word applies far more widely than common usage suggests, and so I use 'neurosis' in its broad sense to cover all the outcomes of a person or group's defensive attitudes and behaviours, that hide from their consciousness some aspect of the truth about themselves and about the situations in which they are involved.

Disordered emotion and will

It is relevant to add here that people's capacity to amend their personhood is critical both for their individual growth and in the social dimensions of life. But whereas it is difficult for the individual to summon up the motivation for a change of heart, making that sort of change in society is even more of a problem. Consequently in those universally common situations of neurotic bondage, where community life is in disorder just as surely as individual lives, humanity stands in need of psychological understanding and appropriate social policies. In both dimensions but particularly in the social and political aspects of neurosis the role of Christian faith is of great significance today, since the rigidity of inherited religious and ideological convictions perpetuate the worst of the disorders that divide communities and nations. By his interest in the religious implications of psychotherapy Carl Jung pointed towards these corporate aspects of neurosis, but I shall argue that the tradition he established took the matter forward in a mistaken way. For this reason I shall look at Jung's teaching about the unconscious in order to suggest a weakness of Jungian psychology and why his interest in religious myth has been unhelpful.

A major emphasis of this chapter and of the whole book has to be on the necessary conjunction of emotion and will in the strategy God employs to meet human need, for without sustained attention being given to the combination of the two any degree of healing will remain partial and ultimately insignificant. This is because there is no neurotic condition, no emotional disorder, which does not involve the will of the people concerned. Individual therapy has to begin with the emotions but can only proceed with a very definite commitment of the client's understanding and will. At particular points when buried memories of mental pain have to be recovered and explored, the will to go further and to persist is important. For this reason some level of faith in God is called for, even if it is not conceptually declared or even discussed.

Therapy and faith
Being willing to acknowledge the distress and disorder of one's present situation is vital for emotional healing – willingness to be pre-dominately open, passive, receptive and to some extent self-critical. Readiness to let go of some of the defensiveness that has fed a person's neurotic view of himself and others, indicates his positive response to the support of the Holy Spirit and not just to that of the therapist or the theraputic growth group. Such openness of heart will need to become eventually a changed attitude towards all who stand within the life-situation where the person acts, and where in some way he continues to suffer. For that situation, with all its preceding history, may continue to provoke neurotic behaviour.

Since some if not all of the emotions underlying a neurotic situation will be painful, trust in divine goodness can help people endure the theraputic process whether that trust is religiously expressed or not. Religious profession may promote or retard healing. It is here that the intellect must play its role, because what the believer sincerely holds to be true may be inconsistent with God's healing intentions, and without sober intellectual appraisal, strength of belief can harm as much as help. Notions of justice, for instance, when conceived in harsh terms against those who have harmed the person concerned can sometimes hold up that person's growth into wellbeing. Because issues like this are so much involved in all aspects of healing, increasing clarity is needed about the content of Christian belief. Without that, Christian mission at any depth may be frustrated. The Church's contribution towards mental health should not be doubted, but whether she is prepared to become fit to fulfil her role is much more questionable.

Ann Belford Ulanov's study of Winnicott's thinking in relation to Christian faith[5] and her experience as a Jungian analyst presents an interesting contemporary comparison with Lake's research, teaching and therapeutic practice. The following paragraphs taken from the early pages of her book indicate some common ground, in particular her strong sense that, however his being is understood, God does impinge on human beings in some sort of direct and personal way. These sentences, however, already prompt some unease. They remind us that the pioneers of modern psychology did their work in an intellectual climate of increasing scepticism about the validity of the Christian creed, and indeed, because of the Church's own confusion, they were largely ignorant of what the Christian doctrine of God really meant. Consequently in reading this passage we have to bear in mind that the language of psyche and archetypes does not refer simply to the field of psychological observation but brings to that field an interpretative scheme that Jung borrowed in large part from religious sources markedly different from historic Christianity. Theoretically they may be none the worse for that, but we have to scrutinise them with our eyes open to the differences.

> By psyche, I mean all those conscious and unconscious processes that enable or disable us to be persons in relation to ourselves, to others, to God. By soul, or religious impulse, I mean that mysterious willingness to be a person in all those relationships ... what religious tradition has always known as an unlockable doorway through which God, or whatever we call our highest value, can come and touch us at any time. When we walk through that doorway, we enter another perspective ... Here something addresses us, prompts us, calls us, pushes us, pulls us into a relationship with itself.... We can refuse this call, but we cannot evade it.... The psyche displays a ruthlessness, what Jung describes as 'steel on stone', as with the heaviness of lead impressing on us what will be. The process of analysis amounts to learning how to align ourselves with this impulse in the psyche to become what we are meant to be, our being. The surprise that awaits us is that we can trust it. (p.8)

To make the connection between Ulanov's words and Christian orthodoxy it is essential to understand Jung himself, and for this purpose I am indebted to two writers, Richard Noll and Anthony Stevens, as well as to his own 1935 Tavistock Lectures in English. I look first at Jung's place in history and then, referring again to Ulanov, I discuss his ideas about the self and about the nature of what is spiritual.

Jung as historical figure
It is not surprising that there was a suspicion of psychology among orthodox Christians lasting throughout the twentieth century. This

might have been stimulated as much by Jung's life and teaching as by the sexual aspects of Freud's theories. By the end of 1912 Jung had repudiated Christianity, although his doubts about it went back to his student days. His hunger for religious enlightenment remained profound throughout his life, and his personal history vividly illustrates the spiritual turmoil through which Europe was passing at the end of the nineteenth and the earlier years of the twentieth century. Richard Noll's research into Jung's life, recorded in his book *The Jung Cult: Origins of a Charismatic Movement*[6] provides a valuable account of his significance, negative and positive, in relation to politics and religious culture as much as to psychology as a scientific discipline. The predominant character of the tradition in which he stood is noted in these words.

> As is evident in the writings and letters of his first sixty years, Jung undoubtedly felt part of the community of Germanic *Volk* united in its faith in a field of life-energy, with all of its accompanying transcendent spirituality and pantheistic beliefs. (p.21)

Noll sees Jung's essay *New Paths in Psychology* (late 1911) as

> the first public evidence [of his intention to form] his own psychoanalytic movement based on Nietschean metaphors of liberation and self-sacrifice.... Those who wish renewal and rebirth through the new agent of cultural and personal transformation – psychoanalysis – 'are called upon to abandon all their cherished illusions in order that something deeper, fairer, and more embracing may arise within them'.... Neurosis is ... nothing less than an individual attempt, however unsuccessful, to solve a universal problem.... 'the problem of present day sexual morality'. (pp.199-200)

One may sympathise with Jung's enthusiasm and hope, but we have to look soberly at his ideas to observe where he wanted to go, and what these ideas really amount to. In fact the speculative and mystical side of his thought has come to little of lasting value as I hope to show, but it has had much adverse effect through encouraging the self-indulgent individualism of contemporary spirituality.

The unconscious; individual and collective
We have to bear in mind, as Noll makes clear, that "what Jung published or said publicly in medical or other scientific forums was vastly different from what he was saying and doing in private".

> While minimally maintaining his credibility as a psychiatrist or psychologist in his contacts with the outside world, in Kusnacht-Zurich he was privately building his own religious movement.... Jung's familiar psychological theory and method, widely promoted in our culture today, rests on this very early neopagan or volkisch formulation – a fact entirely unknown to the countless thousands of devout Christian or Jewish Jungians today. (pp.218-220)

Jung had moved from Freud's essential perception of what constitutes the unconscious. Resisting the communality of Christian civilisation, Jung stressed private self-formation by making *individuation* the goal of psychological development. He also made the assumption that there was a fixed substrate of universal inherited material in the individual's *psyche* on which that person had to build her idiosyncratic self. In contrast to the then-prevailing stance 'that the individual began life as a blank slate':

> Jung took the contrary view – that the whole personality is present, *in potentia,* from birth and that the environment does not grant personality but merely *brings out* what is already there. Every infant is born with an intact blue print for life, both physically and mentally, which has been granted not by the present environment but by a combination of selection pressure and heredity, operating in the context of the previous environments to which the species has been exposed.... [W]ith behaviourism triumphant in the universities, this was a most unpopular position.... [7]

It will be seen that by confining personhood to individuality, Jung's division between personal and impersonal unconscious makes some sense, but only on that assumption. Instead the position I defend on the development of the individual is neither blank slate nor archaic, but thoroughly personal and rooted in the family.

Mapping the unconscious

If we have been mistaken in thinking that human personhood is *solely* to be understood in terms of individuality, then the concept of the unconscious has to be interpreted differently. Certainly consciousness in respect of any one human being has its location in the physical organism of the individual, but what lies beneath the conscious, impinging on mind and behaviour, has wider sources, and to that extent I agree with Jung. Consequently, we need to think of the person's body as that person's centre of action and point of access to a mental field that is of broader range, because it has a shared, spiritual dimension. Thus a person's life is not simply experienced within the individual's subjectivity but is intersubjective. The term unconscious means that which has been filtered out of the mind's consciousness or that which has not yet come into full consciousness. In each case these have the characteristics of living experience, a combination of emotional, intellectual and conative elements that belong to a particular personhood and the community setting in which the person lives. So talk of symbols and archetypes, although meaningful, tends to separate as general what has taken on a particular form that is both individual and communal.

In accordance with Freud's original perception, the consciousness of the individual varies in openness along a spectrum, through degrees of awareness (the conscious) grading down through states of lesser wakefulness or sleep into layers of deeper hiddenness (the unconscious). He was not the first to be aware of the phenomena; it had been familiar to many ancient communities. It featured in the thought of Leibnitz and then was 'a central issue for the nineteenth-century thinkers, von Schelling, Hegel, Schopenhauer and Nietzsche' all of whom influenced Jung. But Freud committed himself to study it in a clinical way. He saw that the conscious mind can to some degree deliberately restrict and reorder the input of experience (by suppression), while further restriction of consciousness can be effected involuntarily and spontaneously by splitting-off and then burying (repression), because the mind, having already decided to suppress some memory, has deliberately turned its attention away. In this way the conscious mind encourages the unconscious mental function of repression to proceed in a compulsive way.

It becomes apparent then that this Freudian view of the unconscious is narrower than the one that Jung developed. This is not to say, however, that Jung's division of unconscious material has no meaning. As I see it, he was alert to something that proves to be of immense importance, but he saw it in a mythical way that is less rooted in personal experience. It seems to have been Jung's early fascination with religious myths that quickly settled the presuppositions that were to govern his clinical thinking, as his Tavistock lectures strongly suggest (*Analytical Psychology* Lecture 4). The positive value of his observation lay in recognising the communality of so much that we absorb mentally and spiritually, but because he formulated it in abstract, impersonal and evolutionary categories, this thinking has actually ended up contradicting its intersubjective character through encouraging the individualism of our culture instead of drawing out the importance of community. Jung's influence, as well as much else in contemporary culture, has left twenty-first-century society with an urgent challenge to face the epistemological question which Kant had avoided: how do we know what is essentially personal?

Collective but not impersonal

Putting the question in terms of the essentially personal might seem to focus on its philosophical aspect, but its psychological and socio-political elements are just as challenging for the Church and for society. In order to respond in that more practical manner one essential first step is to develop Freud's original and psychodynamic account of the unconscious, but to do so in a way which ensures that the intersubjective and communal dimensions of consciousness are not ignored. What we absorb into the mind and the memory is not just the experience of living in our bodies and of engaging with other embodied individuals and with things, but is also the intersubjective spirit of what is going on in the life of communities. This reality must not be treated as if it were impersonal and could be accounted for abstractly in purely conceptual terms, that is, as ideas. The shared life is occurring in two interlocked layers. Firstly there are the areas of life in which individuals are taking part actively, say in politics, religion, sport and in family life. But secondly, there are deeper dimensions of community which are not easily identified and which may infiltrate people's mental and emotional lives in subtle ways below the threshold of normal consciousness. At this sub-conscious or unconscious level corporate experience is shared by the individual with many others and over generations. Jung was aware of this but I think misinterpreted the evidence. Here Christian faith points believers to give critical attention to prevailing cultural trends and, in contrast, to the counter-leading of God's Spirit. This attention will include considering how worship and intercession can be better understood as an activity which goes deeper than thoughts of private devotion and public celebration seem to do at present.

At this point of the discussion the full significance of psychodynamic psychology begins to appear, for it is about understanding ourselves in relation to the One in whom 'we live, and move, and have our being' (Acts 17:28). For this reason I now return to what I began to say about Ulanov in her study of Winnicott as 'representing the British Independent tradition of Object relation theory of psychoanalysis', because by realising the importance of presence she looks beyond her Jungian experience to see something of where a theological psychology is taking us. She picks up from Winnicott the notion of 'mysterious cores – of self-experience and the unfathomable God [which] resist not only definition but also communication'. In conjunction with 'core', Winnicott uses the notion of space which, however, is 'illusory'. His ideas are not very clear, and this affects Ulanov's presentation, but of the core of self she says significantly 'we find and create [it] in the space between us and others'. Winnicott's words continue their usual individual reference but he was pointing to the nature of interpersonal communication, giving rise to his strange statement about a 'non-communicating central self' yet 'out of this (non-verbal) communication naturally arises'. Ulanov expands on this concept, stating that there is an 'excitement and inward gladness of being (arising) from this core of ourselves (which reflects) the unspeakable energy of God that only the word *love* captures' (p.130). This perception seems to be the most promising aspect of her book. Posing the question how 'does this core communicate itself?' she answers 'not through direct contact, not in words but in presence' (p.31). Although the notion is affirmed, there is a contradiction as it seems to me in saying 'not directly' because it is precisely in words that human communication is indirect while in spirit and by personal presence it is direct!

Awareness of the divine

Ulanov takes bodily existence seriously, saying that we are aware of presence and spirit 'through psychic elaboration of bodily experience'. She gives a helpful example of how a person, guided by a skilled counsellor, can come to appreciate the meaning of a dream.

> Sometimes we feel [addressed] through a dream that appears to speak exactly to a question that has been bedevilling us. The dream does not answer the question in words but responds in an imagery that may help us assemble an answer through association and interpretation. [Then follows a particular example.] To be answered this way confers on us a sense that we do not live randomly, undetermined, the toy of impersonal fate.... We sense something calling us in a specific direction ... we feel called into collaboration with this presence that takes a hand in our lives.... In the space between us and the mysterious other we feel the mysterious core of our self must unfold. If we pursue the sense of spirit rigorously, we engage an Other who increasingly makes itself known through bodily feelings, in spontaneous

archetypal images that arise from our unconscious, and in
emotional perceptions that we experience as the Creative
creating us. In so far as Winnicott expresses any belief in
God ... [he] believes in the silent integrative processes of
the psyche. (p.132)

The way I understand Ulanov's phrase 'psychic elaboration of bodily
experience' is that human experience of presence and spirit, as well as
every other experience, is necessarily discerned by 'the mind' within
the setting of the embodied person as a whole. Although I think every
person as spirit will survive the death of the body, it remains the
case that while the body lives any awareness of spirit that we have
is mediated through the brain and so is a function of the body as a
whole. Thus in the embodied state people's capacity to discern God's
presence will be *through* normal body-based consciousness. This
does not mean, however, that what we discern of God is any kind
of *thing,* however unique, nor does this discernment need symbols
representing God or some aspect of the divine, for it is a matter of
spirit with created spirit. Where 'we feel the mysterious core of our
self' unfolding, or are moved by 'bodily feelings' or 'images that
arise from our unconscious', these are but features of our selves,
evidence no doubt of 'the silent integrative processes of the psyche'.
But they are absolutely *not* indicative of the divine *within* the human
psyche, in any sense that obscures the distinction between created
and uncreated. If we do discern God, we discern One who is personal
and thus transcendent, infinite and truly Other. This understanding of
spirit is critical.

Ulanov shows that she is moving away from the kind of view
that I am questioning and it is a most welcome feature that her book
seems to breathe an air which is not confined to Jung's pantheistic
presuppositions. This is apparent when she writes, after referring to
Paul's expression in Romans 8 that nothing can separate us from the
love of God,

Large implications arise for clinical work if this religious
perspective is real.... We cherish the theories that guide
our work, perhaps more so because we also see through
them. They are not ultimate; they may be wrong, or opposing
theories may be just as good. (p.142)

And a few lines later, with particular reference to the therapeutic relationship of analyst and client and what can occur in the course of it,
she notes in thoroughly orthodox fashion

> The religious perspective invites meditation on an addi-
> tional presence in and through the psychic reality of the
> transference-countertransference relationship. This presence
> is not caused or cancelled or authored by the analytical
> couple. It introduces a radically different view, of something
> given, not earned; of something that establishes connection
> based on acceptance.... Such action of God crossing the
> gap to us reverses our usual perspective. And so people talk
> about such an event as a radical before-and-after: I was dead;
> now I live.... The One who creates me, knows me. (p.143)

I have quoted Ulanov at some length because she expresses from
her own clinical experience the character of counselling and psychotherapy that is conducted with deliberate openness to religious/
Christian belief. Openness to the divine when it is set in the context
of the therapist's unconditional acceptance of a person in need leads
to healing outcomes, as clinical theology also emphasises. It is
ground on which to build.

Towards agreement on the unconscious
With that much in common we should now look again at the concept
of the unconscious, because unless there can be a movement towards
greater agreement on this subject it seems that progress towards co-
operative policies in the field of mental health could be frustrated. It
will be widely agreed among psychotherapists that the unconscious
mind is of critical significance in directing human conduct, so surely
there is now the prospect, at this distance in time from Freud, to benefit
in a more concerted way from what the whole pioneer generation has
bequeathed. If so Lake's work will be particularly helpful, since he
was constantly learning from all quarters and incorporating all that
he found relevant into his practice and teaching.

I have argued that Jung's distinction between personal and
impersonal unconscious is misleading since what he referred to as
impersonal he also acknowledged to be collective. He saw the collective unconscious as archaic and so presented it in rigid, symbolic
terms. If we avoid that assumption and the language which conveys
the sense of abstract, impersonal material, we can distinguish between
two closely interwoven aspects of a person's life; the one is localised
around the individual's bodily life and parental histories, while the
other arises within the vastly extending arena of communities and culture. These have both conscious and unconscious areas, but it was the
accumulations of emotion – often forms of fear, possessiveness and

the desire to control others – hidden in the unconscious of humankind generally that Jung was rightly concerned to explore. That work still has to be done, but, I suggest, on the more particular basis of communities rooted in history rather than in the physical nature of the race as a whole. Since the range of the unconscious is so great many questions arise. Evidently these questions concern one immensely complex whole, the aspects of which have to be tackled piecemeal and at different levels, but all are relevant for the promotion of mental health.

The personal both individual and communitarian

When Frank Lake came out of hospital psychiatry he turned his attention away from mental illness (the psychoses) to concentrate on training clergy, and lay people in other professions, to understand the neuroses and to become competent in counselling those who seek a measure of healing in the field of interpersonal relations. The course he designed enabled people to recognise the influences that promote human wellbeing and the way a significant degree of failure to meet the needs of the person at a particular stage of her development will retard and distort proper growth. The teaching and counselling practice focused on the relational deprivations that give rise to emotional pain, the defensive strategies of denial that individuals develop to lessen and ward off the continuing influence from half-buried memories of hurtful experiences in the past, and the consequent formation of neurotic behaviour patterns. Since these behaviours, which strengthen and stabilise the defences, develop out of disordered relationships with others, the real patient is always more than the individual. Everyone's problem has an interpersonal dimension. I shall draw out some of the detail of this in section D of this chapter, but the point to stress here is that in following this path Lake was working from Freud's original insights into the mechanisms of defence and repression.

Because it is increasingly evident that human beings are social creatures even when dominated by an ideology of individualism, we can now see Jung's work as well as Freud's in a more accurate community-based setting than was the case two or three generations ago. The community and individual aspects of psychological material, in relation to the unconscious, are intertwined and interdependent. Lake did not reject the notion of archetypes but was inclined to relate them to biblical contexts rather than to the fertility or creation ideas which were of more interest to Jung. He was not discounting the universal occurrence of these images, but directing attention to the emotional deprivation of the schizoid and other neurotic positions where the images arise. Of the wilderness theme in the Bible he wrote

[n]ot until every man who had reached adult life in Egypt had died off, a period of forty years, did they enter into the Promised Land. Isaiah saw this as a parable of God's chastening method. [The wilderness] is the place where the theriomorphic or beast-like, and the anthropomorphic demons roam. The Seraphim were demons in serpent form whose bite burned into a man.... Beside the serpents are the Se'irim, 'the hairy ones' which inhabited ruined sites. At first they were goat-like gods, later degenerating into demons, whereas the Seraphim began as demons and ended as angels. This is a neat way of describing the degrading and refining potentiality of all demonic experience, in the wilderness of the schizoid position.... (Only yesterday a young homosexual patient under LSD felt that he was having his stomach torn out by a horrible rapacious bird).... To complete the picture the wilderness contained demons in human form who leapt out on a man. Lilith was there; she still is, the seductive and destructive woman, the archetype of all terrible witch-like mothers, she is a winged hag of the night.... Children are her chief victims.... Among the male demons is the 'midday' demon ... traditionally associated with the evil spirit of acci-die or depression. When our Lord ... was led ... into the wilderness ... He, too, encountered these wild beasts of the mind and heart of man under stress, during his forty-day fast. This is the intrinsic pattern of spiritual development. (CT original edn. pp.882, 883)

In effect Lake was applying the idea of archetype more strictly than Jung had done, to what can be observed in the historical and present behaviour of particular people. This avoided the hypothesis of a pre-existing psychic structure, the impersonal collective unconscious which Jung thought could not be resisted.[8]

In a similar way the time is ripe for an extensive critique to be made of Freud's thought in order to separate out the essential foundation that he laid from the system of interpretation he developed which obscured the most critical elements of his first discovery. Evidently he changed his ground to make his position a little more acceptable to his contemporaries. In the next section with reference to the work of Alice Miller I try to show how damaging that change has been, and how necessary it is now for psychotherapy to make a decisive break with its consequences.

C. Freud's anxious withdrawal

To appreciate Frank Lake's contribution it needs to be set in the context of the whole development of modern psychology and its impact on world society. The therapists who had the broadest influence on him included Bowlby, Fairbairn, Guntrip and Winnicott; they all stood on the ground that Freud had cleared in his original discoveries. So Lake's work was rooted in the perception that under stress painful memories are suppressed, split-off and then unconsciously repressed. That basically Freudian view of the unconscious makes a vital contribution to the theological anthropology on which Christian orthodoxy has to be restated. Freud's narrow focus on the infant's sexuality and his speculation about religion in *The Future of an Illusion* are not convincing, but the essence of his position remains secure. This affirms that the particular events of a child's life in its home and community will do much to mould that person for the future, along with the influences of other relationships and interactions as he grows. The adult consequences of those earlier circumstances and the spirit that pervades them are often where the person needs healing. There is, however, a major difference between the school of psychoanalysis, which sees itself implementing Freud's teaching, and the tradition of psychodynamic thought and practice in which Lake stood with the practitioners mentioned above. The former quickly became inflexible in that the psychoanalyst attends to the present condition of the client, making reference to the person's past infantile life only indirectly by means of theoretical explanation. In contrast, Clinical Theology and similar approaches aim to help the client identify what really happened in his early life and so to recognise its effects on the adult's life in the present. This kind of therapy is less bound by theory, and, we would argue, is more humane in giving people the opportunity to renegotiate their difficulties in the present from a whole-life perspective which they themselves explore and authenticate.

Another difference between the two stems from Freud's conclusion that the deepest levels of mental pain could not be reached, whereas Lake and others have been convinced that they can be touched and healed in many instances, if the person finds the divine resources to face them. Freud's thinking was limited by his narrowly neurological perspective that ignored the essence of personhood. Lake's faith gave him a broader interpersonal view and a focus on very early infancy. Not only did he go further in discovering how much of personhood is being laid down before birth, he also showed that the deepest levels of repressed pain could be uncovered and healed.

Whole person healing in community

In *Clinical Theology* Lake was writing against a widespread background of suspicion in associating psychiatry with biblical doctrine and much of this anxiety remains today. We still have to convince people that spiritual growth often happens through emotional turmoil.

> God works well with near-broken or broken people whose defensive delusions about themselves are already on the way out.... it is not the whole but the sick who need Christ as physician.... Time and again, patients have said to me at the end of a course of treatment, 'I do thank God for this breakdown'. (p.33)

In a real sense breakdown can be welcomed as the opportunity for breakthrough. But in parallel with that we have to affirm as being of equal importance and relevance for today that 'the common life of the Body of Christ is the indispensable resource in pastoral therapy'. In pointing out the difference between 'psychiatrists who help (patients) from those who do not' Lake wrote

> [i]t is the power of being, the power of acceptance, the spiritual strength of the therapist which is his main curative resource. Technical skill alone is inadequate.... Deeply broken personalities ... require therapeutic relationships which are beyond the capacity of any one man to provide.... In such cases a therapeutic team is required.

The Church disabled for ministry

Healing emotional disorders is not peripheral but at the heart of ministering the gospel of reconciliation. Intersubjective life, damaged both by neurosis and by sin, requires God's 'ontological resources' for its healing. These resources are given generously and widely but can only be fully realised in the *koinonia* of the Spirit, and through the discipline of living in relation to the crucified and risen Christ. So we come to Lake's lament on the condition of the Church as he found it – and as we so often find it – which is why he had resolved to spend the rest of his life doing all he could to rectify the Church's failure in this quite central matter.

> Therapy has to do with the communicable 'power of being' and 'well-being'. [Considered in this way] it becomes clear that Christian pastors and laity alike ought to be engaged in the care and cure of the disorders of personality and human relationships. The maladies of the human spirit in its

deprivation and depravity are matters of common pastoral
concern. It is a pity that the clergy have been educated into
ineffectiveness in this area…. Many have sadly relinquished
hope of any fundamental change of personality in any member of their congregation. If our Lord had been limited in His
human stint to the regular attenders at synagogue, He would
probably also have relinquished hope of any fundamental
change there. In effect, in turning to the extortioners, to tax-
gatherers and other bad characters, to women of the street
and to any needy, devil-possessed person who sought him
out, He was passing judgement on the intransigence of the
standard congregation. (*CT orig edn* pp.36-37)

Moving on from Freud
In the conviction that Lake's assessment of Jesus' ministry is still
relevant, and that its challenge to the Church is needed to strengthen
Christian commitment today, I have already laid stress on two features. There is a recognition that heart-healing is always God's work
in reliance on his personal presence, and in harmony with that, the
observation that God has made human personhood to be a corporate
reality. Healing an emotionally disturbed individual is a matter of
restoring, or bringing into existence, healthy communal relationships
in that person's life. For this reason the therapy that occurs in small
groups is often more fruitful than one-to-one counselling because
it brings out more clearly the psychodynamic situations in which
people have suffered disordered relationships in the past and may
continue to do so. The clinical theology movement has been alert
since its inception to the fact that the empathetic listening of group
members can facilitate the awakening of painful memories. But to
be successful this form of growth group work needs experienced
and skilled facilitators who understand the importance of the group's
shared sensitivity to the divine presence and healing purpose.

To clarify these twin features I illustrate the shortcomings of the
Freudian approach, as it has developed in psychoanalytic practice,
by taking up the testimony of the Polish philosopher and therapist,
Alice Miller, living in Switzerland. She practised for twenty years
in Freudian psychoanalysis, and then from 1979 devoted herself to
writing with reference to the roots of neurosis in childhood distress
and to the effects of misguided parenting. Because of her disillusionment over the treatment of parenting and abuse she resigned
from the International Psychoanalytical Association in 1988. Her
books enable an instructive parallel to be drawn between her work

and what Lake was doing, since they shared a deep concern over children's suffering and to a large extent the same view of its cause. Freud was a committed materialist in philosophy and by his original scientific training a neurologist. His materialism and his study of neurology are both relevant in understanding the physical focus of his and much modern psychology. Freud's bias meant that, in common with so many intellectuals of his time, he had no concept of humanity's spiritual status that was compatible with his scientific approach. He could focus attention on the mechanisms of pleasure-seeking and reality-testing, but what or *who* enjoys, or is denied, pleasure is a matter that for him remained in shadow. It is not that Freud would have been uninterested, but that he did not have the conceptual understanding to make the question intelligible. Lake, however, because of his lively faith, began his psychiatric training with a profound concern for people, and so his attention was from the outset focused on the existential condition of the person who suffers, not narrowly on the material causes and symptoms of suffering. That difference for psychotherapy becomes particularly significant in regard to babies. To a large extent their hidden lives can only be uncovered through the mediation of the adults that those infants have now become, and this was still uncharted territory in Freud's time.

Drives or needs?
Consequently the character of explanatory theory which is chosen to interpret the infant's psychology makes a decisive difference. Is the psychology of very young children only a matter of the organism's developing through innate directives, that is, its instincts or drives? Or is a baby also motivated in a personal way to respond to people? We have seen in the last chapter that the dilemma over these alternatives has been given its answer by the observations of developmental psychologists; that from before birth (and indeed, in the view of clinical theology, from much earlier), the child distinguishes emphatically between things and persons. For this reason we have to take care over the use of such words as 'impulse', 'drive' and 'instinct'. Certainly there are built-in directives at work that are grounded in the physical constitution of the human organism, but this does not mean that these various impulses are all of a similar kind. Because of this need for differentiation between them, a psychological understanding of personal sensitivity requires an adequate theological anthropology underlying it. Indeed, the evidence for such a concept of acute sympathy in human nature appears not only in recent research, but can also be seen in hindsight to

have existed as an undetected undercurrent in Freud's findings, and in those of all succeeding therapists, regardless of their school of thought. Only the presuppositions of physical science have stood in the way of the necessary perceptions. When a baby is impelled by hunger to cry for mother's breast, it is not just the need for food that is driving him but the need for the person who meets the need for food. Because the two aspects coincide it is not at once apparent that the child is driven by a combination of two different kinds of need. One springs from the physical needs of the organism, the other from the subjectivity of the person, who has been created and sustained through the presence of God and other personal subjects.

Self-esteem and warm personal acceptance
This is where we can see the most significant of the features which distinguish the personal nature of human creatures, their extraordinary sensitivity and vulnerability, and *what that sensitivity is centred on* – the need for every person to be respected and appreciated by other people. It has been shown in research that the one factor without which personal therapy cannot be expected to succeed is the therapist being able to accept the client with accurate empathy and with 'non-possessive warmth and unconditional positive regard'. And while this is an essential need of adults it is even more significantly so for small children.

People come for psychological help in order to overcome some difficulty of which they are partly aware, and when they are warmly received and carefully listened to, some ignored or hidden disturbance in the past or present may be uncovered with the result that the difficulty in question can be healed. Even so, a great deal of unconscious material that is relevant may be left untouched if it does not seem to trouble the client's life, possibly leaving a wider neurosis which both the individual *and the community* cling to with damaging consequences for all concerned. Miller was aware that such a corporately retained neurosis could keep in place the defensive behaviours and attitudes of individuals and cause frustrated growth in children and so in the adults they become. She was pointing out that in the area of child-rearing severe problems can lie not in the child's past suffering itself (often no longer recognised by the victim) but in the culture that adult society maintains on the subject of childhood for its own satisfaction. This can be imposed on parents and on the children who suffer the misguided discipline that is thought to be appropriate.

Unconscious fixations of attitude and idea can be active in this wider way where large numbers of people have similar life-styles and live according to values and concepts which they accept because they belong to the widespread cultural whole. This is the thesis Miller develops in her various books that focus on traditional practices of bringing up children. Beginning with *For Your Own Good: The Roots of Violence in Child-rearing*,[9] she traces the tradition of what she calls 'poisonous pedagogy' in Europe with copious quotations from eighteenth- and nineteenth-century texts, mostly collected by Katharina Rutschky and published in 1977. She points out that 'this revered tradition ... crushes spontaneous feelings' in a systematic way. In the preface to the original edition of that book she wrote

> the general public is still far from realizing that our earliest experiences unfailingly affect society as a whole; that psychoses, drug addiction, and criminality are encoded expressions of these experiences.... I see it as my task to sensitize the general public to the sufferings of early childhood. (pp.xiv-xv)

The child so easily damaged

Miller knew that some aspects of the situation were slowly changing as she wrote, but also that the assumptions about, and prescriptions for, disciplining children rise from deep places in the collective unconscious. Significant elements of shared cultures (as we see today in every continent) change only marginally unless and until the will to change is mobilised at a sufficiently deep level of public opinion. Miller's insights are penetrating partly because of her intellect and strength of character, but in equal measure because she was able to verify her own involvement in what she was describing.

> I first became fully aware of what pedagogy really is by experiencing its complete opposite in my second analysis. [The] analyst, Gertrud Boller-Schwing ... never tried to 'train' or instruct me.... As a result ... I was able to ... become sensitive to the pedagogical atmosphere surrounding us all.... Countless conversations with my son ... played an equally important role.... Again and again he forced me to become aware of my internal compulsions, internalized during childhood and stemming from the upbringing common to my generation.... [M]y own liberation from these compulsions ... could be achieved only after I had developed an ear for the sophisticated ... nuances of the pedagogical approach. (pp.xvi-xvii)
>
> The conviction that parents are always right and that every act of cruelty, whether conscious or unconscious, is an

> expression of their love is so deeply rooted in human beings
> because it is based on the process of internalization that takes
> place during the first months of life. (p.5)

How relevant is Miller's work now in the twenty-first century? Although much has changed in recent years there remains a cloud of incomprehension about the acute nature of infant suffering, about the child's defensive measures against pain, and even more so about the unconscious agreements that can sustain the corporate mind in unhealthy and untruthful ways. To that extent the world is still gripped in the predicament of which she wrote. Like Frank Lake's, her views were dismissed by her fellow professionals and many in society at large, yet her argument remains firm. The very fact that in the second part of *For Your Own Good* she recounted 'the childhood of a drug addict, a political leader, and a murderer of young boys, all of whom were subjected to severe humiliation and mistreatment as children' (Christiane F., Hitler, Jurgen Bartsch) indicates its relevance for today. Thus a vast change of perception is called for, in which we have to consider with new and urgent seriousness, unconscious processes that we would prefer to think only tangentially apply to ourselves and other ordinary citizens. Miller brings to light the verifiable evidence that apparently 'normal' child-rearing can involve acute suffering, and this evidence is constantly being authenticated afresh in relation to all stages of childhood. Both Miller and Lake were pointing in their different ways to the almost universal failure of *societies*, even today, to appreciate the highly sensitive openness of babies, and their need to be treated as persons who belong consciously to the family. Every child is designed to be a responsive person and expects his status to be respected. But if he has been deprived of the respect, care and comfort he needs, especially if this has happened in early infancy, when his understanding of the pain he is feeling is so absolute, his reaction to being hurt will be similarly massive. In cases where the suffering has been severe and prolonged, the reaction may remain so buried that the hatred against those responsible will be pent up and probably can only be released with its full fury in adult years. A malign outcome of the innocent suffering may then be extreme. This we see happening today, as throughout history, in horrendous and often criminal behaviour, as the victim seeks blindly to deny to others the benefits of which he himself was deprived in such tender circumstances.

At this point, however, there is a difference between Miller's account of the healing situation and the Christian one, which is seen in the slight difference of emphasis on the place of the therapist or companion who is alongside the injured adult to witness the child suffering and to assure him that the suffering is now at last being recognised. Lake realised that the human helper mediates silently the presence of the Creator. In the long term this is important because it alters the perspective in which emotionally healed people are able to face the future and help others to find their own healing in the context of the divine purpose. That Christian approach to emotional healing keeps in mind that human destiny is directed to transformed community life and that wellbeing for people needs the personal resources of the divine Trinity as well as the presence of other human persons. Help from beyond the individual who has suffered is critical but Miller appears to suggest, in the passage quoted above, that becoming sensitive to what she had felt as a deprived child is enough to restore the stability that she needs in order to 'live with that truth' (see also her words quoted below). My conviction is that the *adult* needs personal affirmation in the present which is more than the internalised confidence established before the infant deprivation occurred, and more than the respect and support of other adults in the present. This is the security that only God can give.

Miller's campaign

One of the most significant passages in Miller's books is to be found in *Breaking Down the Wall of Silence: to Join the Waiting Child*,[10] where she writes, with reference to leading analysts who were aware that Freud had drawn back from the rigour of his own findings.

> In vain they waited for their colleagues to confirm their find-ings on the consequences of repressing childhood traumas, consequences that they discovered in patient's histories. Because they lacked the experience of their own child-hoods, they allowed rejection by their peers to divert them from their goal. Had they found their way back ... they would not have needed this confirmation from outside. To live with one's own truth is to be at home with one-self. That is the opposite of isolation.... Since feeling the almost unfathomable isolation of my childhood, I myself no longer feel isolated. This ... allowed me to free myself of redundant opinions and lay aside the blinkers that had become unbearable to me and prevented me from fully living. As a child they were crucial to my survival. Had I seen and felt as a child how my parents mistreated me and

what consequences that had ... I would probably have died.
As an adult I can live with that truth. (p.52)

As I go on it will become apparent how relevant that testimony is
to understanding the healing process. When it is qualified as I have
indicated above, Miller's argument is fundamentally consistent with
Christian faith and is needed in the Church, for without adult trust in
God further breakdown may occur.

A therapy of listening and empathy

In the early pages of *Thou Shalt Not Be Aware*[11] Miller contrasts the
practice of psychoanalysis in terms of *dogma,* in which the treatment
is in effect an educating of the patient, with a psychotherapy that
begins with the patient's *experience* and stays with that attention
throughout. The latter approach, which Miller affirms to be the
only way anyone can find the psychological freedom we all need,
is also the one that clinical theology follows. What is important
is whether people 'are led to regard themselves as a subject or as
an object'. Miller repeatedly explains that psychoanalysis as she
found it, applied in inflexible and doctrinaire ways, had developed
a practice which was strangely partisan in the sense that the analyst
stood, if only unconsciously, in alliance with the authority figures
under whom the patient had been brought up. Miller is identifying,
as the obstacle, Freud's drive theory which he adopted at the end of
his first phase of practice to replace his original trauma theory.

> If I as an analyst direct my interest and attention to finding
> out what drive a person ... is suppressing at the moment ...
> I will listen sympathetically when he tells me about his
> parents and his childhood, but I will be able to absorb only
> that portion of his early experiences which is made manifest
> in his drive conflicts. The reality of the patient's childhood,
> which has been inaccessible to him all these years, will be
> inaccessible to me as well. It remains part of the patient's
> 'fantasy world', in which I can participate with my concepts
> and constructs without the traumas that really took place
> ever being revealed.... If... however I confront the person
> who enters my office with questions having to do with what
> befell him in childhood and ... consciously identify with the
> child within him, then from the very first hour events of early
> childhood will open up before us that would never have been
> able to surface had I based my approach on an unconscious
> identification with the parents.... [I]f the analyst directs his

attention to early childhood trauma and is no longer compelled to defend the position of the parents (his own and those of
his patient), he will have no trouble discovering the repetition
of the earlier situation in the patient's *present* predicament.
If, for instance, the patient should describe with complete
apathy a current partner relationship that strikes the analyst
as extremely painful, the analyst will ask himself and the
patient what painful experiences the latter must have had
to undergo ... without being permitted to recognise them
as such, in order to be able to speak now so impassively
about his powerlessness, hopelessness, loneliness, and constant humiliation in the present-day relationship. It may
also be ... that the patient displays uncontrollable feelings
directed towards other neutral people and speaks about his
parents either without any show of feeling or in an idealising
manner.... [B]y observing how the patient mistreats himself
[the analyst will also see] how the parents once behaved towards the child. In addition, the manner in which the patient
treats the analyst offers clues to the way his parents treated
him as a child – contemptuously, derisively, disapprovingly,
seductively, or by making him feel guilty, ashamed or
frightened. All the features of a patient's early training can
be detected in the very first session if the analyst is free to
listen for them. (1990 edn, pp.11-12)

I have included this long excerpt to show the nature of Miller's own
working and its particular emphasis on the predicament of children's
suffering in the home. From its beginning in Freud, modern psychotherapy has had to grapple with this area of child distress, but only in
much more recent years has convincing evidence of the horrifying
scale of that distress and its life-long blighting effects been brought
to public notice. In February 2006 I watched a TV programme docu-
menting the sustained self-harm of women held in Styal prison in
Cheshire, and the valiant efforts of the staff to keep them from suicide.
The results of child abuse range from its severest consequences as in
the lives of those people who are unable to live effectively with the
rest of society, through to the majority whose lives may have been
spoilt in one degree or another because the way their emotional life
was manipulated in childhood continues to affect their ability to relate
well to others in adult life. The great problems that society faces in this
regard concern the nurture of family life since it is children mistreated by
significant adults in early years who are likely to adopt and carry with

them a repertoire of reactions to pain that they endured passively at the time. Taking the examples of notable tyrants, Miller shows that abused children are being unconsciously conditioned to mirror their parents and to perpetuate the actions from which they have suffered when they have the power to hurt others, in later childhood, in adolescence and eventually in adult positions of responsibility and power.

The task is to identify with the victim
To meet the needs of anyone in therapy a major feature of the treatment has to lie in the therapist or counsellor being whole-heartedly attentive to the condition of the client as she was in the vulnerable state of being an infant or child. Miller refers to the way many colleagues found in her first book a difficulty over whom she considered 'the guilty party' in cases of parent-child relationships.

> They could not grasp that I blame neither children nor parents. You cannot, some said, absolve parents of all responsibility; after all, someone must be responsible for the misery. Others pointed out how difficult some children make it for their parents... you have to be fair and assign guilt to both sides. (p.58)

Miller was 'struck by the frequency with which analysts dispense moral judgements' and saw in this the extent to which the tradition of 'poisonous pedagogy' that she had exposed at length in *For Your Own Good* had infected psychoanalysis. It was because she realised that leading figures in the movement, who had perceived where Freud had wavered and had not given full weight to the evidence of child-suffering, were still doing the same that she withdrew from the analytical association. They had, she wrote, 'remained until their deaths in the dark labyrinth of analytic theory' (*Breaking Down the Wall of Silence* p.52). For her the seriousness of the situation was aggravated since it was not just within the psychoanalytic fraternity that the age-old customs of harsh child training were being condoned. There are now new psychotherapeutic organisations springing up that also support something of the old ideas within a more modern setting. In these circles, much emphasis is being put on the idea that therapists and counsellors should tell their once-abused clients that they need to forgive the parents or other adults who had mistreated them in order to be relieved of the guilt they are carrying. Some of these therapeutic associations have specifically Christian motivation and often claim biblical views of forgiveness in support of their teaching. But this kind of guilt, built up in someone who is still coming to terms with his infant suffering, is neurotic and does not call for forgiveness at all. In no sense can it be resolved by reciprocal forgiveness (as that is expressed in the Lord's Prayer).

Although claiming not to blame either side, Miller does by implication give attention to the undoubted facts of parental guilt. This is needed. It is fundamental for real healing that those abused in childhood should come to realise how severely wrong the abusers were, even when they acted at the time in the belief that what they were doing was necessary and right – for the child's good. She is also right however that blaming does not help. What is needed is exposure of the whole truth. Moreover what enables healing is bringing the child-feelings into the consciousness of the adult who once suffered those wrongs. When that work of exposure has been completed and truly absorbed into the person's adult subjective experience, self-condemnation and projection of blame onto innocent others can be withdrawn, and after all that the prospect of proper reconciliation opens up. Only then is it appropriate for the therapist or healing group to speak, when the client is ready, about forgiveness, the future and the restoration of good relationships. Paramount in this process is the client's new ability to see that her sense of 'guilt' ('it must be my fault') was mistaken and self-imposed. Certainly children become blameworthy in many specific instances, but if their faults are not addressed appropriately the responsibility passes from them to the ones who fail to meet their needs. But any facts of their own moral responsibility cannot be recognised by clients until the memories of the past situation have been recovered and they are able to *feel the original hurts* within the warmly accepting and affirming relationship that the therapist or group offers. The will is involved, however, because willingness to acknowledge the truth of one's original situation is critical.

But there is a caveat to be added which Miller does not mention. There is a limit to the extent that this kind of deep therapy is possible without further harm to the client. The therapist should always refrain from leading anyone into this method of healing (Lake called it 'primal integration') unless there are signs that the client in her adult personality is strong enough to endure the exposure of infant pain without breakdown. Thus the process has to go forward only gradually. There is always the potential for either a breakthrough to real psychological freedom, or for breakdown if the defences have been dismantled in too hasty a way or without the active adult participation of the client. It is relevant also to stress that the uncovering of unconscious memories of pain is always the client's own work, in which the therapist is a facilitator, not the agent.

The sense of guilt hides its cause

Although public opinion has changed for the better over recent years, Miller's protest on behalf of infants in a desperate state remains valid.

> The baby's whole being would like to shout out its anger, give voice to its feelings of outrage, call for help. But that is exactly what it may not do.... If no witness comes to its aid, these natural reactions would enlarge and prolong the child's sufferings.... Thus the healthy impulse to protest against inhumanity has to be suppressed. The child attempts to extinguish and erase from memory everything that has happened to it.... What remains is a feeling of its own guilt, rather than outrage that it is forced to kiss the hand that beat it and beg for forgiveness.... When all its attempts to move the adult to heed its story have failed, it resorts to the language of symptoms to make itself heard. Enter addiction, psychosis, criminality. (*Wall of Silence*, pp.129, 130)

To some it may appear that Miller (and Lake) overstate the case to gain our attention. Not so, because the severity of some infant suffering cannot be exaggerated, nor must we allow ourselves to be persuaded by easy assumptions that the root cause of major behavioural disorders in present time could not be in infancy. The evidence is abundant that it is. The world was not and to a large extent still is not paying attention to the real message: that the tragic dysfunctions she mentions here in the last three words are *caused by deprivation*, partly physical but mainly emotional in the infancy of the people concerned. So deep is every person's *original* sense of the Creator's goodness that often a victim of abuse is driven to blame himself.

> He may be wracked with pain, but the child still clings to the hope that the torture is no more than a response to his own guilt, that he is being chastised out of love. His own guilt is the mistreated child's only comfort! (p.124)

Thus all of us who stand in whatever degree within the main religious traditions, whether european or asian, need to recognise that it has taken a free-thinking philosopher and psychotherapist to show where conventional morality can go wrong (especially in the Judeo-Christian-Islamic tradition) in respect to guilt feelings and the care of small children. (The failure is actually wider than that, but this particular aspect of ethics provides an opening through which to review religious morality as a whole.) So Miller writes 'we cannot resolve the consequences of the traumatization they have suffered'

by offering the victims traditional morality. She includes an instance
of a woman who wrote of her own childhood and the release of her
repressed feelings which was eventually successful.

> This took place during her training as a massage-therapist....
> Gradually she discovered in detail events that she had totally
> banished from consciousness: that she had been sexually
> molested by her grandfather at the age of four; that she was
> subsequently grossly abused by a perverted uncle, and that
> she was finally raped by her step-father. As the pattern of self-
> destructiveness was not resolved simply by this knowledge,
> she went to a woman therapist who [worked]...with her on
> the horrific journey of self-discovery.... 'If you don't forgive
> your mother, you will never be able to forgive yourself'.
> Instead of helping the patient to resolve the guilt feelings
> that had been imposed upon her...she was burdened with
> an additional demand, a demand that could only serve to
> cement those feelings of guilt.[12] (pp.131-132)

Corporate dimensions of neurosis

The shape of Miller's career, like Lake's, prompts us to explore the
way prophetic insights are usually resisted by the climate of opinion
entrenched in a community. Biblical history in particular makes the
pattern familiar. So we can learn from the way Miller reached her
conclusions, and what the opposition was which forced her into a
wilderness position. Through the period of writing her awareness of
her own personal suffering increased, until eventually it became most
vividly present to her through the primal therapy she underwent (using
the method outlined by J. Konrad Stettbacher in his book *Making Sense
of Suffering* NY 1991). In consequence she was able to realise even
more clearly what was wrong in the community of psychoanalysis
than when she had begun to dispute Freudian developments.

> Finally, my own experiences helped me to grasp that psy-
> choanalysis will never be able to take up new insights into
> childhood because it is, *sui generis*, incapable of doing
> so. Indeed it owes its raison d'etre to the camouflage of
> concrete facts by abstract, diversionary intellectual con-
> structs.... I wrote...three books while still a member of
> the Psychoanalytical Association and...never encountered
> unbiased, constructive criticism.... The fear my conclusions
> evidently induced...remained unstated...prospective psy-
> choanalysts knew very well that my name was not to be

mentioned if they wanted to pass their exams. As I radically challenged Freud's theories by treating a subject that he wished to bury under the weight of taboo, I clearly aroused many people's fears. [B]ecause Freud could not bring himself to confront the truth about his own childhood, he made his students suppress the truth about child abuse wherever it raised its head. The consequences were appalling.... If patients do begin to notice something, they often allow themselves to be talked out of their tentative findings.

The character of those consequences is well illustrated by this instance.

A forty-year-old woman witnessed with her own eyes her husband sexually abuse their twelve-year-old daughter. Alarmed by the emotional consequences, she sends her child to the same analyst with whom she had been in therapy for the previous eight years. After the first session her daughter returns home distracted, saying, 'I never want to see that woman again. She is terrifying, Mom. She said there was nothing wrong with fantasising such things. Children often invent stories. But what I need to do is find out why I want to cause my Dad problems'. (op.cit. pp.42-47)

Here there was a glaring case of corporate neurosis in the association where Miller had worked for twenty years. But how do the Church and other major institutions in society respond in similar situations? Is it with the same closing-of-ranks and blinkered vision? Miller interprets the terrible history of these behaviours using frequent references to Judeo-Christian literature: Lamentations, and Abraham's offering of Isaac in particular. This is understandable and relevant. I am glad she did so, because Christians, Jews, Muslims and others need to face the reality of corporate neurosis at work within their own hallowed traditions. The texts which record God's revelation in Christ are themselves not immune from the effects of human weakness and partial knowledge.

Courageous love counters corporate neurosis
The media response to Miller's writing was at first positive, but it seems praise for her first book was often followed by rigid, contemptuous dismissal and distortion of her arguments (see chapter 5 of *Breaking Down the Wall of Silence*). This showed her how massive was the resistance to the facts she wished to make known. A corporate neurosis was indeed operating. In a letter written in 1986 Miller had

indicated her conviction that because Hitler, who misled so many people, had not

> experienced even a glimmer of friendliness and kindness on the part of his parents ... he [became] the greatest criminal in the history of the world. The inflexibility of his attitude ... that knew neither pity nor exceptions in its desperate fury ... made of him ... ultimately ... the absolute incarnation of evil.

After quoting from the letter, Miller tells, by way of contrast, of the instance of Manfred Bieler who wrote *Quiet as Night: The Memoirs of a Child* (1989).

> In the book he takes the child he once was by the hand and leads it back through the forgotten horrors of its childhood. He ... becomes [the child's] enlightened witness. He is able to do this thanks to a grandmother who sometimes protected him from his parents and ... so was his helping witness. On one occasion ... she even turned against his father ... [and] showed the child that an injustice was being committed against him.... Bieler's grandmother also demonstrated with her affection that he was worthy of love (pp.68-69).

The care of his grandmother was the decisive factor that led to healing and a life fulfilled.

Pain and distorted creativity

Taken together these passages indicate the two possible outcomes of childhood suffering. In Hitler neurosis was complete, but in Bieler the potential for neurosis was overcome and the freedom to grow creatively secured. What made Hitler what he was began with his terrible childhood resulting in the repression of emotional pain, which prevented him from feeling and knowing how his parents had treated him and what they were like. But on the deprivations of his childhood he built a compensatory life obsessively committed to achieving his own grandiose significance in controlling and inspiring his nation. For this he was able to take hold of past and current fantasies of Aryan superiority and so forth. In all this we see how important it is to keep in mind the central human need for care and for self-esteem.

Miller's reference to Bieler's autobiographical account shows the results of precisely this same need being satisfied in childhood if only marginally. The effects of actual emotional pain in infancy and childhood were overcome in later life because the child had had the strength to hold on to his true status as a person, which in Christian

language is being a child of God. That status cannot be confirmed
by the individual's own exertion but is given in relationship. So here
the capacity to empathise, almost entirely absent in a character like
Hitler's, is in Bieler's case able to grow, because it was evoked by his
grandmother's love for him. This insight strengthens our confidence
that corporate neurosis can be overcome. But is the Church of today
able to apply that wisdom?

Corporate distinguished from individual neurosis

Both individual and corporate neuroses have a shared character for
they are patterns of compulsive behaviour which have been formed
as ways of escape to ward off the uncomfortable effects of past
mental pain. The unconscious memories of the original suffering are
carried by individuals, but if similar fears of the pain recurring have
been felt by many people living together their common anxiety can
establish a shared way of defending against that recurrence. This
constitutes a collective neurosis. The two forms show themselves
differently. Individual neuroses appear, at least to the trained eye, in
characteristic defences which cover up some raw emotion not very
deeply repressed. Corporate or collective neuroses on the other hand
appear differently because in each case the leading edge is an idea or
shared ideology held compulsively as if it were the most natural thing
in the world. Every corporate neurosis has as much emotion behind
it as the individual disorder has, but the emotion is attached to and
led by the ideas that makes it distinctive. In individual neuroses some
conceptual thought will also be evident, but there the thinking serves
to bolster the individual in her own more or less separate defence
system. Such systems betray the individual's isolation, for each is
locked unconsciously in a painful situation where she originally felt
alone. Her thinking therefore helps to disguise the pain but the isolation is barely hidden at all. It may even be held on to obstinately.
In contrast the corporate neurosis looks very different since the idea
it incorporates has been adopted by a very large group of people, all
of whom keep their individual sufferings more strongly repressed
by holding on to the shared idea and the practices that are associated
with it. The shared emotional drive is disguised in intellectual and
cultural concepts held and enjoyed in common.

I am now in a position to bring Frank Lake's work into the main
stream of my argument, and put it into relation to all I have explored
so far. His teaching on this corporate dimension of clinical theology
is less extensive, but it makes Lake's work of even more importance
for the twenty-first century.

D. Mental suffering and defensive lifestyles

The seminar programme in pastoral care and counselling that Lake launched in 1958, initially for clergy of the Church of England, starts its exposition of the psychodynamic understanding of human nature with the model of the 'dynamic cycle' mentioned in the introduction which traces the individual's participation in relational life. It is often said that the model is the most important element of his teaching; this could be slightly misleading if it is not realised that there are three aspects to its significance. Certainly a large majority of seminar members and many others have found the model illuminating, and it remains as helpful today as it was originally. It links psychological learning with theological reflection, because it presents in a clear visual way the idea that Jesus Christ was in a sense the only psychologically normal, or properly functioning, member of the race. From this model all the other diagrams that Lake drew follow logically, but on the basis of careful, clinical observation.

> Our need in a clinical theology [he wrote] is for a model which correlates the biblical material concerning Christ and of the Church's witness to Christ and obedience to him on the one hand, with the sum of our knowledge of human personality growth and development and the disorders that affect them on the other. Most of the models developed by pastoral and ascetical theology tend to be as sin-dominated as the classical psychiatric models are sickness-dominated. We need a model which will correlate the dynamics of relatively well-functioning personality and of spiritual health, in its formation and maintenance, before it turns to the clinical conditions in which this integral wholeness is lost and replaced by deprivation, anxiety, conflict, distress, defences and various forms of disorder. By inference, the model must point the way back to health and wholeness, showing why the various therapeutic factors are effective and at what point. (*CT* p.29 abdg. edn)

It will be seen that the model and its derivatives really do achieve this purpose. The three aspects of the matter which make the dynamic cycle so valuable, are first in expressing personal dependence on community, second in understanding the neuroses as distortions of the cycle, and third in showing that the healing of these distortions in earlier life makes possible growth towards spiritual maturity and humanity's ultimate destiny. The first has been emphasised in the first chapter, the second is the main subject of this chapter, and the third will become evident in its last section.

But to get a balanced picture of Lake's seminar programme we should notice that the work concentrates on the first two aspects. The basic form of the model represents the optimal sequence of *growth through dependence,* initially that of the infant on his mother (fig. 1). The cycle is to be understood as continually repeated, and its four-fold form is applicable to all stages of life from conception to death. The quadrilateral shows a sequence that begins with acceptance and ends with achievement, and by its widening and then diminishing shape it indicates that with the depletion of strength and wellbeing the person has to be renewed again from the source person on whom he depends. As life goes on the finite sources change and the capacity of the person to internalise personal gifts increases; but even with age human beings remain dependent on others for all that characterises their personhood. Faith perceives that in fact the need to depend on the divine Source remains fundamental. It continues in such a way that full maturity cannot develop unless that deeper dependence becomes conscious and deliberate. If it does not, old people die while they are still spiritually deprived children. Human personhood which is intersubjective from the first shows itself increasingly to be trinitarian in its underlying structure. Throughout the process the two phases of input followed by output (and again input) characterise the nature and purpose of life, that is, to develop the interrelationships of community and creativity.

Secondly, the basic model is used as an ideal template from which disordered patterns of growth are seen to be departures, and this is where the most valuable insight of Lake's conceptual scheme lies. Disturbances in the actual relationship with the infant's source-person are the cause of later psychological weaknesses, and these are shown as starting at the beginning of the four-fold sequence, before a satisfactory form of *acceptance* has had time to become settled. The exception to this is in the case of the paranoid neurosis, which is recognised as being rooted in a failure of *sustenance.* For the rest the disorders are seen to be the consequence of difficulties in building up and maintaining the fundamental partnership between mother and child. These disorders fall broadly into two categories; in the one the child has already been affirmed emotionally and physically cared for, at least in the womb, so that when difficulty comes she is able to protest actively. In the second category, however, withdrawal of presence and lack of support have been the baby's lot from an even earlier time. In such a case the infant is prone to protest only from a relatively passive position and to establish defences accordingly.

Separation anxiety

Lake's recognition and explanation of these patterns of malformation and the way they continue in various adult forms, marks out his brilliance as a clinician and as a teacher. That way of understanding these disorders in oneself and in others is remarkably fruitful in practising the care and therapy needed by those who suffer from them. Because his approach begins with a grasp of what human 'normality' is like, it has the great advantage that it does not disguise the basic perception that *all people* have a common humanity and that all are prone towards these disorders. One of the discoveries that almost all students of clinical theology come to at an early stage of the course, with some amazement, is that they can hardly avoid noticing that something of every disorder is recognisable in some measure within themselves. This recognition helps to make it clear that neurosis, in some form or other, is the broken condition that we all share, and is not only a matter of some people's disabilities.

What holds together the entire logic of Lake's exposition is the perception that the root disturbance underlying all the neuroses in one way or another is the suffering of personal separation from the source person. This fits the situation described earlier in terms of persons having their origin and destiny in the intersubjectivity that God's presence creates. Accordingly Lake explained that beginning in 1955, while still working in a hospital setting, spending

> many hours alongside patients re-experiencing the first year of life, whether normal or abnormal, under the psycholytic drug LSD-25, I found that none of the classical psychological or psychiatric models seemed adequate to organise the facts which were emerging. The work of John Bowlby and the neo-Freudians was obviously tending to conceive of the first year in terms of interpersonal relationships. This was more cogent than Freud's own model. (pp.33-35)

He knew when he began the seminars that many clergy were 'suspicious of this mixture of oil and water, of spirituality and psychology'. Rapprochement between the two, he wrote,

> was not possible while psychoanalysis wandered uncertainly from one hypothesis to another about the origins of anxiety on too-late, oedipal levels.... It was not until the definition of the schizoid position, within the first half-year of life, made it clear that the primary anxiety is ontological and that the basis of existential trauma is despair or dread,

that an effective correlation could be made with Christian theology ....

Whereas Freud did not reckon the deepest conditions, involving the threat to being as well as wellbeing, were open to analysis,

> the Word of God in the cross reaches down to identify him-
> self with the desolation which is almost in despair of life's
> renewal (what we would call the hysterical position). He
> reaches down beyond that to dread of life itself, to the final
> despair that death is not possible (which we call the schi-
> zoid position).... Each [of these] constitutes a dilemma....
> To state this dilemma, as the existentialists have done, and
> as psychoanalysts now can, is to invite all those whose th-
> ought is centred on the cross of Christ to come alongside
> and speak with poignant relevance to the human condi-
> tion.... It is my wish that those clergymen who regard the
> study of psychopathology as the strange occupation of a
> queer and unreliable profession should not turn away from
> this opportunity of discovering the Lordship of Christ in
> these particular hells which we and our patients inhabit.
> (pp.73-74)

We have to remember now, over forty years since his writing was published, that the Church did very largely what he hoped she would not do. Most of the official Church turned away and remained in-different. Fortunately there were at that time many exceptions; the number of clergy who did respond and take part in the first seminars was significant, and many of them needed therapy for themselves. They got that in generous measure as well as the benefits that flowed into their pastoral ministry from the seminar work. But apart from a very few bishops the hierarchy and the theologians were not willing to do more than express their misgivings, and this situation has not yet changed very much. As far as I know only one theological college has made a sustained attempt to take advantage of the opportunity that Lake and the association he founded was offering. College courses have not entirely neglected the subject, but the perspective has been relatively shallow. At the time the climate of opinion in Britain was averse to psychology, theologically, sociologically and personally. Not surprisingly many clergy at all levels were themselves locked in those very conditions of defensive withdrawal of which Lake spoke and wrote so much. Despite some change there still remains reluctance to face these difficulties. I return then to separation anxiety in infancy as the prime root of all the personal deficits which give rise to neurosis, and to every spiritual malaise, in one form or another. The diagram Lake used to show what he saw to be the dangerous progression in suffering that a baby might be forced to endure during mother's over-long absence is eloquent in itself. As the baby's capacity to manage without her *presence* diminishes, his separation anxiety increases, until at the very worst the margin of tolerance may be reached (fig. 2).

Four basic disturbances of personhood
Since the person originates and exists in relationship with the personal Creator it is inevitable that her wellbeing rests in *being with* her Source in an embodied way that is suitable for her current mode of receptivity. Thus for the baby before and after birth, the immediate presence of parents or their surrogates is essential. In reading *Clinical Theology,* either the original volume or its abridged form, one cannot escape the theological content of Lake's psychology. Encountering it must have been a shock for any reader, whether Christian believer or not, who preferred to keep the scientific and the devotional in tightly separate compartments. So the book's reticent reception was not surprising. The dynamic cycle was expanded by a series of quotations from the Fourth Gospel. Lake's exposition of every emotional disorder also put the psychological features in parallel with theological implications. In the chapter on depression he gives warning of later themes by summarising the four basic positions of neurosis that he is tracing from their roots in mounting separation anxiety.

> In the depths of memory our spirits are surrounded by many strange and puzzling faces.... There are two vital needs of every child in these foundation years (the first three years or so), which could be summed up as the face of the mother and the voice of the father; the smile of loving recognition and the word of guidance.

Although the child can have no concept of God it

> has learned to expect a welcoming face or a rejecting, scornful, angry face, with corresponding powerful defensive manoeuvres to mitigate the encounter which promises to be too terrible. When the loving face of the mother, by which the baby lives and without which its spirit dies, is absent for too long, the mental pain may be too severe to be retained in consciousness. The loving face is obliterated from the

mind by prolonged absence but the threatening faces which take its place cannot be tolerated.... They undergo splitting off, repression and fixation and so remain for ever a threat to the security of the inner world. Unfortunately for God, though perhaps fortunately for the offending parent, this 'death mask' usually becomes one of the faces of God, if not his only face. Disbelief in his existence and hatred of his 'providence' arise here. (p.58)

If Christians gave attention to these words they would make a better job than they usually do, not only in commending their faith generally, but also in the Church's ministry of preaching, teaching and pastoral care. It is an understanding of unbelief to be kept at the back of one's mind in every opportunity for witness, but especially when ministering to the sick and dying, in conducting funerals, and wherever believers have contact with young people.

Violence attributed to God
It is not only disbelief in God's existence which is liable to result from very early infant distress, for people can believe in God and yet suppose that much about him is harsh and barely comprehensible. The most common form of neurosis, that of depression, begins the distortion by giving rise to pathological images of God in adult life. When the neglectful parent provokes angry responses from the baby, the eventual outcome in adults may be a form of religion which interprets God, by the simple method of *projection,* as punishing and controlling. The faith that God is good can be qualified by convoluted theologies which attribute to the divine Source those moral/immoral impulses that have distressed infant experience. (This psychological feature requires the Church to give fresh attention to her atonement doctrine.) Accordingly depression is formed in disappointment: and the 'reaction pattern formation' of defensive behaviour which it provokes covers up the infant's rage

against the absent, and therefore supposedly merciless face of the mother.... [I]t seems ... to this split-off buried self, as if the source of life itself, by demanding the impossible waiting, distorts its face, the face of 'god' into hard, pitiless lines. The infant fantasy sees its own rage reflected in greater rage on the face of an presumptively angry 'god'.

In the *second,* hysterical position, the infant, tried beyond its capacity to be patient, may fix its inner eyes on substitute fantasies of the loved persons, or parts of them, of a lovely face and shapely breasts distorting reality by the acceptance of mere fantasy, friendly and always accessible, but phoney ... often [with] a sense of guilt at having done this lustful thing, so that the face of 'god' takes on the punitive ... gaze of the accuser.

The *third,* 'most terrible' face, the schizoid

is the faceless face of dread and fear.... We meet patients for whom the 'face' of 'god', on the earlier levels of being, pressing through into consciousness at a time of illness, is hideous. And behind the hideousness is the paralysing facelessness of an identification with non-being.

Fourthly giving rise eventually to paranoia, the mother's face, when visible, is

so dead, lifeless, and utterly ungracious towards the baby [that] this imparts to the countenance of its own spirit or self-image a sense of worthlessness. The one who could give so much ... is felt to be persecutory. The infant ... looks out fearfully towards a 'god' whose face is full of scorn at its own, evidently contemptible, face.

To this summary of what he will develop at length, Lake adds this important paragraph.

These bitter memories of supposedly or actually unloving faces seen in the foundation year, when the human spirit must come to 'being' and 'well-being' through the 'umbilical cord' of visual encounter, or die, are the root of all compulsive unbelief, of all our neurotic defences, and ambiguously, of much of what becomes our sin. Here are the beginnings of man's distortion of the truth about the ultimate personal reality, God Himself. This is where the first lie is told about God ... which determines our solidarity with the race in ignorance, pride, fear, anxiety, despair, idolatry and lust, unbelief and murderous hatred of God Himself. (*CT* orig. edn. pp.180, 181)

The large amendment: before birth
Early in the year Lake died he had finished in bed his last and shortest book which has only been published very recently. Titled *Mutual Caring*[13] it refers particularly to 'the first trimester (the first three

months in the womb)' where the interaction 'between the mother's emotional state and the needs of the foetus is of greatest significance'. *Tight Corners in Pastoral Counselling* and *With Respect* addressed to Pope Karol Wojtyla (John Paul II) had been published before he died, and in each of the three books he explained how his new perspective on human consciousness before birth had opened up since 1976. It had grown between 1976 and 1980, by which time he was in the midst of four years intensive research by means of residential workshops at his centre in Nottingham. Through these the experience of twelve hundred subjects were correlated by means of verbatim notes and sound recordings at the time. None of the data described in *Mutual Caring* is

> offered in evidence at the bar of pure science for 'proof'. That is impossible and should not be attempted. However, when you listen to foetal persons undergoing the trials of the first trimester, you are struck by a group of statements which they tend to use frequently, and others which flash out from a unique individual experience. This has enabled us to construct their world in a coherent way. (p.16)

Although he was confident that the earlier work was still sound as far as it went, the pre-natal perspective now

> changes almost everything about origins in counselling, and deepens its practice.... When people experience loneliness very painfully, empathy used to have in mind a scared baby and an absent mother. Now... our empathy has also to envisage the likelihood that within this anxious adult is a foetal person, longing for some acknowledgement from the mother of its being there in the womb, ... to know that she accepts, and does not reject the fact that she is pregnant and has a new person growing within her. (p.15)

One immediate consequence of this altered perception is that statements such as those quoted above about the foundation years when being and wellbeing are formed 'by visual encounter' have to be amended. (Of course under 'visual' Lake included the tactile and vocal contact as well.) From the recognition that the foetus is conscious of being a person the reality of that new person's life in the womb was steadily coming into view for Lake and those working with him, as the following account shows. Evidently this rapidly growing organism is an experiencing person from the start, reacting to her environment. It was also becoming apparent, as we shall see, that a mother's responses to occurrences in her own life, and her changing dispositions, caused, say, by bad news or conflict, have an immediate effect on the child. What disturbs mother disturbs foetus. Often the accuracy of foetal memories picked up in therapy by the adult can be corroborated by the mother if she is still alive, or by some other member of the family. All this interaction between mother and unborn child is encountered frequently when primal-integration therapy is practised using deep breathing, just as it was in the workshops referred to. In this way Lake's own findings are being continually re-confirmed.

Sustained trauma in the womb

Another aspect of the pre-natal perspective that Lake was discussing in this last piece of writing concerns the deepest and most sustained forms of infant suffering, a type of distress often termed affliction. He observed

> that many elements of these classical descriptions of afflic-
> tion [he had mentioned Gerald Manley Hopkins' Terrible
> Sonnets] refer decisively to the first trimester, and not at
> all (unless by failure of repression of the primal material,
> 'contaminating' the post-natal scene) to the problem of
> the 'nursing couple'. For instance Simone Weil's recurrent
> metaphor of the nail piercing the navel, sees it as being like
> a moth, pinned alive into an album as a specimen.... The
> nail, spear or dagger metaphor ... is exceedingly common,
> when subjects are reliving a distress-invaded first trimester.
> It is never found as a metaphor arising out of or associated
> with post-natal deprivation, or out of any catastrophe occur-
> ring after the umbilical cord has been cut.... Hundreds of
> our subjects have used these images to express the foetal
> experience of being invaded ... by the black or green dis-
> tress issuing from the mother's circulation, replete with the
> catecholamines, the emotional transfer biochemicals of sev-
> ere and bitter distress.... Though it may ... persist throughout
> the whole of the pregnancy, that is not common. Usually
> there is some relief in the middle trimester. (pp.23, 24)

This kind of foetal distress is remarkably expressed in the drawing I reproduce (fig. 3) which is taken from sheet C 50 printed in 1979. Some of the long term effects of this suffering will be evident in the personality of the adult even after the pain has been healed. But before healing, mediated through therapy or in some other way, the formation of defences will usually have made it possible for that

person to live competently and more or less happily in later life while
being largely unconscious of what life in the womb was really like.
In parallel to the findings of his research Lake placed a wealth of
literary testimony in 'the poetry of the schizoid' and 'the theatre of
the absurd' which has turned the 'pre-verbal images' of the unborn
'into exquisitely accurate words'.

> It is all there … but until now we have not known when
> human beings were undergoing the experiences, so terrible
> as to warrant tortured language of this intensity. Now we do,
> the extension of the counsellor's ability to provide accurate
> empathy, which is the core of his or her effectiveness, has
> reached a new and authentic, because self-authenticating,
> depth of precision. (p.24)

Recall and verification?
My own view is that once you experience the recall of events in your
own very early life, such as your birth, and discover that a particular
sequence of memory is being endorsed by your whole body (in a
manner that is different from ordinary remembering), you view the
experience with amazement and great respect. You realise that it is
not just your brain but all the cells of your body which somehow
carry a record of what you went through in the past. From then on
the problem of verifying how this happens is greatly diminished.
It remains a matter of puzzlement but one that can be left for gradual scientific investigation instead of being dismissed at once as
implausible. It is similarly reassuring when a further outcome of
the experience is a physical improvement. In my case reliving my
birth resulted in a definitely lessened sense of pressure round my
forehead when under strain. I 'knew' then that the pressure I used
to experience must have been an outcome of the very long labour
which for my mother was severe. It was a birth process which made
a slight but distinct distortion of my skeleton at the top of my spine,
in the formation of neck in relation to chest. Repeated sessions of
therapy have eased the discomfort of these pressures as well as giving
emotional release. Lake reported that often

> the effect of full primal re-enactment is to modify the symptoms
> profoundly and in some cases cut them off at source so that they
> cease.… The most convinced person is usually the subject. His
> closest relations are also convinced, as they find him or her
> now able to revise many life-long, automatic refusals, totally
> out of the power of will formerly to change. (p.27)

Concerning the actual transmission of meaningful experience in an organism so undeveloped, Lake writes

> taking it all back to conception, is it conceivable that in the protein molecular structures of that single cell, there is a capability to react to internal and external, good and bad, pleasurable and noxious stimuli? That the single cell can do so much is evident to anyone who has studied the analogous single-celled amoeba. We watch them expand their pseudopodia to enjoy a congenial medium, then suddenly draw in, and even encyst when the environment changes to an uncongenial one.

In the human being there may be

> in some protein molecular structures such as the ribosomes, not only recording ... but transmitting capacities, so that significant information present in the zygote is still present in every cell of the blastocyst, and, after implantation, is carried into every cell of the rapidly developing embryo. This must ... include the cells of its enormous ectodermal invagination, the primitive brain, which is beginning to be recognizable in a couple of weeks. These neural precursors must be capable of transferring coded data, as cells divide and differentiate, maintaining the continuity and identity of this particular organism in time. (p.28)

Roger Moss on Lake's pre-natal workships

What I have reproduced in the last three sub-sections was taken initially from my duplicated copy of Lake's manuscript and concerns the third of three phases in his exploration of foetal life to which the psychiatrist Dr Roger Moss refers,[14] explaining that Lake

> came across the little-known works of Francis Mott, an analyst who had been this way in the forties and fifties through painstaking research into the analysis of his patients' dreams. That part of Mott's work which was based securely in embryology and physiology ... has proved remarkably accurate when the same material has been investigated ... through deep-breathing techniques. Mott revived a term first used centuries before – 'umbilical affect' – to denote the feeling state of the fetus as brought about by blood reaching him through the umbilical vein.... Frank Lake began to recognise this was the predominant mechanism by which is transmitted to the

fetus the mother's positive emotional regard, or the absence
of it.... The latter 'negative umbilical affect' [appears] to be
the source of much of the deepest of adverse feelings that
are felt to derive from experience within the womb. From
the umbilicus, the bad affect, according to Lake, diffused
through the body in a severe, overwhelming fashion that
seemed to correlate with the schizoid position; or when not
quite so severe, it might be displaced into any of the organs
of the body, including the skin, the gut, the respiratory tract,
the limbs, the muscle groups and so on, in such a way as to
give a valuable clue to the possible origin of psychosomatic
and hypochondriacal disorders. (pp.7, 8)

Moss, a leading member and sometime Chair of the Clinical Theology Association (and then Bridge Pastoral Foundation), was asked
by its Council after Lake's death to prepare a report on the primal
therapy aspect of his work, and it was this that he presented to the 1st
International Congress of Pre- and Peri-Natal Psychology in Toronto.
In brief his conclusion was that

the theory provides a useful basis for some new approaches
to the aetiology, therapy and prevention of the functional
psychoses and neuroses, psychosomatic and personality disorders, and merits further research.

Widely varied experience put into words
Fully aware that they had no language then, those who re-live their foetal
experience nevertheless have no difficulty in translating it into speech.
Lake writes of a 'pre-cursor of language' being present in the foetus
who is communicating through the adult he or she is today. Not only
is it present in rudimentary fashion, it is capable of carrying nuances
of meaning, and changes of meaning, and the vast range of emotional
states present in those (who take part in the workshops). '[E]ach ... is
convinced that what they are saying now is an accurate report, couched
in such language as they can find, of the deepest experiences of their
life. So clear and convinced are they ... they may say, as one did: 'I felt
that intensely then, and I can feel it just as intensely now. It has become
basic to my being me. That is how I am, and that is how life is" (*Mutual
Caring* p.47). In reporting on the workshops Moss included excerpts
from a selection of scripts. The details are vivid in each; I indicate
here the gist of a few of them. The setting for the work was of several
groups of four being together within earshot of the leader who in a
neutral voice 'rehearsed the well-known anatomical and physiological

facts from conception, through implantation to the establishment of the umbilical circulation'. Moss noted that each

> response is highly individual, and the possibility that the resulting material is *mainly* suggested by the leader is quickly discounted. This fact makes for some difficulty in selecting representative statements.

I list them, as he did, in four sections.

(1) Beginning with sensing their parents' sexual union by which each was conceived, the experience was sometimes very joyful and exultant for the foetal subject. For others it might be alarming and violent, and in one such case with a drunken father, this was the seventh of eight supposedly traumatic conceptions. The foetus could sense the mother being nauseated by 'the smell of beer'; and protested at the conception itself, and then went on to experience her mother's attempt to abort. 'She doesn't want me. Let me out!'... and then 'Stomach pain. She wants to get rid of me!... It's horrible this stuff.... She shouldn't have done that to me....'

(2) When 'in the first week after conception the fertilized egg has divided again and again until it has formed a hollow ball of cells, known as the blastocyst.... Time and again, this stage elicits responses which are remarkable and beautiful'. One man said, 'Feel good. Suspended. Yellow. Luminous. Floating. Shining. Power-potential'. 'At this point his body began to move for the first time'. 'Frank Lake noted that this sense of being, of awareness and joy, was often spontaneously associated by his subjects with having God and the universe within their being'. But again this 'stage is not joyous for everyone. Even this may reflect the mother's mood'.

(3) Implantation two weeks after conception is also experienced with very wide differences of feeling. For some it is most satisfactory, but for another person, whose mother's marriage was in disarray, the prospect was daunting. 'I don't want it. I don't want to be part of this person.... It's all bad, there's no good place to be'. 'Her body tensed and shivered'. One man's 'mother was bedridden throughout the pregnancy, she had lost a previous baby, and her grief was unresolved.... The fetus was pushed beyond the limit of endurance into trans-marginal stress'.

(4) The general experience of life in the womb is also marked by variety and by instances of specific memory. Some experience the time as perfect. 'She's pleased'. Of the umbilical cord: 'It's giving to me'. 'It's lovely. She likes to feel me move inside her'... then after a while... 'There's extra food. Something orange, fruit and apples. She feels a little bit guilty because she can have the orange. There

are people who can't. [This was wartime.] It's good for her to have it because it's good for me'. Quite common is 'the sense that the fetus is receiving nothing from its mother emotionally'. 'Here is a man who even in his fifties still acknowledges that he has a lot of self-doubt and is self-effacing. His mother had no sense of her own worth as a woman. In the womb, he is saying: 'She doesn't know I'm here. She doesn't feel anything. Perhaps she's working hard, and that's all. It's so silent and lonely. It's comfortable enough. It's well supplied. It's plain and dull. There's no encounter with anyone. No sense of communication. I've got nourishment, but apart from that a cloud'. And again we come across an instance of quite vivid attempts at abortion.

> A man of 40 ... suspected his father would not have welcomed the pregnancy. During his work on the first trimester ... he encountered a familiar tight feeling in the stomach, and then a nasty metallic taste in his mouth which he would often notice on waking. 'Afraid ... of death. Metallic.... Fear of not being'. He shook and convulsed.... 'I see a long silver thing, pushing in ... I shrink away. Oh! Death.... Can't get away.... Don't want to be here'. But a little while later this has passed. 'Can breathe now. Want to stay. She likes me. She wants me to stay.... Almost like early bliss', he sighs. Unfortunately, this man's mother died many years ago, so this could not be confirmed – though in some cases such discoveries are admitted by the mother when she is asked directly. Recently this man said these experiences had ... illuminated and brought together all otherwise unconnected strands of his personal growth.... 'It made complete sense of my life and all my problems, totally, in terms of their overall relationships. I found out where things all began'. (pp.12-15)

Occasionally people have expressed what they experienced in vivid pictures; figure 3 is one that Lake distributed in the course of his teaching.

Further comments by Roger Moss
Endorsing Lake's confidence that 'the maternal-fetal distress syndrome and the methods of personal integration that go with it' do point to a needed revision in understanding and in the therapy of the major disorders of personality, Moss wrote

> Frank Lake used his very considerable experience of primal integration work to formulate some preliminary ideas about

the pre- and peri-natal dynamics of the main disorders. These included the roots of anxiety-depression and phobias; the psychosomatic disorders and hypochondriacal states have particularly useful light shed upon them by this theory; hysterical and obsessional splitting can be recognised; and the mechanisms of paranoid defences and schizoid orientations can be unravelled. Frank Lake also felt that some of the processes underlying allergies and addictions, and not least alcoholism, could be better understood from the new perspective. He provided some initial formulations of these dynamics, but there is much work to be done to authenticate and develop them.

With respect to the '*implications for therapy*' Moss also reported on the benefit of focusing on 'the inner 'Child' (in the terms of transactional analysis) at its simplest and yet most vulnerable stages'.

The existential truths of the basic feelings and relationships of human existence can all be focussed here. Much of the symbolism of dreams and of psychosis can be related quite easily to aspects of life in the womb. In the process of integration, there is much from later in life that has to be worked through as well; but the basic themes that emerge from one or two leisurely journeys through the nine months of pregnancy serve as a useful map or agenda of the work that has to be done. So often the satisfaction derived is the feeling of having got to the foundations. (p.17)

Moss ends his report with words of caution about the use of primal therapy methods in particular instances, on the lines of what I wrote earlier. People

with deep problems and questionable ego strength need very careful preparation and assessment, secure therapeutic support, and the availability of adequate skilled help afterwards. Those who have been in a position to continue the work in peer groups who have all shared this kind of experience (amounting to 33.5% of this sample) seem to have gained more than those who did not. (p.18)

The continuity of Lake's teaching
It will be helpful at this point to notice that Lake's work on foetal experience truly complements the bulk of his earlier work – not only that published in his books and pamphlets but also what is contained

in the unpublished materials used within the Association. At the end
of his life he did not have to abandon the main thesis about Trans-
marginal Stress as set out in the 'tome' of 1966.

> I find it all, still, astonishingly true, well-conceived as theory
> and practice, and relevant resource material for Christian
> Pastoral Care. What I do have to admit has turned out to be
> a serious mistake was the assumption that the nine months
> of foetal development in the womb were free of significant
> incident, a blank without possibility of psychodynamic con-
> tent. Four years of research … have totally broken open the
> bland assumption of pre-natal bliss, or, as the abortionists
> would have us believe, of a merely biological product with
> none of that self-awareness which we call personhood. Foetal
> life … is as eventful as the nine months that come after birth.
> (*Mutual Caring*, p.21)

He went on to remind his readers of what many of us had heard
him rehearse frequently, that his work as a hospital psychiatrist and
in later practice had repeatedly shown how babies suffered from
the 'failure to effect maternal bonding soon after birth'. Patients
were recovering an awareness that as infants they had been driven
into 'despair of making any progress into self-hood'. They had been
given a sense of their own 'unloveability', as a result of a systematic
practice of 'four hourly restricted attention'. It was a deliberate feed-
ing policy 'ruled by the clock' popularised by Dr Truby King.

> He was knighted for his services in giving clear consciences
> to coldly professional nurses and mothers who had too much
> else to think about and disliked cuddling babies anyway.
> These post-natal catastrophes could be conclusively shown
> to be occasions on which trans-marginal reversals took
> place. [The reversal was] from 'hysterical' clamouring for
> the mother to come … and restore peace by her presence, to a
> sudden flip of all the life switches, [when] the pain tolerance
> limit was reached, into 'schizoid' terror of the mother.

The baby was now 'demanding only that she keep her distance' and
was 'driven to distraction to avoid her touch, that had so recently
been longed for'. A baby in this position was now

> happiest when left alone to find whatever goodness can be dis-
> covered, by introversion of the heart turned in upon itself and
> the mind ceaselessly active in compensatory fantasy. (p.4-5)

As we have seen this terrible predicament was being experienced by some long before their birth. The same suffering, and the same patterns of defensive behaviour in reaction to the suffering, were occurring in the foetal situation as in the 'nursing couple' situation after birth. A dramatic diagram (fig. 4) represents the psychodynamic crisis that occurs when a person reaches, and may be pushed beyond, her margin of tolerable mental pain, and is plunged for a time into mind-shattering dread. This is one of a range of fifteen large composite 'charts' which together with a multiplicity of lesser diagrams and tables are used in the clinical theology teaching programme. It is more picturesque than the majority which are simply diagrammatic.

Not all seminar members find the charts helpful but they have the great advantage over written texts, in that they show in a visual way the complex inter-connection of event and responses to the event. A large range of clinical observations can be set out on one sheet of paper. This particular diagram pictures the situation which demonstrates what can happen when the attenuated capacity of the baby to bear mother's absence (on the scale represented in fig. 2) reaches breaking point. By this time, if the waiting had become a recurrent experience in the relationship, the child has already been forced into passivity. She is no longer protesting actively at mother's neglect (as in the depressive position) and is already on the edge of despair. In this passive frame of 'mind' the infant (or foetus), feeling starved of precious relationship to the person she depends on, is being moulded towards one or other of two neurotic positions: the hysteric or the schizoid.

The clinging hysteric, who has despaired of being given love and attention, from then on devotes her energy to a defensive behaviour pattern of getting people's attention by her own exertions, of excessive self-advertisement and so forth. In contrast another infant who may have been driven into passivity at an earlier stage, when repeatedly in such desperation, may very easily react paradoxically. He too falls into dread but when the worst of the crisis passes he climbs out defensively in the opposite direction. Instead of taking the hysteric's way out he commits himself to himself in isolation. No longer making a pretence of trust and relationship, as the hysteric does, the schizoid turns emphatically away from relationship, and into an interior fantasy life of self-sufficiency and the illusion of self-sustained power. Lake was prompted into the formulation of these perceptions by remembering Pavlov's experiments with dogs early in the century.

About the time that I was searching for interpretive concepts to provide a basis on which these paradoxical reactions

to stress could be explained...I came upon Dr William
Sargent's *Battle for the Mind* (1957). In the war years he
had encountered similar reactions in soldiers and civilians
suffering from battle or bombing. In the course of prolonged
exposure to nervous strain they were apt to break down
into strange patterns of behaviour, discontinuous from their
former attitudes. He found that Pavlov's work ... gave him
many of the formulations he needed.... The question for me
was, 'Did it apply to infants?'

He realised that there was 'no inherent reason' why not. 'In fact, all
animal experimentation has shown that it is precisely in the very
young animal that this kind of conditioning is most vividly and deeply
imprinted upon the character' (*CT* p.610). So in presenting his new
findings Lake remarks on the way his hypothesis had been neglected,
with his conclusions as a whole, at the time they had been published.

Those were the days of Kleinian and neo-Freudian ascend-
ancy, when the best of British psychodynamic writers ... were
focusing on problems generated by mishandling of the
intimate mother-baby relationship. None of them took up our
insistence that all our severe and endemic hystero-schizoid
personality difficulties could most elegantly, economically
and accurately be accounted for by seeing them as mirror
images, exact reversals of each other's perspective, on either
side of and in flight from the moment of supra-maximal
pain, or dread. This hypothesis, which we have not been
able to nullify, stands, in my view, stronger than ever, and is
immensely fruitful in therapeutic discussion and germinal in
interpretation. (*Mutual Caring*, p.22)

Defensive life-styles, individual and communal
Throughout this section the focus has been on the suffering of
infants before and after birth which does a great deal to determine
the character of the adult's life. Space does not allow more detail of
the consequences, but it will be evident that these defensive features
of the person's behaviour are what indicate the form of neurosis.
The neurotic person's attitudes, behaviours and life-style tend to be
inappropriate, in the sense of untruthfully relating to reality. For
example one manifestation of the depressive personality is in being
compulsively compliant. As in all neuroses, the unconscious core
experience that prevailed in infancy, is denied by the adult who
presents a reaction pattern of an opposite kind, in order to keep

the original experience out of sight. In the case of the compliant adult the infant is likely to have indulged fantasies of 'dominating and compelling the mother and father to fall in with (its) will.... [But the] super-ego has compelled the raging ego to turn the rage back on itself'. The adult therefore exhibits 'an inability to feel or express anger ... [having become] an intense supporter of every point of view mother espouses'. (*CT* abd p.154)

In order to show something of the large range of disordered behaviour that 'reaction pattern formation' causes in individuals and consequently in society I reproduce the last of Lake's broadsheet charts (fig. 5). This should be read in conjunction with what I have written earlier concerning human communality and corporate neurosis. Entitled 'a model of the human predicament', it indicates the broad character of human normality, a 'normality' characterised by large elements of avoidance, pretence and compensatory self-preoccupation. On the basis of the first-line defences of splitting off and repression people make life as tolerable and satisfying as possible by denying even the possibility of unconscious mental pain, so leaving it as little provoked into awareness as may be. Secondly and on top of this more or less substantial barrier of compulsive yet unconscious hiding, there are the person's ways of life that are actively and openly espoused and pursued. These are outlined in the 'balloons' of the top half of the diagram. Although they are features of individual life and behaviour, many are regarded as socially acceptable and the rest are treated as normal human traits because followed by many others. In adult consciousness they can be comfortably chosen for life in the present, with no awareness that their purpose is to negate what the person suffered in the past. Because people are social creatures their goals in life are adopted in their daily interaction with others. Thus their choice of life-style, social consciousness, moral standpoint and philosophy of life, together with characteristic forms of tension-relieving behaviour, may be determined by the unconscious origins of the tension, and by the individual's alliance with others who are motivated in similar ways. Most of these behaviours become features of public life promoted in society under the influence of the chosen interests and unchosen motives that people have in common. In this way the sufferings of individuals, which when they occurred were relational in character, lead in their gradual outcome to wider relational consequences, namely shared cultures, corporate endeavours, common beliefs, and the setting up of community institutions and aims.

E. Promoting reconciliation and transformation

Having in mind the whole social dimension which that chart (in fig. 5) refers to, this section raises the question of how Lake's work could be developed much more widely than has yet proved possible. Can the theological aspects of it be given greater attention within a broader community approach? The time seems opportune for the church and mental health professionals of all kinds to work together in interdisciplinary, ecumenical and interfaith partnerships for this purpose. With this question in mind I draw some lessons from Nicholas Lash's *Holiness, Speech and Silence: Reflections on the question of God,*[15] in which one encounters an academic theologian's perspective on the search for an answer. By following Lash, I begin to draw out the significance of Lake's work for the Church's future, and then in the last section of the chapter I refer to Rowan Williams on spiritual maturity.

There has been a tendency to disparage Lake's position by calling him an 'amateur' theologian. This was unfortunate because his study of the subject was often far more extensive and sustained than that of his critics. Lake always made a point, in speaking of a 'clinical' theology, of emphasising that learning to think theologically is a duty of a baptised Christian, if she or he has the capacity for it. The reluctance to encourage that duty in the Church at large is symptomatic of a wider problem to which Lash draws attention.

> I never cease to be astonished by the number of devout and highly educated Christians, experts on their own 'turf' as teachers, doctors, engineers, accountants or whatever; regular readers of the broadsheet press ... occasional visitors to the theatre who usually read at least one of the novels on the Booker short-list; and who nevertheless, from one year to the next, never take up a serious work of Christian theology.... It is difficult to avoid the conclusion that devout and educated Christians who refuse to acquire a theological competence cognate to the general level of their education simply do not care about the truth of Christianity or ... do not care sufficiently to seek some understanding of that Word through whom all things are made, into whose light we have been called, and which will set us free. (pp.4-5)

Having myself worked as a priest for most of my ministry in underprivileged areas and for my last period of service in an urban priority parish where there was but one university graduate in the congregation, apart from my wife and myself, it is particularly remarkable to me now, retired in the country alongside a high proportion of able professionals, to see how marked is this feature of today's Church. The avoidance of intellectual commitment on the part of responsible citizens including Christians is severe. The evidence is not obscure, yet few Church leaders seem to notice the nature of the problem. Meanwhile the consequences continue to mount as the Church's capacity to fulfil her mission steadily deteriorates in this respect.

The avoidance unconsciously rooted
The great importance of Lake's work lies in attention to exactly this kind of problem, problems of deeply buried resistances against facing the truth. Here we see why the Church and society at large need to be helped out of the blindness that holds well-intentioned, conscientious people in uncritical compliance. There is so much untapped potential still readily available on the edges of the Church's life; and in the population as a whole there is much intellectual curiosity, but everywhere it is strangely limited. The limits are tightly bounded by emotional avoidances that often have their roots in buried hurts from the past, reinforced collectively. These emotional factors are often diverting the Church's intellectual energies into channels that are too narrow, with the result that Christian leaders are missing the deeper aspects of the problems they are trying to solve.

And now there is a further dimension of the ecclesial situation to be taken into account, to which Lash also draws attention in his chapter 'Cacophony and Conversation'. Observing the undeniable facts of commercial globalisation he discusses the need to develop a 'global imagination' and 'sense of solidarity with the whole of humankind: past, present and future' for which it would be necessary to encourage 'something like a common *conversation*' (p.52). Immensely difficult though such a project is bound to be, he argues that it is certainly not impossible, as some have claimed by the theory of 'incommensurable conceptual frameworks'. The hope that international solidarity could be realised constitutes for many people a threat to the way they see the world and want to live in it. Yet that self-regarding resistance must be confronted in the confidence that humanity has an ultimate destiny that lies in community. Preoccupation with difficulties of communication between cultures (and religions) 'may mislead us into supposing that the recognition of our common humanity is something which first happens, as it were, inside our heads; that 'recognition' is a mental act'. Instead we are to realise that *it is shared vulnerability* that shows us what we are and how we are under obligation to live with all others.

> The recognition that the stranger is a fellow human being entails an element of mutually acknowledged vulnerability, a requirement that a kind of *trust* be mutually offered.... Ours is ... quite evidently a world in which such trust is, especially by the rich and powerful, regularly and systematically betrayed – from the countless millions we spend on weapons to the nauseous spectacle ... of wealthy middle-class communities being transformed into well-protected fortresses against the supposedly dangerous poor. (pp.52-56)

Trust and truth–speaking betrayed

Being under obligation is what our common humanity is about. So Lash looks beyond the threats to shared life and the hope of global conversation towards 'an even more fundamental betrayal' which is a breaking of the contract or covenant between 'word and world', for true human being involves responsibility for 'giving voice to the world of which we are a part'.

> The webs of cause and consequence, of interaction and relationship which bind the world into a single, complex whole become [in us] relationships of duty, of ... the ability to say 'Yes' or 'No', to make our contribution to the story and the drama and the healing of the world.... [We have] the responsibility to attempt to speak the truth in an almost unbearably dark and complex, almost ... unutterable world.

Lash sets out and commends in his discussion the views of George Steiner,[16] explaining his thought that 'the matter of *music* (is) central to ... the meanings of man'.

> The world makes music before we do, and the music that we make is, as it were, an articulation of the music of the world, a giving *voice* to things. In the music that we make, the truth of things (if we make music well) sings, and celebrates and weeps.

To the question: when was the contract broken? Steiner's answer is 'during the decades from the 1870s to the 1930s'; although Lash sees it 'in medieval nominalism or undoubtedly in the ... 17th century'. Whenever it has happened the loss of historicity has become critical;

and Christians particularly have to play their part in its recovery. Continuing to expound Steiner's thought Lash writes

> forgetfulness of temporality entails, in the last analysis, forget-
> fulness of God.... Steiner is highly critical of Wittgenstein. 'For
> the *Tractatus'*, says Steiner, 'the truly 'human' being... is he
> who keeps silent before the essential'. Such insistence... now
> so pervasive... may wear the masks of modesty or even 'mys-
> ticism' to disguise our abdication of responsibility. We 'keep
> silent' before God, and truth, and justice. We 'hold our peace'
> and, in this silence, millions starve and die.

What Lash is affirming is that our society has forgotten that 'the
fundamental form of speech is conversation', and keeps silent 'about
things that really matter'. We try to 'settle for some modest, homespun
humanism, some comfortable common sense'. But that 'is not... how
things work out'.

> Increasingly, in place of serious conversation, cacophony
> takes the form of an unholy and exceedingly dangerous
> combination of, on the one hand, strident and destructive
> *monologues* – the political, scientific and religious funda-
> mentalisms that boom at us from every side – and, on the
> other, of what Steiner calls '*kitsch* ideologies'.

Instead we have to affirm that 'serious speech', which is 'response to
the one Word through whose utterance all things are made, is what
makes... us human beings, and hence serious speech is our defining
duty'. (pp.57-60)

It is ironical that the nations can be so largely united in matters
which depend on research in the physical sciences, but so indifferent
to rationality in those which concern the emotional and moral wellbeing of every community.

> Our impatience with debate, with difficulty, with ambiva-
> lence and paradox is, 'at heart an impatience with learning'
> [Rowan Williams].... Good learning calls... for courtesy,
> respect... reverence for facts and people, evidence and
> argument, for climates of speech and patterns of behaviour
> different from our own. (p.62)

Even when we claim to seek divine help in this we find ourselves
unable to treat each other with that respect. Our best intentions are
unfulfilled until in some measure we are emotionally healed; and that
is where Lake's work comes in.

Religions subservient to the Kingdom

The last thing I need to do in this section is to stress the universal worldliness of reconciliation and personal change. God revealing himself as Creator and Redeemer is one activity. Within this single divine activity, reconciliation and transformation through the suffering and resurrection of Jesus is to be recognised more widely than in the confines of institutional religion. Lash affirms that it is

> within the world, in *all* the world, in all we think and do and say and see, achieve and suffer, and by no means only in some small margin of the world which people, these days, call 'religion' that we are required to be attentive to the promptings of the Spirit, responsive to the breath of God (p.40). God does not say many things but one.... God speaks the one Word that God is, and in that one Word's utterance, all things come into being, find life and shape and history and, in due time, find fullest focus, form and flesh, in Mary's child. (p.66)

So Christians must have an answer to the question: if God gives himself to all people everywhere in Jesus of Nazareth who is identified in the context of Israelite history, how does God overcome the gap between that particular self-giving and his universal self-giving? The answer has to be that there is no gap, because the personal presence which was enfleshed in Jesus is the Creator's presence in creation as a whole. Perceiving this depends on growing into a new humility, on eagerness to learn from each other, and on the development of practices of openness through which people of all faiths or none engage to share with others in 'a common human *life*'. The shared work nationally and internationally to which all peoples are called is one of healing and release for all. This means that as Christians we should be addressing the atheists from a different standpoint, insisting that the assertion that there is probably no God only diverts attention from the common obligation to live as citizens in dialogue with each other. In his reference to Isaiah 61 in the Nazareth synagogue (Lk 4:16-21), in referring to himself as Son of Man, in speaking of the temple (Mk 11:17), and in describing how he was tempted to betray his Father's commission (Lk 4:3-8) Jesus showed that his challenge was to people simply as people; it was international and universal. The Kingdom he preaches is not a matter of one religion having precedence over others but rather one which transcends religion. In both testaments, God's kingdom concerns life as a whole without partitions between sacred and secular.

How then are we to encourage and teach the practical way forward in this direction? We might sketch a broad image of the world of time and space as a theatre in which God meets with his children through their involvement with each other. He places us as members of a huge theatre company in a way which ensures that engagement with each other is unavoidable. To disengage is barely possible, yet the freedom to give or withhold mutual support according to individual and community wilfulness is immense. In that situation the Spirit is able to give us eyes to recognise that Christ offers his hidden presence to advance his reconciling work among those who as yet are unable to recognise him. They are there in the theatre but do not know what it is for. When people are ready to be together in facing the suffering and confusion of a troubled situation there is the opportunity for more fundamental forms of co-operation to begin. Through working together on limited objectives the common recognition of need and responsibility may encourage people to rethink matters of deeper disagreement and non-comprehension. This, the believer recognises, is because God is present. Writing about the meeting on the road and at Emmaus, Lash points to this kind of change.

> What the stranger does … is to give [the two disciples] an entirely new sense of what has been going on.… [T]hey discover, when they are at table, that it is *they*, … who are the guests, recipients of hospitality; and that it is *he* who is the host.… (pp.70-71)

But to keep our feet on the ground we have to remember that the resistance against any such recognition is massive. This is the defence of retention by which people cling to the status quo wherever they feel their personal stability may be threatened. So the question has to be faced: how can that tenacity be surrendered?

F. The stages of dispossession through Christ

With John of the Cross

This last section of the chapter integrates the theological and psychological sides of personal growth in Christ, a subject which exercised Lake's devotion for most of his life. His wide reading enabled him to integrate his professional learning with broader studies in theology and spirituality. What he called transitional states in the Life of the Spirit had been part of the seminar syllabus from an earlier date, but as revised in 1978 it included the results of his increasing attention to the pre-birth relations of mother and baby. Then, over the years 1979-80, he brought out a series of summarising sheets that brought together the thought of other authors to develop 'an interdisciplinary model' which integrated his research into the pre-natal origins of psychopathology 'with existing observations and ... theories in Anthropology, Sociology, Urban Ministry, Community and Family Therapy, Literature, Art and other disciplines'. The sheets that focused particularly on the exposition of a Christian theodicy were collected under the heading 'Studies in Constricted Confusion'. Some of these noted the lives and teaching of Ignatius (died AD 110), Augustine, Luther, Bunyan, P.T. Forsyth, S. Weil and more recent authors, all of whom stressed the significance of death and suffering in NT spirituality. The sheet I reproduce and discuss (labelled by Lake as T11) is the last of four on John of the Cross (fig. 6). Lake found John's account of spiritual progress particularly illuminating because it relates the stages of spiritual growth towards Christian maturity to the process of release from the psychological fixations (or neuroses) that are the result of repressed mental pain that had been resisted, actively and then more passively during the times when it was first endured. The aim is to draw out the relevance of this traditional teaching, showing why the fundamentals of Christian spirituality are still liberating in today's world. In this diagrammatic table of emotional and religious development, level II indicates defensive reactions, and level IV the unconscious layers of painful memory against which they react. The defences aim to control the impact of those memories on conscious life.

The lefthand column distinguishes the levels represented horizontally across the table. Then follow three pairs of columns which detail in sequence the development of defensive reactions and their successive dismantlement. The process whereby repressed emotion buried in the unconscious begins to break through the defensive barriers of previously satisfying behaviour and thought is traced by the blocks 1-15, with each pair of columns referring to one of three levels of 'breakthrough'. Through experiencing more of his mental pain in each case the person can begin to develop a more truthful relationship with God. The pain is first represented as unconscious (left of each pair) and then as becoming conscious (right of each pair). Although the process will dig deeper, at each of the first two levels a characteristic form of spirituality is found which encourages religious complacency and strengthens the resistance to further pain. Eventually the defensive spirituality that is characteristic of the schizoid personality (right hand column but one) is acknowledged to be an even stronger barrier to full dependence on God; but this too can give way that the deepest levels of past mental suffering (represented by the right hand column) may be faced again. Having done so the person will be free to grow towards maturity, without being held back by his defences.

As believing people pass through the three stages of this development their spirituality can mature so that they feel less need to disguise the truth about themselves, and so their capacity to receive from God increases. They see him more realistically and become more responsive to the Spirit's work in themselves and in other people. Through the sequence of emotional healing they find deeper fulfilment as individuals, but are also enabled to share more effectively in corporate life and meeting the spiritual needs of others from the faith position in which they stand. Surely God intends all who seek spiritual truth to be drawn to him through a healing and maturing process of this kind, in which they will come to recognise that it is the Trinity who makes it happen.

Breakthrough or breakdown

The diagram relates Lake's analysis of the neuroses to John's perception of spiritual maturing in the conviction that the three transitions belong to the necessary growth sequence that in varying ways *every human person* needs eventually to pass through. In the light of the foetal observations we can understand that traumatic memories of pre-natal and later experience now repressed, are likely to be a complex mixture in which traces of hystero-schizoid reactions will be combined with memories of less severe suffering. That realisation helps to reinforce the conviction, which is central to Christian faith, that all share a common humanity in which suffering as well as pleasure shapes our personhood and our capacity to engage in God's purpose of love. The vast range of human talents and achievements does not override this commonality but rather indicates that the variety is intended to contribute towards the eventual transformation and interdependency of individuals in community. Similarly the relation between an individual's consciousness and his unconscious suggests that everyone's multilayered personal history can be healed and integrated, making possible a quality of community life at present only glimpsed in moments of inspiration. On this view it is intelligible that everyone must undergo the three transitions although the experiences involved for each one to get through the process will be different. If we reflect on the movement that the table describes, it becomes clear that there is no lasting resting place between the three phases. Each of the first two transitions leads on to the next, and only some experience of the third sets a person free to live as God intends, within a suffering world and finally to participate in eternal life (John 6:54). Even so, in reaching the third stage of release we will still be in a position of incomplete and continuing growth, for these transitions are being worked through repeatedly as we mature.

Already in 1966 Lake was writing that those who appear as 'prone to anxiety depression', actively defended against, are also found to 'have roots in hysterical and at times, in repressed schizoid positions', and so they are grounded in earlier deprivation passively endured. Although a baby may now be strong enough to protest, in the more active style of the depressive, his ability to do so can have been weakened by the previous experience of suffering:

> acutely in silence, giving the mother the impression of an undemanding and unnaturally contented baby (p.168). [Thus with] antecedent conflicts and defeats such as these ... the infant is handicapped in any attempts he may make later to use his growing sense of personal status so as to react actively and somewhat aggressively against later frustrating circumstances. (p.170)

It follows that the distinction between more or less active and more or less passive defence mechanisms must not be allowed to disguise the fact that all the neuroses of our 'normal' human condition are rooted in the passive suffering of infants whose needs have not been adequately understood and met. For these reasons the entire sequence represented on this model (from 1-15) is relevant for all to grow into maturity 'measured by ... the full stature of Christ' (Eph 4:13). If as is most likely many readers protest that they cannot recognise in themselves, or in other people they know well, any trace of this range of mental suffering then they should consider the fact that surprise is to be expected. Those who undergo primal integration therapy continually discover to their amazement how much very strong painful emotion has lain hidden from their consciousness. They had not realised how much suffering they had been through and how violent may have been their reaction to that suffering at the time it occurred. Only when the memory is released in therapy do they regain contact with the past experience, which is usually from the earliest periods of their lives. Most often they discover they felt violent negative emotions against their mothers of which they were totally unaware. Lake wrote that the roots of each of 'the basic positions of the human ego when it has fallen away from simple human relatedness to its personal source', are for the adult

> all covered up.... There is no resemblance but only a dissemblance.... The hidden face of rage wears a mild mask. A face full of hate contorts itself into a winning smile.... Deepest of all, the wretchedness and hollowness of dread become the dungeons below the ivory tower ... [which he] builds as high as he does to be able to live well away from – the truth – his personal nothingness. (p.178)

We should also bear in mind that any person's capacity as an adult to recover and reown repressed memories of past experience is bound to be partial. Healing those memories can certainly make anyone markedly different in being more open and free as a person, but that growth can only continue through a long-term process of deepening response to God's grace. The diagram of this model traces the contours of these psychological and spiritual changes but not the gradual and subtle movement through which the Spirit inches people towards making those changes. We have to be aware of the resistance which tries to keep unconscious material locked away, and the limitations under which it can be released. Often it is only when the intense provocation of life-situations in the present begins to disturb long-lasting defence mechanisms that repressed pain starts to show itself. In those circumstances one of these major transitions could be initiated. Even then the crisis may amount to breakdown rather than breakthrough unless there is sufficient caring support for the process to go well. The very fact that John of the Cross is taken as an outstanding guide to the spiritual dimensions of personal growth makes it plain that what is happening even in the smoothest instances (and thankfully there are such) involves a series of distinctly painful changes. The details of John's early life makes this understandable.

Depressive religion is tenacious

Taking account of the resistance represented in the diagram by the shaded 'repressive layer', we have also to note a further aspect of the matter that the diagram does not represent. Not only may there be breakdown rather than healing, but the disturbance of defence mechanisms may lead only to more self-concern and diversion.

I shall now review the three transitions and trace the continuity towards healing and personal maturity, in contrast to the ways in which the process can go wrong. Considering the first transition we have to remember that the defence of denial in respect of repressed aggression (as at block 1) is extremely common and easy to practise, although it can require the expenditure of much emotional energy. Denying how extremely angry he ought to be (and was), the depressed person presents himself as socially compliant, as he once learnt it was politic to do in order to get the comfort for which he craved and which he was too often denied as a small child. Of this depressive condition Lake writes that there has been a 'fall from the unity of the personality of the infant ... a fall from the original gracious relationship to the source of being in the mother'.

> The mother is still needed as a supplier of this and that, indeed as the supplier of love. But the centre of concern has shifted from her to the place of anxiety, the point of contradiction within the self. The need to split off, repress and deny lawlessness leads to a painful, self-scrutinising adherence to the law, which, it is imagined rightly or wrongly, mother requires for acceptance. The inclination is still to lawlessness, but the obligation is to law-abiding virtue.... Lawless drives continue to rage and hurt within the split-off areas ... He is therefore never secure.... Love is no longer a simple response to the love that comes unfailingly.... The unity of personality has been lost.... Deep in the heart of every such person is a sense of guilt because the mother, whose absence caused the innocent fall, by her previous comings and her eventual return establishes her case as one who ought to be loved. (pp.165-166)

Because of the predominantly aggressive and guilt-ridden tenor of the hidden impulses, this depressive psychological position is immensely resistant to any kind of therapy, and also to conversion. Today we need to acknowledge that much church life conforms to the narrow elementary and self-justifying religious stage, marked by block 1. Thus personal growth beyond that first level of religion or spirituality, described in the second column of the diagram, is comparatively rare, and few of those who are attracted to its moralism are inclined to go beyond it. Very often therefore it is only when the deeper levels of repressed pain are strong enough to make their presence felt in consciousness, or in symptomatic disguises, that crisis threatens and unconscious processes demand attention. I must add, however, that it is not only religious conformity that provides defensive citadels for *obstinate self-sufficiency*. It can appear just as readily in the guise of a liberal humanism or of a conservative commitment to 'traditional values' in society. Fortunately liberation from those habits is possible but only when people have been dislodged from their comfortable stability, and so can start to move on towards the maturity that human nature is intended to reach. Lake's work is of theological importance in several respects but none more so than in this, for without the combination of psychological and spiritual insights the full significance of sanctification and ascetical theology will be missed. The fact that the Church has shown considerable reluctance to take this seriously is a sign of precisely the tensions represented on the diagram by blocks 1 and 2.

Divine grace is repudiated

What is at stake here is the issue which the Reformation tried to resolve by going back to the scriptural distinction between faith and works, but the outcome of that history has hardly been a clarification of justification by God's grace. Converted believers as much as pagans are still largely confused about the priority of God's activities. It is vital therefore to understand how our disordered psychological make-up resists God's call to live in dependence on his gracious presence.

As Lake's model of the dynamic cycle and its successive charts demonstrate, the basic human need for unconditional acceptance and sustenance had not been sufficiently met in the personal history implied by 1 and 2 on the diagram. Parental support had been experienced as grudgingly given, and it seemed to the infant that what was needed was extorted in response to the child's own vociferous and repeated protest. This depressive psychological position is one in which a person sees himself as undeserving and guilty, at least in relation to God, while at the same time obliged to be religiously active. The mere acknowledgement of God only promotes (at 3) that 'over-active restless, never-ending struggle, actively to purge "badness" out of the character'. Therefore the gospel is not appreciated when a sense of condemnation remains dominant in the unconscious. The believer may want to be faithful to a doctrine of salvation by faith alone but surreptitiously the need to present himself as conscientiously striving often gets the upper hand. From there religion is naturally perceived as rule-keeping, conforming to codes which emphasise moral diligence and compliance. I note here that this feature is as common in Catholicism as in Protestantism. When this interpretation of scripture appears to support this view of religion in general and of Christianity in particular, its theological errors as well as its futility in healing mental pain are able to go unnoticed so long as its adherents feel successful in projecting moral failure on to others, condemning them more severely than themselves.

Irreligious conformity as well
The positions represented by both 1 and 6 apply not only to theistic spiritualities but also to pantheistic and agnostic belief systems. For example, and again with respect to the depressive position and its characteristic defences of denial and the presenting of a false personality image (as with a mild outward demeanour disguising rage underneath), this protective behaviour can flourish as abundantly among militant humanists as among religious people. In the former case it shows itself across a wide range of scepticism and energetic social action – for example in campaigning for human or animal rights – commendable causes in themselves, but for some they become vehicles for projecting unconscious or partly conscious aggression. The defensive behaviour can appear in a multitude of religious practices, often but not always in fundamentalisms of one kind or another, for it may equally well take the form of aggressively 'liberal' theologies. In both religious and anti-religious people the common factor is rigidity and the determination to control others or at least keep them at arm's length.

In summary of this section so far, I offer now the general observation that all of us in passing through the first stage of spiritual development have either actively helped to construct, in our own hearts and in the community life that we share, a distorted view of God's goodness and of the righteous behaviour he requires, or we have been content to tell ourselves that because God must be intolerantly demanding, therefore we do not believe. Lake was saying that the distorted view of God's demands that religions often take for granted has been developed in human consciousness from the widely shared sense of being trapped in a world that is unreliable. This sense of God actually arises from the disturbed, suffering life of infants whose deepest needs were significantly left unmet or only addressed on unjust conditions. When infant lives are moulded by the buried memory of such injustice, the adults they become cannot but find themselves obliged to see God (whether they believe in him or not) as if he did conform to that false image of parenthood under which they once felt themselves to be suffering. From this kind of belief many unchristian ideas get attached to Christianity.

Interaction of God and creature

The question now is how the first healing change (from 5 to 6) can take place. Lake writes (block 5) that we 'offer to God our rage against "god". We open our lusts to him. We come to rest in Christ's work'. He has a notable passage about this which is important in relation to atonement and the meaning of God's 'wrath'. Under the heading *Vent your Rage into His Bosom* he wrote

> I came upon a letter from the saintly Robert Leighton, a Presbyterian minister for many years, and then Archbishop of Glasgow in the uneasy years of unsettlement in the Scottish Church, a letter written to a woman suffering from depression. Some people have thought that I was advocating something new and strange when I urged depressed people to let God carry the destructive burden of their rage upon Himself, crucified.... I seem to remember that Luther's spiritual director pointed out to him that he was full of rage against God and that he should show it. The Archbishop, writing in the centuries between Luther's time and ours, gives the same counsel.
>
> As a father pities his child when it is sick ... though it even utter reproachful words against himself, shall not our dearest Father both forgive and pity those thoughts in any child of His, that arise not from any wilful hatred of Him, but are kindled in hell within them? ... Thus, or in whatever frame your soul shall be carried to vent itself into His bosom, be sure your words ... shall have a most powerful voice and ascend into His ear and shall return to you with messages of peace and love in due time. (pp.368-369)

In this Lake gave us the guidance the Church and society greatly need at this time, with respect to theological understanding and to practical action. The need is for training at several levels of the Church's ministry, first to understand these concepts and then to enable selected members to put the therapeutic methods into practice. In this process the foremost necessity is to recognise that it is God who is at work. We cannot remind ourselves too frequently that God himself is present to mediate his grace through us. This gentle interaction of God the Trinity

with his creatures is at the heart of humanity's life and shows why
the incarnation is so fundamental to the whole process of creation-
redemption. But the problem that the intending disciple so often stum-
bles over is how can he discern God's presence and his influence and,
most critically, that of the risen Jesus himself.

Emotional freedom and the Resurrection

In the chapter entitled 'Talking to a Stranger' of his book *Resurrection*,[17] Rowan Williams expounded the crucial character of Christ's
resurrection in making human transformation possible. The process
that Lake was mapping in this diagram is realisable because the Spirit
is enabling people to pass through these stages within the particular
conditions of their own life-story. Usually without any awareness of it
they are being drawn into relationship with the risen Jesus. Williams
writes that 'proper proclamation of the Easter gospel' points 'to a
hidden and elusive Christ with whom we can never simply and un-
conditionally identify', and of a 'decisive rejection of ... fantasies of
gratification, undifferentiated dependence ... '. This is certainly true,
but it does not mean that a child-like dependence is properly excluded.
On the contrary, as we have seen, true humanity has to grow from a
genuine experience of dependence, one that consists in the original
building base of personal relationship with God *being restored,* however
damaged it may have become. One way or another this experience of
relationship has to be slowly absorbed *before* adequate adult maturity
is secured. This is why the ministry of the gospel has always to start
with the aim of convincing the believer that he is loved before he is
judged. Williams refers to infantile fantasies that are projected by the
adult onto the private screen of his own chosen religion. Individuals
and whole congregations, when indulging such fantasies, are demanding to take over and control the relationship like the suffering infants
they once were. This is a state in which many Christian churches exist
at present, because they are often poorly led and nourished. By and
large ordained ministers have not been trained to work according to
the delicacy of the situation. On the one hand church members in
sophisticated cultures often do not want an experiential knowledge of
God through response to the Spirit, yet without that grounding their
psycho-spiritual growth cannot develop. Resolving this dilemma is a
matter of restoring confidence in the immediate closeness of God.
That Christian experience, so familiar to many African and Asian
believers, is often an embarrassment to clergy and lay people in the
West because they are cut off from a large measure of their emotional
capacity, especially in matters categorised as 'religious'. The sense

of community that they may readily respond to in the pub, in sport or the theatre they find offensive in church. On the other hand those who are comfortable with ebullient religious emotion *may* be in danger of indulging equally infantile fantasies of grandiose self-satisfaction and superiority. What is needed is a disciplined blend of emotional assurance with self-critical realism, and the recognition that in Christ the aim of spiritual life is turned away from individual possession to the fulfilment of interpersonal life centred on God.

Psychological wellbeing grounds theology
For these reasons it is vital for the Church to wake up to the situation I am discussing, if the faith is to become meaningful again in westernised communities and if the real maturity of the Christian life is to be pursued. For that to happen it becomes evident that growth in holiness can only proceed if there is that healthy rootedness in childlike dependence on God, the ground of our personal being. That phrase usefully recalls that John Robinson's *Honest to God* was popular precisely because it awakened for so many that almost familiar sense of God's immanence which conventional church life had smothered to so large a degree. So we come to the connection between this deep-rooted sense of God and his existence as Trinity. This sense begins the recognition that an individual is constituted in God as a person who is cherished. The foundational experience of God the Father that was available to him before he had any capacity for conceptual knowledge is being awakened. Infant being is completely *given,* for at that stage human beings are persons but not in the sense of being independent. Individuality was still in the process of being formed. We have seen that the process is easily disturbed by degrees of failure in the mother-infant relationship, but such deficiencies can be lessened or aggravated as the child grows. Any remaining awareness of divine goodness can be either upheld or submerged by the ethos of the family and wider community in which the individual is brought up. So only from a restored confidence that God intends the world to be a benign environment for growth does it become possible, for child, adolescent or adult to start *thinking* coherently about himself as an individual in community.

Relating to God under the compulsion of fear
How then are we to perceive the connections between people's development in rational thought about the world as created and the underlying psychology of which so much is unconscious? Understanding the diagram with this question in mind is illuminating. The left-hand

column we can say represents human experience in its natural fallen condition in relation to God *after* the primitive foundational experience at conception has been broken or obscured. Notice that only a small fraction of the column, at the top (level I), indicates where traces remain of a healthy relationship with the living God. The 'Positive Dynamic' with its drives and motivations is what the dynamic cycle pictures in its undistorted form. Lake saw this as occurring properly only in Jesus, the Word made flesh. In contrast our attention is directed to levels II to IV and the negative compulsions they involve. These are responses (level II) to less than satisfactory experiences unconsciously registered and held (level IV) in the person's memories of early and later life. What is shown at level II refers both to an individual's spirituality and to the kind of religious forms a society may develop. In describing this Lake has put great emphasis on denial, because of the intense need to compensate for the suffering and disappointment that marks human experience throughout history. God as the Source of life is sensed as partly good and partly bad. Both perceptions motivate us but the negative experiences are so prevalent in nature and in human relations that religion is largely constituted socially as a way of coping with the negativities. All religion includes features corresponding to the three aspects that are listed here at II: (a), (b) and (c).

When we come to the second and third columns we are thinking of religious development as beginning to move in a slightly less compulsive way and in a more self-critical direction. Rationality is starting to play a greater part. The prevailing sense of negativity remains but people may be moved by the Spirit to counter their fear-driven sense of guilt and of God's disfavour by a better spiritual discipline than the mechanics of denial. The need is to activate the positive dynamic which people subconsciously 'remember' from their origin. Reflection on their experience and on what they observe of human behaviour in community may lead gradually to the realisation that the natural compulsive religion of simple denial, fantasy and moralism does not meet the need. This perception and the spiritual disquiet that goes with it are healthy (blocks 3-5). The ambiguity registered by the two blocks 1 and 3 characterises the kind of Christianity that much of the Church upholds. People have begun to affirm an elementary awareness of God's grace, although their focus is still on human action, on religious remedies, as at block 6.

Disturbance leads to disclosure
The startling nature of spiritual growth has begun to show itself. When change comes eventually, it can emerge unexpectedly, under a pressure

that is far more emotional than intellectual. The underlying depression and self-condemnation may have resulted in aggressive iconoclasm or zealous innovation. That the sequence of transitions is marked by general instability is to be noted. The reformation prescriptions are unbalanced in so far as they are relying on human effort and judgement. I am referring here to the social and to the specifically religious aspects of spiritual development in communities, but at the same time to its appearance in the individual – to which the diagram refers directly. What we see very clearly in the individual is that unless there is willingness to allow buried or half buried negative emotions to surface and be integrated into the person's ongoing relationship with God, that person will not begin to mature. But if she is ready to take the risk, as it will seem to be, the benefit will eventually lead on towards the fullness of God's purpose. A more open-hearted relationship with him enables the suffering that has been uncovered to become instrumental for her spiritual growth and wellbeing. And exactly the same is the case with the reforming process within the Church's community and denominational life. The immediate outcome of reformation is never more than a stage on the way towards the spiritual renewal and missionary adequacy that God intends. The point to stress is that the whole process of life-enhancing growth (cf John 10: 10,11), for individuals and the Church, depends on the gradual opening up of the unconscious suffering.

The person's pilgrimage
I will now follow the sequence of the diagram imagining a newly awakened believer who intends to take seriously her faith as a member of the Church. Her starting point at block 1 is a position in which, however negative, indifferent, fearful or uncertain her previous feelings and ideas about God may have been, she is making a deliberate effort to be definite. There is a conviction that after all God is good, and this conviction is being upheld in the believer's determination to prove that her belief is right by the way she is energetically pursuing a path of moral rectitude and goodwill to others. Whatever emotions there are to contradict this position (represented below the bold line) are largely but usually not totally unconscious. The believer in this position understands herself to be keeping faith with what she knows of God's fatherly goodness. However as time goes on that form of religious devotion will prove to be less satisfying than the believer was led to understand, or assume. If and when she is plagued by doubts or with emotional misgivings which arise from the blocked or partly blocked-off rage, anxiety, lust and despair, there will come

a point when she finds herself being moved into a different position (represented by block 3). Here there is pressure, which hopefully she will be honest enough to acknowledge; a pressure to admit that the 'badness' which in her unconverted days she could blame on God, or his world, is somehow part of her own make-up as well those of other people (block 5). If she recognises something of this, the Holy Spirit will give her, when she is willing, the grace to release those negative feelings, as explained earlier, directing them into God himself.

The second transition
The outcome of that first transition into spiritual realism is that the person will be found positioned (as in 6) such that she is now obliged to exercise her will actively in order to make critical decisions about her life-style. There has been a first measure of conversion. Still it should be kept in mind that although her church life in this fresh place may be more self-critical and therefore more perceptive than before, it should not go on indefinitely in this tenor. The second transition comes into prospect when that first stage of eager and energetic church life is seen to be characteristically more focused on human action, ideas and interpretations than on God himself. This realisation may be forced on the believer because that form of Christian spirituality now leaves her once more unsatisfied, even tempted to despair of the Church, or to turn to a secular enthusiasm. There is, of course, no certainty that any of this will happen, since the first settled religious position may remain highly resistant to questioning, but prompted by the Spirit she may recognise that the Father is not being honoured and that she remains starved of what God promises in Christ. If so, she will need to exercise a deeper self-criticism, and be ready to learn an unaccustomed passivity by depending on the Spirit's strength to 'reach down' and to 're-own' her own compulsive attachment to the kind of religious practice that she has been following. She comes at this point to perceive her behaviour as unreal and immature because other negative subconscious and unconscious memory traces are beginning to break through into awareness in some way or another (9). It is likely that her conscious knowledge of Jesus' suffering and the centrality of the cross in Christian belief will have been helping to bring on this crisis, and if all goes well she will admit that there is nothing for it but to trust the Spirit of Christ to enable her to endure in her own circumstances some little part of what Christ suffered on behalf of all in loneliness, emptiness and dereliction.

The Christian is being invited to face the fact that NT Christianity is *very far* from being a relationship with the Father which can be truthfully represented and lived straightforwardly, in a way that can be made consistent with the culture of 'normal' life. Her previous church practice may have been a compromise with the assumptions of modern individualism to such an extent that conversion and the new life in Christ had in some way to be fitted into those assumptions instead of turning them around. It is a practice of Christianity which leaves the Church too readily as a happy company of those who have chosen some sort of comfortable and over-simple version of the faith. In that way people can be content, as many are, with a basically private spirituality, which stops short before there is any willing encounter with the mental pain to which the 'reaching down' from 8 to 9 refers. Once we take the plunge of being serious in the Christian way (as at this mid-point of the diagram), however, we dare not turn back without making our crisis worse. At this juncture we have to look to God as he is in Christ.

Beginning again: endless responsiveness

In the chapter I referred to earlier, Rowan Williams was pointing to one of the strange features of the resurrection narratives being 'the otherness, the unrecognizability of the risen Jesus'.

> Three major stories (Luke's Emmaus episode, John's account of Mary Magdalene at the tomb, and the 'Galilean fantasia' which concludes his Gospel) underline the point.... [I]t is hard to deny that ... the encounter with the risen Jesus began as an encounter with a stranger.... [I]t is one of the most important pieces of evidence counting against the suggestion that the risen Christ is to be seen as a projection of the community's own belief.... Jesus condemns the inadequacy of their earlier understanding: he is not what they have thought him to be, and thus they must 'learn' him afresh, as from the beginning. Once again, John crystallizes this ... by presenting the disciples in their fishing boats, as if they had never known Jesus: they must begin again. (p.83)

Christians may betray the faith by too shallow an idea of resurrection. So the challenge of these lines is to allow the scriptures to deepen our relation with the risen Christ. Christianity is always being rejected because it is misunderstood on the assumption that it is naïve. Often the critics are right in this because that is the impression that Christians communicate. Williams points out that we may avoid discipleship by 'struggling to interpret *his* story in the light of *ours*'; instead we are 'to interpret ourselves in the light of the Easter event' (p 84). The first disciples had to begin again to get to know him, and so do we – when we think we already understand him.

> The Lordship of Jesus is not constructed from a recollection but experienced in the encounter with one who evades our surface desires and our surface needs. [He] will not subserve the requirements of our private dramas.... Christ is with the believer and beyond the believer at the same time: we are in Christ and yet face to face with him.... Jesus grants us a solid identity, yet refuses us the power to 'seal' or finalize it, and obliges us to realize that this identity only exists in an endless responsiveness to new encounters with him in the world of unredeemed relationships....

So Christ demands that we give up 'imagining that we have finished the making of ourselves, that we have done with desire and restlessness'. (pp.83-84)

Recognising the risen Christ
Williams was noting the critical point where in practice the distinctive character of Christian believing is being tested as people grow spiritually. Do we realise that the Church does not just stand on the conviction that the NT is a reliable record of Jesus being raised to new and eternal life, but rather that the risen, ascended Jesus is present, active and recognisable today?

Before coming to the last columns of the diagram I add a further quotation from Williams' *Resurrection*, as commentary on Lake's work, and also in leading towards my closing chapter on God's holiness.

> We rightly shrink from a hasty response to Easter morning which blandly says that Jesus, our God-in-Jesus, has triumphed over pain and death, has done with it, so that what seemed tragic is really not so.... So far from pain and death being bypassed or 'transcended' in the usual sense, they are presented to us as now interwoven with God as we encounter him.... [T]he question of my 'salvation and significance' becomes a question about my response to the fact of pain generated by violence. To discover, to grow into, a reconciled identity for myself, I must go by way of this response.... [T]he problem of suffering is never going to leave us alone.... In the resurrection, it is presented as the 'unconditional', the universal question. I shall not be

asked at the last day whether I have 'suffered well', I shall
be asked how far I have allowed Christ's questioning to
transform my life into compassion, and how far, therefore,
I have allowed compassion in me to transform the world....
Understood thus, the resurrection becomes the moment
which overthrows an idolatrous view of grace, idolatrous
because it sees grace as serving *my* needs as I define them.
(pp.86-88)

The deepest transition

Looking at the two right-hand columns of the diagram I am conscious of no longer being 'thoroughly at home' with the experiences
that Lake and saints like John of the Cross are dealing with. Although
I know that I have something of the schizoid personality in me, being
someone who can endure a small amount of being alone without distress, and who is prone to keep his distance in company, I do not
know what it is like to come close to dread. I can sense enough of the
schizoid position to empathise, but am certain I never came anywhere
near the transmarginal stress which Lake defines or the ontological
affliction to which Simone Weil gives eloquent expression.

How then can I be confident that everyone must pass through all
three transitions and only the completion of the third sets a person free
to live with fullest freedom and creativity? I think the reasons I have
given are sound provided we remember also that 'our' pilgrimage in
this life will remain unfinished. Nor is pilgrimage on the Christian
view, to be seen in terms of each individual's personal history only,
but that of other people as well, and so of communities and the
entire race together. In this we should keep in mind that 'universal
question' of compassion. Here we see why empathy matters so much
and why the role of the Church in developing this capacity is one
of her particular contributions. The clinical theology movement has
recognised this since its foundation; and its seminar work has always
shown that even those who have a natural disposition for it find
that they need training and practice in how to listen and empathise
accurately.

Active-passivity in the Spirit

Earlier I used this phrase – Lake's own and distinctive of his teaching
– about how through openness to our own buried mental pain, we
learn to let God in Christ sustain us in a passive state of emotional
suffering (our own and others') so as to give attention to what would be
intolerable if our attention were fixed on our own lonely endurance of

deep distress. The difference between a breakdown and a breakthrough situation most frequently lies in there being empathetic companionship for the sufferer, although secondary factors such as good health are relevant also. Certainly the gift of divine presence in suffering – which can only be enjoyed to the extent that the sufferer has learnt to be actively passive – is of greatest significance in situations where these deepest wounds of 'paranoid fears and persecutions and schizoid detachments and revulsions' (14 on the diagram) are being faced. It is a matter of experience and frequent testimony that only with Christ's presence in the Spirit does it become possible to 'endure, in loving attention and active abandonment to God, the pain of having trusted a 'god' [the human mother or carer] who proved to be destructive' (15).

Now it is pertinent, towards the close of this chapter, to observe again the trinitarian character of God's action for human wellbeing. God's varied activities complement each other, and show the tri-personal co-ordinates of his being. Through the prayer of deliberate and learned passivity, especially as focused in eucharistic worship, Christians are called to be witnesses and intercessors in the world, affirming their confidence that God desires to act through his believing people where others see only human inadequacy.

Dethroning emotion in favour of feeling

In 1988 Rowan Williams gave the Frank Lake Memorial Lecture on the subject of *Christianity and the Ideal of Detachment*.[18] Acknowledging that spiritualities of detachment and dispassion have often distorted the Christian message, he urged that 'the ascetical tradition of Christian faith can still be retrieved.... [T]his tradition is essentially proposing not a reduction but a relaxation and enlargement of the spirit and its liberation from the melodramas of anxiety'.

> The reconstruction of our own definition of our wants and needs is fundamental to the Gospel. The crucifixion of Jesus represents the human preference for darkness over light.... In St John's language, it convicts us of the untruthfulness of our ordinary perceptions of ourselves and the world. We need to be renewed, remade, in truth, and that will occur only as we dispossess ourselves of the identities we have made for ourselves and cling to.... But this dispossession-and-reconstitution implies two other elements.... First ... what so preoccupied Augustine, the 'attractiveness' of Christ.... if dispossession is called for in order that we may see truth-fully, it is not so that we should 'see' the immaterial God

or the eternal ideas, but that we should learn to listen for and to encounter God in the life and death of Jesus.... [In consequence] the believer [comes to understand] why conversion is dispossession.

Secondly, Williams was saying that the preaching and the resurrection of Jesus

show us a God who is 'dispassionate' in that he is not deflected from his love by human failure or even by human rejection: he is causeless and measureless agape.... To surrender the struggle to master the world, and to be open to what it gives (or even imposes), to act without paralysing fear of consequences ... to be in every sense *patient* with the world of time-bound particulars ... all of this is possible only if the final nature of the reality we confront is not perceived as menacing. (p.12)

What he is saying 'comes down to a reflection on conversion and faith', provided we are prepared to see how revolutionary conversion and faith have to be according to Jesus. Jesus summons believers to be liberated from 'the melodramas of anxiety' and to live the kind of detachment which sees 'faith as a simple and comprehensive passion'. (p.13)

Early in the lecture Williams had referred to Jacob Needleman meeting Metropolitan Anthony Bloom and the latter's startling statement that we 'have to get rid of emotions ... in order to reach ... feeling'. Bloom was saying that prayer is vulnerability. 'You must be not enthusiastic, nor rejecting – but only open'.[19] Explaining what the Metropolitan was getting at Williams gives the instance of music performed.

An 'emotional' interpretation of a work of music, say, would be one in which we became more aware of the performer than of the music; but to say 'She played with great feeling' ... should be a testament to the transparency in the performance of the form and quality of the music.... Christian discipline looks towards this kind of transparency. (p.4)

What comes out as the substance of this lecture is a considerable warning against the neurotic desire to control and take for ourselves, as well as an acknowledgement of the fact that *emotion* as well as its absence can be defensive both in individuals and 'at the group level'. He takes racial prejudice as an example of situations in which people and nations who exercise imperial power can seek 'precarious security by cannibalizing the other... when claiming to be acting in love or benevolence'. Instead of prejudice and fear we must learn to abandon self-images which serve 'essentially self-bound ends'.

> Feeling, passion, vulnerability stand as the real alternatives to the passionate domination of emotive attachment. The musician who plays with feeling is giving space to what is not her own; the journalist reporting with passion is some-one who has listened hard enough to be able to speak for an experience not directly his own.

It is a message even to politics and commerce – in fact, to every area of society.

Dispossession and the Kingdom

All this is relevant to the meaning of empathy and the non-possessive, warm regard which reliable counselling and psychotherapy seek to practice, objectives shared by the Church in her wider healing and reconciling ministry.

> Our love should be love of the world *as it is* – temporal, cont-ingent, existing in the purpose of God over against us and our self-directed interest. Among modern writers, it is undoubt-edly Simone Weil who has given profoundest expression to this in her analysis of consent to the order of 'necessity'. 'To accept that [persons] should be other than the creatures of our imagination is to imitate the renunciation of God; to accept simply that they should be.... Passion [is the] renunciation of [the act of] creation transposed onto the human scale.... To put up with the discordance between imagination and fact'.... Passion here seems to mean something closely akin to the 'vulnerability' of Anthony Bloom.... Simone Weil's detachment is especially striking... because it is in no sense an effort to avoid the disturbance of the inner life by deep feeling; it is, rather, an attempt to be educated and changed by deep feeling.... [In] Simone Weil's terms, dispassion is not a strategy of disengagement, but the condition for serious involvement with the world, unfettered from the fears and projections of the ego. (pp.6-8, 11)

Thus in Bloom and in Weil dispassion is 'being redefined: instead of being the state of the soul protected from all disturbance, it has become the exposure of the self, freed from the compulsion to keep itself safe, or to keep itself in control' (p.11).

It will be appreciated that this is a considerable departure from what had become, apparently, something of a consensus among modern writers on catholic spirituality. When Frank Lake's psychological interpretation of John of the Cross first appeared (in the 1966 volume) such writers seemed to have disparaged it, yet there are now signs of a much more positive sense of common ground, as Kevin Culligan writes in *A fresh approach to St John of the Cross*:[20]

> contemplation, as John of the Cross understood it, is by nature psychotherapeutic ... because it enables us to see and feel the effects of sin and the deeply rooted, unconscious disorders present in our soul. [Freud and John] both ... see the healing of the unconscious as coming through enlightenment, in making the unconscious conscious.

The discussion fostered by writers such as Culligan, point to the hope that the interchange between theology and psychology will become yet more fruitful in the near future.

In this last section of the chapter it has appeared that the goal of spiritual healing and growth in Christ, as traced in these stages, is the individual's dispossession so that true personal freedom and increasing community in God may result. The life of the crucified and risen Jesus, into whom we have been incorporated by the Spirit, sustains us as we learn the way of dispossession. But as I have said the transitions are not negotiated just once and for all; they have to become *the groundwork for a way of living* in this world through which God works.We are all involved in all that he does because we are not saved for ourselves in separation, but in community with humanity as a whole. Hence the significance of the 'dispossession-and-reconstitution' discipline Williams described in his lecture, a discipline we can expect to be increasingly fruitful. Williams wrote in *Resurrection* that since Jesus' risen life

> embodies the paradigm of merciful reconciliation, it enables men and women to be at home with themselves and with one another as well as with God. It is in this way that the resurrection gospel speaks of the last things, of a completion of history ... the resurrection community shows humanity in its ultimate reality. (p.91)

That ultimate reality is being revealed in the small changes which appear in people's lives. The resurrection community has existed since Jesus rose, and continues to grow. It is extended when sufferers willingly re-experience what has occurred in their lives, but now do so with hearts and wills enlightened in the Spirit as they discern that God was suffering with them and also with those who caused their suffering. Members of Christ are being equipped to serve the Kingdom when they make this discovery for themselves. As they minister with growing effectiveness in the *koinonia* of the Spirit, their awareness of being part of the corporate Christ increases, and they begin to glimpse the transformed community that God is making.

The great theological importance of Lake's work is that he gives us in effect a deep trinitarian perception of what is involved in the spiritual process of justification-sanctification-transformation. It shows how the intersubjective life develops through gifts of empathy. These spring from people's lives in Christ through the Spirit, and enable them to be truthful with each other and free to live day by day as members one of another. The transitions that Lake identified mark a structure of development towards spiritual maturity that the Church's mission in the world is to facilitate. As Christians go on renegotiating these developments in their own lives, they appreciate the dynamic cycle more deeply as the life to which they have been introduced. In that cycle it is the Father who accepts and sustains us, giving us the comfort we all need; this is the input phase. It is then the Son in whom we are called to live the output phase, being enabled to do so in a more and more disciplined way, as Williams explains. Thirdly it is the Spirit who facilitates our passive reception of both these two forms of divine self-giving, enabling us to respond to the triune action and to live out God's creativity actively in the world.

Empathy, we might say is the divine principle of relationship that Christ lived and died to nourish in all humankind. In the light of that perception we see that Lake was exploring a fundamental feature of human functioning and of NT theology. What becomes apparent is that through the empathy of his self-giving in Christ God redeems his children into the community of his Kingdom. That community flourishes because the Spirit enables her members to relate to each other and to all people with the empathy of Christ Jesus. In this perspective the reconciliation of sufferers is not to be separated from the redemption of sinners, for the two are necessarily bound together. The former is the condition on which the latter can be realised. Unless we choose to share actively in God's care for sufferers, and in particular those who suffer on account of our sin, our own repentance and redemption will not be genuine. That is why, in the rest of the book, I shall give much attention to the missionary and intercessory nature of the Eucharist, for it is in the formation of Christian congregations as agents of vicarious, Christ-centered worship that the world's life can be changed. Here we discover that the Church's worship embodies God's mission.

Appendix to Chapter Two
The 'transpersonal' self

I draw attention to the recent publication of *Spirituality and Psychiatry* edited by Chris Cook, Andrew Powell and Andrew Sims; London; Royal College of Psychiatrists Publications 2009. This is a wide-ranging collection of essays reporting research, and drawing tentative conclusions, in the field of spiritual belief and practice as it impinges increasingly on the professional attention of psychiatrists. Christians and all believers will find it interesting and often wise in respect of healing, forgiveness, prayer, pastoral care, community life and the connectedness of humanity in the natural world as a whole. The chapter on "Neuroscience of the spirit" by Peter Fenwick is particularly illuminating in noting experiments which suggest "that consciousness is a field" and that individuals meditating "enhance the field effect". Similarly "mind may not be limited to the brain" (pp.180, 186).

That highly significant result is relevant to the discussion presented by Tim Read and Nicki Crowley on "The transpersonal perspective". I refer to this in the context of my own argument for personhood being understood as an intersubjective phenomenon. If my case, for the subject self being always in harness with the person's extended personhood, is moving in the right direction there may be a problem in using the term 'transpersonal'. While it is good to "bring together the Eastern and Western concepts of mind" (p.221) in order to see where they support the search for a reliable account of the human spirit, it is vital, in my view, to uncover what personal and transpersonal mean in relation to "levels of consciousness".

Powell and MacKenna refer to the universal realm of "superconsciousness" and the "transpersonal self", in which we "recognise that ultimately we are all one", a realm "characterised by social cooperation, altruistic love and a transpersonal vision of spiritual evolution". This is similar to what I have represented as God's purpose in creating 'a community of communities' yet the latter cannot be conceived as "composed purely of consciousness and will" (p.112). Similarly Read and Cowley speak of "all sentient life, experience and awareness only being possible through activating the life force that flows from this Source" (p.230). If so in searching across the spiritual traditions the aim must surely be to clarify what is intended by the term transpersonal. Does it simply mean beyond the individual person, and if so what kind of participation in that 'beyond' is being suggested? Even if judged only by the material gathered in these chapters the evidence suggests that the individual has to become in some degree passive in order to move into this wider realm. We know this already from both eastern and western traditions; that it is not so much a matter of the individual 'activating the life force' but rather of being activated. Thus it is the Source who plays the major part. In saying this I stress that the Source is personal, that the transpersonal is not beyond the personal but the accentuation of it. The warning I make, therefore, is that while it is good and necessary to welcome the perception that human consciousness is of primary significance and will come to be enjoyed "independently of the brain" (p.221), it is inadvisable to encourage the use of the word transpersonal in connection with spirituality because it can obscure the intersubjective character of human nature and human potential, by reducing it to the sub-personal. It is evident that in the present climate it is easy to over-emphasise the phenomena of expanding states of consciousness and to forget the other essential ingredients of personhood that the word spirit embraces.

Chapter Three
Identifying the Spirit's coaxing

A. Judgement and liberation in one action

The first section of this chapter aims to draw out some practical implications for church reform that arise from the psychology discussed in chapter 2. I start with a contrast between two books, *The Cost of Certainty* by Jeremy Young[1] and *The Sacred Neuron* by John Bowker.[2] Having been a parish priest, Jeremy Young is now a family therapist. His book covers much of the psychological ground that I do, but his treatment is heavily influenced by Jungian theory in a way that I think weakens the theology of his thesis. I share his concern about the serious abuses of Christian faith to which he draws attention but fear his approach to reforming the Church abandons the distinctive role for which the Christian community exists. I argue that it is in the congregation and its smaller groups that emotional healing and growth towards Christian maturity in faith and mission is best developed, although it must be supplemented in other settings when therapy is needed.

Young's argument arises out of experiencing painful consequences of going through the first stage of his developing faith in the setting of a conservative evangelical congregation. His conversion occurred at the age of sixteen during a school trip to see the Oberammergau Passion Play.

> I experienced an overwhelming sense of the presence of Christ and was convinced that I had found the meaning of life. When I returned home I made my family's life miserable by trying to convert them. Unaccountably, they did not immediately see the light and become Christians. Life gradually settled into a new pattern.... The teaching which I received at my church, and at the Christian house parties that I attended, stressed God's love for us. However, we

were also told that God is holy and just and that, apart from Jesus, he could have nothing to do with us, because of our sinfulness. Holiness and sin cannot mix.... Christians who believe this account ... have to find some way of minimising or excluding from their awareness the punitive and terrifying aspect of God's character, namely, that he will condemn to eternal torment in hell those who do not accept Christ as their Saviour. (pp.8-9)

God's competence to complete his purpose

I discuss *The Cost of Certainty* at some length because it instances a series of difficulties for the would-be Christian that can be provoked on the basis of misleading teaching. What Young heard misrepresented the gospel and obliged him, as time went on, to reconstruct his faith in a way which took his theology even further from the NT original. He concluded that, instead of God's unconditional love being made clear, believers were being deceived into thinking they could receive God's forgiveness only on conditions they feared they would not be able to fulfil. His psychological studies showed what abusive complications can follow in these circumstances.

Fortunately Young did not abandon his faith as many do after such an experience, but in reaction to the contradictions of what he had been taught and under the influence of postmodern criticisms he assumed that there is a 'fundamental dualism at the heart of orthodox Christianity ... between the elect and the reprobate' (p.127). In that perspective he built up his alternative version of Christian belief, and his proposals for church reform. I believe Young is right to pay attention to the impression so often given that salvation is conditional, for unless we are convinced that God's love is truly unconditional our conversion will remain incomplete. We shall suppose that in the end it depends on us; not just in the sense that we are free to accept or turn down God's offer, but that God has no other way of drawing the world to himself than to lay down terms and conditions with which he requires us to comply. On that basis we would be confronted with a 'take it or leave it' option. That is the kind of choice people understand and sometimes prefer, but it is not the choice that the Church is commissioned to expound. What Jesus presents to the world is not like that at all. The remarkable message of the NT is that God has taken responsibility for dealing with sin and that the saving faith which the Spirit elicits is trust in God, who has already taken the decisive action in Christ and will bring it to completion through his own initiatives, worked out in people's lives

with their co-operation. Christian orthodoxy stands on the revision of
Judaic faith that we find in Jesus' teaching (contained in the gospels
and Acts). The rest of the NT supplements our understanding of that
revision, although at points makes for some confusion. Affirming the
distinctive character of God's working that we see in Jesus is critical
to the Church's mission, for we find that the ignorance and opposition
that resists the gospel can be entrenched as much in people who claim
correct religious knowledge as in those who regard all religion as a
dangerous delusion. Like Gordon Lynch's and that of so many others
who have suffered similarly, Young's story needs to be heeded and
its lessons learnt, in *every* denomination and school of thought. As
his book shows, it can be conservative catholics as well as conservative evangelicals who allow these misunderstandings to continue. In
either case the outcome for a new believer who has suffered a similar
experience is that, feeling let down by one traditional position, he
or she may find nothing better than some form of conservative
liberalism. Whether the end point is a compromise or a fresh structure of belief within the 'sea' of faith, the prospect for the people
concerned will be that they are less able to relate comfortably within
the wholeness of Christ's Body. Their authentic Christian growth in
the Spirit will have been badly disrupted.

I can readily empathise with Young's predicament without finding his prescriptions for overcoming the problems at all convincing.
In following up this criticism of Young's position and in tracing
Bowker's different approach I continue to follow Tom Wright's lead
in emphasising the teaching of Jesus as a *revision* of Israel's understanding of herself and her mission. I am entirely in agreement with
Young about the persistent failure of the Church to present the gospel
of God's unconditional love consistently and intelligibly, and on the
need to guard against distorted versions of God's dealings with sinful
humanity. But in his concern for those outside the Church he does
not explain the coherence of God's activity. He sees, for example,
a major problem in Christianity's 'covenant theology derived from
Judaism', as if the claim that salvation is for all were cancelled by the
'exclusive' claim that only those who can accept 'Christ's death as a
sacrifice for their sins will be saved' (p.12). He is right that the cross
is widely misrepresented and Christians frequently fail to bring out
the paradoxical way God works to set people free from themselves.
But the prophetic outlook of the old covenant and the apostolic gospel
of the new are emphatically at one in the belief that the privilege of
belonging to the people of God is given to those who trust God as
Abraham did for the definite purpose that through their witness the

same gift may be received by all humankind. This *recurrent* theme in Genesis, starting with 12:3, taken up in Jeremiah 4:2 and by Peter in Acts 3:23 is clearly also at the heart of Paul's message and ministry, explicitly so in Galatians 3:8. But most significantly of all it is implicitly declared by Jesus in his choice to call himself 'son of Adam'. So it is less than accurate to say that

> Christians believe that God's favour rests on them in the same way as it used to rest on the Jews and in a manner in which it does not rest on other peoples. (p.12)

Because of his unconditional love for humankind God calls a particular community to be the first to move out of paganism for the benefit of all who are still pagan. The Church's theology sees God's intention revealed in both Testaments in the light of their fulfilment in Christ. Any restatement of the Church's thinking, if it is to be genuinely orthodox (that is, a true discernment of the Spirit's leading), will seek to express the revised missionary vision that Jesus himself formed and fulfilled. Living out that revision of the Israelite tradition is the one task to which the Church is called; it comprehends all the different aspects of what it is to be Christian.

Called and accepted for mission
If that is so we must not only be bold in acknowledging the Church's past and present failures to be faithful to Jesus' reform of the covenant with Abraham's people. We must also show that under the Spirit's guidance *the biblical scriptures do make clear,* to those who are willing to use his gifts of discernment, the nature of God's judgement in Christ, the present reality of his redeeming activity and the Church's part in that activity. As I have sought to bring out, God is continually present to accept, support and enable all human beings so that they may together grow up into Christ and so fulfil their destiny. That growth and fulfilment requires all of us *to undergo judgement as much as to be healed.* Therefore much of what Young has written does call for immediate action because he is pointing to major factors in the Church's present decline.

> Instead of being equipped to discuss [theological questions, Christians] are frequently upset when anybody in authority in the Church gives anything other than the teaching with which they are familiar. They should not be blamed for this reaction; *it is the Church as an institution that is at fault for failing to educate its members....* The last thing [many

> churchgoers] want is any sort of challenge to the status quo,
> let alone a prophetic voice.... People will accept a challenge
> to do better ... or even the denunciations of their sinfulness in
> general terms, provided the challenge and that denunciation
> do not question the structure of their moral outlook, their
> political convictions or their understanding of what it means
> to be a Christian. (pp.49-53)

This observation is greatly needed, so I want to emphasise the value
of what Young has written, especially with respect to the problem of
personal rejection and condemnation. Affirming the baby's variable
sense of personal identity, as I have done, he says that the adult may
struggle to keep a secure sense of being. For 'it takes a great deal of
emotional energy to preserve a false self... but for many people this is
the only way to survive emotionally' (p.80-81). Because of feelings of
rejection and inadequacy carried from infancy, any believer accused
of being different for whatever reason may suppose other people's
animosity shows that he is guilty on moral and religious grounds.
All he may feel able to do by way of protest is to reject or radically
amend his understanding of the faith itself. But this does not heal the
original sense of condemnation. So Young takes up James Alison's
plaintive cry as a gay Christian.

> At root, I myself believed that God was on the side of
> ecclesiastical violence directed at gay people and couldn't
> believe that God loves us just as we are. The profound 'do
> not be' which the social and ecclesiastical voice speaks to
> us...was rooted in my own being, so that, *au fond*, I felt
> myself damned.[3]

This kind of predicament helps to explain the remarkably strong and
lasting aversion many believers nurse towards the Church's institutional life, thereby failing to live as active members.

Tension between acceptance and judgement

Against this background Young attributes the tension between God's
acceptance and God's judgement which had been so painful for him
to a dualism imposed by the religious pride and possessiveness of
the Church to keep ordinary believers in subordination. Under orthodoxy as he perceives it, the believer is necessarily victimised by the
institution in that the Church claims for herself the authority and
superiority of God over against sinful humanity. Such a distortion
of the NT is certainly harmful, but instead the message is that God

himself has resolved the tension by entering the human situation to bear the pain of all who suffer it. Believers are not to hold power over others. Nor does Christianity privilege a source of spiritual knowledge which is mediated through 'the finite and conditional world of ordinary human experience' (p.134). While I agree that Christians often attribute to God their own desire to coerce others, and also that this misuse of the concept of revelation has been persistent in Christianity, doing much harm, I am unhappy with the argument that there are two sources of knowledge and that this justifies the development of 'A Spirituality of Uncertainty' (the title of his closing chapter). By using the notion of duality I have sought to show that Christians can avoid making a sharp 'distinction between the visible tangible created realm and the hidden intangible realm of the divine mystery', for God acts from within his created world.

Two faculties of knowledge in one world

On the distinctly Christian view, the world of present experience yields knowledge both of what is visible and tangible, and also of what is intangible and mysterious. Consequently there are not two different sources of human knowledge. It is the one 'world of ordinary human experience' through which God makes himself known. Certainly it is true to say that there are two faculties of human knowing, but it would be a mistake to see these as belonging to separate 'realms'. I am referring on the one hand to the knowing which is mediated chiefly through the physical senses, and on the other to the knowing that involves the faculties of personal spirit and intuition. Both of them belong to the ordinary condition of the human being, and while people live in their physical bodies they use the two faculties within the compass of a brain-dependent mind.

Human fear overcome by divine Presence

I emphasised in chapter 2 that various forms of fear and anxiety are the driving force underlying defence mechanisms, and similarly Young shows that drive to be at work in alienating aspects of church life. Most frequently it is the fear of other people and the repressed memory of feared situations, at work in the unconscious, which sustain the defensive behaviour. The unconscious memory of early anxieties, of the oppressive presence of those who caused pain in the distant past, can maintain in the adult certain habits of personal disposition and response to people, and these are often reinforced by continuing social pressures, religious as well as secular. Early established habits may be followed in the present when situations occur which seem to that adult, in her unconscious mind, to be threatening in the ways that caused distress in infancy. This rule of fear provoked from the unconscious results in dysfunctional relationships and rigid life-styles. Where they have come to prevail in the Church they may affect worship, doctrinal teaching and moral attitude adversely, and can lead to practices that are often explicitly contrary to God's will as expressed by Jesus. I agree with Young that where church members feel forced to conform to a system of belief that should not be questioned, this will do nothing to help anyone understand what God is like. The suggestion that the Church is meant to be an agent of God's coercion, however mild, will just strengthen the defence mechanisms that are already at work, and therefore accentuate any previous underlying fear that God's love must be conditional. People who are engaged in promoting such theology have not been able to grasp what God is offering them; they still need the healing that flows from coming under the influence of God's presence. In order to release this emotional healing in the Church a congregational life needs to be built up in which careful biblical teaching on the way Jesus healed and confronted evil will go hand in hand with ministries that demonstrate the character of God's triune activity in today's circumstances.

The congregation as the place of freedom
The aim of Christian pastoral and healing ministries will always be to help people experience 'the glorious liberty of the children of God'. However that intention will appear naïve unless the teaching and practice of the Church's pastors, ordained and lay, is well grounded in the experience of their own healing and renewal in the Spirit. It is certainly true that defensive mechanisms are frequently at work in the congregational life of anxious Christianity, a situation that I discuss in chapter 4 with reference to the ministry. An intensive formation of rigid behaviours can be built up which Young refers to as 'the Christian neurosis'. Here he follows Pierre Solignac's thought in the book of that title.[4] While this is valuable it may lead to neglecting the fact that the root of disorder in the Church is the one which causes disorder in society at large: that is human nature. The danger in identifying the Church as the culprit is that it avoids this critical truth. Young argues that the tension between the desire to be accepted and the fear of rejection has been made chronic in Christianity by its doctrine of judgement. The collective force of this complex can be strengthened by teaching that reinforces the fear of divine disapproval and implants in church members the conviction that God's love is actually conditional.

How does the Church avoid falling into the state Young describes, so that Christians can live in freedom from the tension
between acceptance and judgement? I believe the answer lies in
distinguishing between the two features of God's activity, positive
and negative, which seem to give rise to the tension, and then in
recognising their necessary connection. What Young describes does
happen. It is manifestly a feature of religions generally because of
the human condition. But Christianity is unique in directing the
world's attention to the way *God is present to liberate* his human
creatures from this very tension. Young draws attention, as I have
done, to the basic human need for acceptance and to the fear of
rejection when acceptance is not experienced. He interprets the
psychology of this in terms of Jung's theory of the 'shadow', those
more hidden attributes of the personality that are not developed and
given expression, and that need to be integrated if they are not to
fester in the unconscious, perpetuating disorder. But taking a step
further Christianity can put the problem in broader perspective,
where theology guides the psychology and communicates a more
radical understanding of redemption than prevails at present. It
seems to me that at its best the Church has not failed in this regard to
the extent Young suggests. She has always known that God's acceptance and judgement go together. When they are in their right mind
all Christians know that they do not live godly lives in order to gain
God's favour. They know that they come to their worship, private
prayer, disciplines of penitence and their charitable practices, as
those who 'have passed from death to life', that any righteousness
they may enact has been effected in them by the Holy Trinity. Even
their faith has been initiated by a divine act in which they were
passive, through new birth from above. Of course we frequently fail
to live accordingly, but we know that we have nothing that we did
not receive from God (1 Cor. 4:7).

Because of this we should not let the shameful abuses that do arise
prevent us from discerning, through the often contradictory appearance of actual church life, that God is at work. The way forward is
not to make the discipline of Christian living less Christ-centred but
to define it more clearly, so that from the start it is experienced as the
way in which God exposes the religious character of much neurosis.
Human freedom is God's starting point even though it takes us into
sin. The tension between God's judgement and his acceptance is not
resolved after an interval. People are not, in God's intention, to be
brought to repentance that afterwards they may enjoy the assurance
of forgiveness. No one can be truly converted to God unless he

knows he is already a forgiven sinner, for it is forgiveness received
in the heart which is God's converting activity. This explains the
order of God's providence. His saving work is entirely conditioned
by the incarnation of the One who dies for all. Only from there can
real human change take place. This gospel the Church has always
known although she has often failed to make it evident, and therefore
her ministry must not be discounted, nor the NT message changed.
The Christian difficulty has very often been in communicating the
priority of God's grace and in helping believers to live accordingly.
There is and can be no conditionality about salvation, yet it has to
be willingly received. 'From first to last this has been the work of
God' (2 Cor 5:18 NEB). One of the great benefits of a psychological
critique in matters of theology is that it can help people see why they
find it so difficult to rest in a position in which God is leading and
has already acted to save.

The gospel heard through mental pain
How then does God use the particular events of people's lives to
bring them into faith, healing and a converted way of life? Each of
the world's religions has a distinctive response to the problem of evil
and suffering, but Christianity is remarkable in seeing that suffering
has a creative function in a more intimate way than the others do.
The apostles' sense that suffering enables us to appreciate what God
has done for us in Christ, and how he enables us to grow accordingly
in the Spirit, comes out in 1 Peter 3:18 with 4:1 and 2. The principle
of his action in the world is that he will do nothing in relation to
people that counters their freedom to act by their own volition or
under pressure from within their own unconscious. Christians can
agree with atheists that the only *exterior* constraints and interferences
people suffer are those imposed by the world of things and of other
persons. God's loving influence therefore – including the restrained
ministry of angels – flows through people as they respond and react
to him and to each other within the world's circumstances. For this
reason I shall argue for greater attention to the Church's ministry
of intercession. The human freedom to act or relate personally one
way or another within the very tight constraints of each situation is
all the room God allows himself to enable his children to discover
the purpose for which he has made them, and how he intends to
care for and lead them. It is only because people have been created
to be freely choosing as well as freely suffering in a beautiful but
disturbing world, that they share the prospect of growth towards unselfish communal love, eventually being willing to be healed of the

aggressive and possessive compulsions that can affect even the most
pacific characters. God has planted in everyone the desire to seek
him and his truth, but that desire needs to be rediscovered, exercised
and developed in community, and of course unbelief diverts it from
its proper direction. The more we are fostered in freedom and self-
esteem, the more we are able to make choices and engage in actions
that are responsive to God and contribute to the community where
we belong. If we find we are given undeserved welcome in the company of God's believing people we will be in a stronger position to
undergo the progressive transitions that were considered at the end
of chapter 2, and so enter into true freedom in relation to others and
in closeness to God.

Where then can we identify the negative, judgmental aspects of
God's activity? If it is not in the Church that we are to find it, it
must be in the pressures of worldly life; and that is precisely what
the scriptures of the Old and New covenants explicitly demonstrate.
With many whose defences are particularly strong it is only when
they are severely shocked by something of suffering, loss and limitation in the circumstances of their lives that they may be willing
to make a decision towards living in dependence, because God's
acceptance begins to look worth having. For others acceptance has
always been urgently desired, but not sought in the place where it
can be found. For all, however, making the right decision only comes
because something of God's judgement is also perceived along with
some assurance of his acceptance. And that, Christianity claims,
only happens when God is sensed to care and to be suffering with
us. Hence the significance of the cross in judgment and in grace. It
seems we go on obstinately if not checked by some sort of judgement
experience, and from this we can surmise that if God offered us only
acceptance we would not change. While our defences remain strong
divine acceptance is not appreciated. Evidently it is in situations
of suffering that a sense of judgement surfaces into consciousness,
as I indicated tat the beginning of chapter two. Then people may
open themselves to acknowledge God, but only if somehow love
stands out above judgement. Otherwise fear and self-concern keep
us withdrawn and prevent us from admitting that divine acceptance
really does matter to us. When that point comes we see our defensive
isolation is counter-productive. Often it deprives people of quality
relationships that they need most. Opportunity for healing may
come when a therapist, a spiritual companion, a caring group can
mediate God's care, guidance and grace. If all goes well it will be
a sacramental uncovering of the Creator's presence. With the pain

exposed, the person's life-situation seems precarious, yet if the right support is being offered it will appear less threatening. Whether or not the person has rejected God's initiatives at earlier times, on this occasion healing can be received and judgement bears its positive fruit (cf John 8:11). It is a slow and intermittent process and the person concerned may have little or no consciousness that God is present and active.

Embodiment the setting for suffering and change

The perspective on emotional healing I have been developing shows that God's complex creative purpose involves the entire universe. The existence of people *living together* in the highly inter-dependent biosphere we inhabit sets the scene for the great range of change in the lives of individuals and communities. A point may come when people can change quite rapidly, and at those times judgement can act like a lever. It only happens occasionally, but if events weaken a person's determination to turn away, God's closeness may touch him a little more easily, through some kind of shock, in fear, sadness, shame or even curiosity. Intense resistance to being moved by God's presence may suddenly give way to the realisation that he intends that person's wellbeing. Where there is a deep-seated fear of criticism there is likely to be strong denial and avoidance, but in other people the impression of judgement may be registered in a far more favourable light as a matter of relief, perhaps because they have been prepared for it by their upbringing. This, I suggest, is because there surfaces a deeper memory of divine goodwill, first inscribed in the origin of the person. It is relevant to note in what kind of community God's presence and will are more readily acknowledged than in others. The Church has a role to play in encouraging a climate of opinion that favours self-criticism, in contrast to organisations where moral indignation is mainly stirred up in order that blame may be projected by the supposedly innocent onto the allegedly guilty. In a community whose members have learnt to be self-aware it is easier to observe the way God acts; that he does not expect people to confess their guilt until they know his loving acceptance. This prior and unchanging disposition of God, most fully revealed in Jesus but mediated by the Spirit in endless life situations, enables people to change eventually in heart and mind. If so, it is not the spoken or written offer of forgiveness which is the starting point but the actual presence and activity of the Trinity. That creative presence of God touching us with love stimulates spiritual growth, very often in the setting of sadness and suffering.

But if people's suffering in the presence of God is the context of their awakening, then we need to recall the importance of the emotions and how they affect personal life. By their embodiment and growth as sentient creatures in community, people have a nature in which feelings and emotions as well as intellect are the raw material out of which their spiritual personhood is constituted, be it in beauty or in ugliness. Because they are acutely vulnerable, people are capable of falling into extreme depravity. That same vulnerability, however, is necessary if God's presence and love are to be discerned. As we have seen it is emotion that stirs the intellect and will, therefore human destiny for good or ill will be worked out more in the field of feeling and emotion than in the dimensions of conceptual thought. What God is working on at the heart of his creation is the fulfilment of human persons in the *koinonia* of his Spirit, and for this their involvement in physical and emotional suffering, their own or that of others, will mark the road that leads to their sharing in God's joy. This primacy of emotion in relation to the human being's capacity to discern the goodwill of others, especially God's, in a directly intuitive way, explains the significance of Jesus' words:

> I praise you, Father ... because you have hidden these things from the wise and learned, and revealed them to little children. (Matt 11:25)

Just how intimately salvation is rooted in ordinary human feeling can be shown in a multitude of examples. Here is one instance: Peter Dobbs, a bricklayer had been a person of extreme violence, willing to ambush a man and shoot him dead to satisfy another family's grudge, although he did not actually do so. By a series of encounters with Christians he reached the point of change when listening to a sermon.

> All of a sudden I had these emotions. I could feel all the stirring inside my body. I didn't know what it was and I didn't like it. Then ... it was as if somebody had literally put their hand inside my stomach, grabbed me round the spine and just pulled me up.... [Going to the front, having] never knelt before ... I knelt down and floods of tears starting coming out ... I stood up ... to get out of the Church. But as I stood it was as if Mike Tyson had hit me ... I went down like a sack of spuds ... I felt so bad in myself as a human being.... For the first time in my life I felt sorry ... I felt pain, sadness happiness – emotions I never knew I had.[5]

Whether the change is violent as in this case or barely noticeable at the time, it is mediated from within the person, on the initiatives of the Spirit. Whatever shape it takes at the start, conversion and growth should eventually involve the whole complex of feeling and emotion of which the body is capable.

Conversion instigates a change of ownership and life
As we develop as persons through childhood, adolescence and early adult life our energy is consumed in, and our appetites are focused on, the various projects over which we can have control in the environment. For the majority of people, especially in the present technological age, total preoccupation with the activities of 'this world' is likely to remain throughout their lives. But for many there will also be dimensions of spiritual desire and curiosity that are awakened in childhood or adolescence, often waning with time before being stimulated afresh, if it all goes well, in the second half of life. This perspective explains why spirituality is generally seen as an obscure if not fanciful and marginal area, and also why it can take so long before faith in Christ grows strongly.

Although God begins and continues a person's spiritual growth by awakening and deepening the sense of his love, he intends to enable the person to recognise and confess the common condition of sinfulness, for without that perception of divine holiness conversion will not go deep enough. That turning to God has to deepen over time, as the implications of depending on him gradually dawn. Shallow to start with, conversion rarely follows its proper course smoothly since the believer may be held back, outwardly by the prevailing culture and inwardly by his own anxieties. While all people, believers and unbelievers alike, share in the disordered and condemned state of the world as it is, the paradox is that every one of us has been embraced on the cross. Christ has taken us in God's intention to a destination we cannot yet conceive. Instead of condemnation, God has offered us unconditional acceptance, which we may receive by identifying ourselves with Jesus who has identified himself with us in his total self-giving. When this is perceived believers are able, sooner or later, to abandon ownership over their lives – and over their church structures – and allow the Spirit to enliven their response to Jesus and the Father. They can realise that they died when Jesus died and so are liberated to live in Christ (2 Corinthians 5:14,15). This awareness takes time to become a settled conviction, but as it does so the Christian will be growing. His concern after conversion will be to serve and witness in the world, but the will to do so should become more deeply focused on Christ in the Church's worship and intercession, for it is from there, chiefly at the Eucharist, that mission out into the world is best resourced. Here psychological wisdom is most needed in the parish situation, where pastors need to be able to perceive what is holding people back from faith and ministry.

Doctrines that divide rather than heal

It is important then for the Church to recognise the danger of her strange-seeming doctrines being taught in an alien, impersonal way that is not sufficiently grounded in the reconciling gift that we are given in Christ. Doctrinal belief can become a religious possession that separates believers from the rest of humanity instead of being the deeper bond which is intended to break down barriers to human community. It is remarkable that when conversion sets the Christian free to live openly with others, whatever their spiritual state, it does so because those who have accepted Christ as Saviour have good reason to know themselves as fellow-sinners, contaminated with the same inherited disposition to betray each other and the One who created them. Where local congregations perceive that by dying for the ungodly, Jesus makes the Kingdom present, *and live with their neighbours accordingly,* there the mission will succeed. We shall see in section D of this chapter how Bonhoeffer was working on this theme.

In Mike Higton's study of Rowan William's theology *Difficult Gospel* (2004),[6] he devotes the first chapter to what Williams calls God's 'disarming acceptance'. Higton's discussion draws out the fact that God takes believers along the route which Jesus has pioneered, by uniting them with his actual historical life, his 'flesh'. Accordingly God has said, 'This is *my* work, *my* life: what is done in Jesus is what I do, now and always' (*Resurrection* p.55). That work is the healing which will increasingly occupy the world's time. It is a healing, writes Higton,

> worked out only in constantly repeated encounter with Jesus, as his disarming acceptance is repeatedly heard afresh and its meaning discovered in deeper areas of our lives, new areas of our world.... Because Jesus is alive, the gospel of his love is not in our control; it is not in anyone's control but his own.... Christians become carriers of the acceptance and the judgement that they have encountered in Jesus, not as people who live fully the gracious acceptance ... but as

> those who point continually away from themselves and
> towards the living one in whom they trust. (pp.29, 31-33)

Williams' account of Christianity can properly be called difficult not
because of his erudite exposition but because it does not avoid any of
the harsh condemnation to which Christ's death commits the whole
family of humankind without exception. The cross which declares
our acceptance and our judgement cannot heal us unless we accept
being identified with the crucified Jesus.

> Williams is painfully aware of the many ways in which we
> dilute the gospel, trying to make it more palatable. We do
> not... wish to live with the implications of a loving accep-
> tance so total, and so universal; we do not wish to see our
> defences and achievements bypassed and rendered irrele-
> vant; we do not wish to be shown up as fearful and deceitful.
> We coat even the cross in sugar.... (p.35)

The need for fresh teaching and realism
If that is true of the state the Church is in, as it is in large measure,
we should not let believers or unbelievers suppose that the situation
is surprising or discouraging. As Christians we must expect to find
the Church imperfect and sometimes recalcitrant. The NT clearly
indicates that God will go on rebuking, correcting and developing his
people as they will always be in need of reform. In particular God's
discipline is needed to guard against clinging to past practices without question and without willingness to listen to the Spirit alongside
other believers.

The fresh teaching is needed as much for those who have long
established roots in church life as for those more recently converted.
For the drive to adopt ideas and practices uncritically can be immensely strong when they are assumed to belong to a newly discovered
faith, and in situations where faith is part of a traditional culture
shared from childhood or early adult life. When a person is converted
it is not only the divine word which is seized on, but in all probability
also a number of the presuppositions that have been accepted in the
milieu where the conversion occurred. These can be assumed to have
a validity that the converting experience authenticates. Therefore the
way we allow the Spirit to lead us in presenting the message should
make it as easy as possible for both new believers and established members of congregations to understand the extent to which *the gospel
subverts the mind-set and assumptions* in which people's lives have
become settled. The gospel involves counter-cultural implications

not just in secular areas of life but also in the Church because God requires his people in every generation to examine inherited ideas and practices, discriminating between the wheat and the chaff that the right reforms may be chosen. It is not only the morals and lifestyle of a person's community which are challenged, but also much of the broader thinking that is taken for granted because it is part of the historical complex in which a community has developed. The lessons of Christian missions in the 19th and 20th centuries have not been well learnt if Church members are not being taught how to discern what in the culture of any society is to be honoured and only gently modified, and what has to be questioned and perhaps uprooted. The challenge in Britain and elsewhere is to recognise whether attitudes, which are deeply rooted in prevailing social custom, need changing, especially where they may have been absorbed into the accustomed way ordained and lay office-holders in the Church have learnt to do their work. For example Christians may engage in regular rituals of general confession, and even sacramental confession, yet when they find themselves confronted by the need to admit failures and faults openly they may be reluctant to do so.

Witnessing to God in the present climate
Lake had a good deal to say on this subject that is akin to the non-religious Christianity which Bonhoeffer was calling for: (see section D of this chapter and Mutual Caring p.68). How then are we to treat the practical issues of Christian discipline and judgement within the Church without betraying the gospel? How do we help Christians grow in faith and obedience in ways that are according to God's example and leading, 'not counting people's sins against them'? God's strategy is healing based on unconditional acceptance since he accepts people *before* they can recognise and acknowledge his judgement. The tactical order of the Church's preaching and teaching should therefore follow the same principle, although like Jonah his servants want to reverse that order. God intends to use his converted people to heal and convert the world on the basis of forgiveness already offered and reparation already made without demanding repentance in advance. But when Christians fail to rest under the shadow of the cross they show that they have not been healed themselves, that their own conversion is too shallow. In that situation the Church's mission fails because *witness* to the gospel is lacking. I am arguing that the Church should give priority to the healing of emotions and motives in the light of Jesus crucified and risen, for only in his love thus revealed can sinners perceive that they are accepted and judged at the same

time. This is not only the message needed by puzzled individuals who are being drawn to Christ in their search for the meaning of their lives; it is equally relevant in relation to the testimony and example of Christians in the presence of the unbelieving public who observe how the Church behaves.

If the debate now raging in the Anglican Communion were conducted on that basis, both believers and unbelievers would be edified. Those who sincerely believe that God has *not* prohibited certain practices (the ordination of women to be priests and bishops, and the legitimacy of same-sex unions[7]), even though they are contrary to previous traditions, are being condemned in the conviction that these practices are self-evidently godless. It is my conviction that we shall only come through this crisis with the Church strengthened and re-formed, if all concerned allow God to lead with his generosity and to reconcile those who oppose each other. Where the proponents of different views are prepared to be together in addressing the question whether these prohibitions are actually God's will, Christian faith shows that the Spirit will heal and make truth known. In looking for this to happen we look for gifts of courage and vision and also a shared willingness to have one's mind changed through the peculiar holiness of God's Trinity. That is the holiness of the One who suffers, who passively endures our gross rebelliousness and self-content, our desire to lay hands on what is his. Indeed, we have just seen an instance of such courage and vision in Bishop James Jones of Liverpool in his change of mind about homosexuality.

Clearly a theological resolution must be found to the tension between God's acceptance and judgement that all Christians can accept, but that resolution can only be built on fresh clarity about God's way that does not involve one party imposing its opinion on the others. Since God's acceptance is the bedrock of Christian living, we can trust him to make possible a disciplined life for church members and also the supervision of ministers on that foundation. But how can the Church establish that trustful discipline? I suggest that part of the answer lies in giving sufficient attention to emotional healing for all members, especially ministers. It is becoming clear that we are now in a period of theological reconciliation in which there could be a much deeper appreciation of the lessons and meaning of the sixteenth-century Reformation. Only the recognition that God is the agent of the believer's self-discipline can overcome the temptation to turn Christianity into a religious activity under human control. Scripture shows that the Church is constituted in Christ to be a fellowship of communities inclusive of *all* who confess faith in Jesus crucified and risen, and who are willing to commit themselves *to each other* to live out their allegiance to God's Trinity. Assessed in the light of modern notions of individual choice the prospect of realising such a unity seems unrealistic. But is it, if God intends to make his freedom and diversity serve the kind of unity he can give? The human capacity for closely integrated community life makes it possible for God's holiness to be discovered in *koinonia.* Turning away from the subjective focus into intersubjectivity underlies the discipline that Jesus made explicit in his teaching, his dealing with people and his entire life of self-giving in suffering, death and resurrection. See for example the parable of the younger son and his brother (Luke 15:11-31) and the parable of the vine (John 15:1-8). The form of life and ministry that Jesus was laying down for his Church in training the apostles is comprehensive and incarnational. It involves teamwork and interdependence under the Spirit's leading. For this reason it can take the work of healing, conversion and empowerment for service much further than is possible through psychotherapy alone.

A spirituality of congregational life
Accordingly it is not enough for the Church to be committed to the importance of emotional healing without recognising that this means also giving more attention to congregation and parish. Whether living in town or country, small-scale living is important if the depth of life in Christ is to be reached. Whatever other dimensions people have to their lives, all need one particular confluence of neighbours, beyond the natural family, that becomes for a while at least the relational nexus in which a person can grow spiritually. Although we can move on to other congregational settings in turn we always need one such centre. People who have come together apparently by accident, and so become neighbours, may remain indifferent to each other, but when some of them respond to one another they have the opportunity to be a meaningful community of concern for each other and for the world. Thus the human capacity to make friends with strangers provides a foundation on which a deeper community of care and prayer may be built. As I have argued, God's presence is significant everywhere, but through conversion to Christ the healing work of the Spirit develops as a function of congregational life. The congregation, with its smaller groups, supported for at least some members by the influence of other associations, is the social context in which God coaxes his children out of defensive self-chosen relationships into ones where he can further his work. Of course emotional healing can and does take place in situations beyond the believing communities,

but Christ-centred congregations, who direct their wills to God's purpose of reconciliation and restoration, provide the best setting in which healing and growth can be advanced and sustained.

Despite all the social changes, the congregation, which keeps to the spirit of parish ministry in locally based clusters as in the past, remains highly significant for today, and for a future in which society may be even more fragmented than it is now. Eclectic congregations gather the like-minded, who insist on their particular affiliation, whether 'Evangelical', 'Catholic' or 'Liberal', usually supposing that in doing so they have chosen what they understand to be the truth. In fact, homogeneity of that kind builds a shared disposition to avoid attending to God as he acts in the present, and to the reality of the world to which the congregation is sent. Therefore the Church needs to go on encouraging mixed congregations in which the plural character of a nation's population is reflected. In that setting genuine Christianity can develop, led by the Holy Spirit, and human tendencies to prejudice God's intentions are kept in check.

The Eucharist as focus of God's mission

When we perceive that the congregation is the chief setting in which God works to conform believers to his judgement and liberation, it becomes even clearer that the Eucharist was instituted as the event through which people offer themselves in prayer for the Kingdom to be realised beyond the sanctuary. Over recent decades there has been in many Anglican parishes a falling away from the vision that had begun to grow through the liturgical movement, now over a century old. The opportunity at this present juncture is to see how strongly both biblical evidence and pastoral-evangelistic need require celebration of the Eucharist to be restored to its true function.

One point at which a simple change of practice could encourage a much deeper reform concerns the title that many Anglicans commonly choose for the service. Referring to it as Holy Communion leaves the impression that communion as such is the main purpose of the sacramental meal. The benefit of receiving these gifts of the Lord's historically grounded life, becoming more aware of Christ in the fellowship and solidarity of the Body, is obviously the joyful and fruitful conclusion of the celebration. But we have to add that the function and significance of the Supper lies in the corporate action of the believing community as it meets to 'remember' the risen Christ, thereby allowing the Spirit to engage those believers in what Christ is doing in the world and intends to do more fully through them. Christians have the privilege of communion in Christ day by day, but what the Supper provides is the tangible focus of corporate prayer whereby the intercessory intentions of the congregation can be directed to the world situations that these particular disciples have on their hearts. They are engaged in a communal task, and are learning to act together, to serve and intercede as the Body of Christ. Christians have to turn from themselves as individuals to wait on God together, to seek his will and do as he does. For all believers, including ministers, there is a priority to curb their own preferences so that more intelligible and accessible ways of celebrating the liturgy can be pioneered which will touch and attract those outside the Church as well as deepen the prayer of those who are already communicants.

How then can this work of facilitating congregations be promoted? Although clergy and lay leaders are working devotedly for the benefit of potential Christians as well as church members, it seems that very often something is missing. With a sprinkling of exceptions to this observation, there appears a general deficiency which leaves many congregations uninspired. My conviction is that it lies in failure to give due attention to the agency of God's Trinity as it is focused in the liturgy of the Supper. Each member of the congregation needs to be growing in sensitivity to the presence of the risen Jesus as the One who inspires believers in unity of purpose through the Spirit. If we continue to assume that the risen Jesus is enthroned 'in heaven' praying for us – and is therefore not here – we shall be unable to take seriously that he is not only present in the world but also active. His promise to be with us always cannot be thought to exclude action. His resurrection and ascension are together the happenings that initiate other diverse events. They actually make Jesus accessible to unbelievers through the devotion of all who give their lives to him if the congregation knows that God intends their prayer, focused at the Eucharist, to be directed for the benefit of those not yet members of the Church.

The risen Christ still leading his disciples
From this realisation there flow other practical consequences for the wellbeing of the Church. As far as we can judge from the style of his leadership and the content of his teaching, Christ gave the great commission to the apostolic band as a whole, rather than to the eleven as officers. In Jesus' mind it seems that the twelve had been chosen to 'be with him' and to stand by him 'in (his) trials' (Mark 3:14,15; Luke 22:28-30). Their authority was explicitly over the powers of darkness, although this authority was being extended to all believers also. Evidently the saying about the 'two or three' who come together in

Jesus' name and 'agree about anything (they) ask for' applies to every disciple because each is called to serve his mission. To each of them he promised his presence and his Father's power (Matthew 18:19,20). Led by Peter, the apostles were certainly expected to exercise leadership but in the different way that Christ had laid down (Mark 10:38-45). Their care for all was to be from the position of serving all. Their primary role, however, was to be witnesses to him and to 'these things', the events which had culminated in the resurrection (Luke 24:48). This too is the task in which Jesus calls every Christian to share. It means that the whole focus of Christian ministry is in turning away from self to the presence of the risen and corporate Christ.

Jesus was not founding a democratic Church, but gave his community of disciples a spiritual polity for the Church to be faithful to her Christ-centred character. But is this a realistic basis for practical change today? How can those who are often stretched to capacity in leading the work be expected to wait long enough, with others, for the invisible Christ to bring them to a common mind? The temptation to make decisions by majority vote in a way that merely confirms long-established divisions must be resisted because it implicitly denies that God is present to act through his people. Although the compromises that are agreed at church meetings allow progress to be made, they leave the Church not only divided but committed to a position in which God is not trusted. So what prospect is there of moving from the present stage of progress in parish mission? Clearly most parishes are in no state to change procedures quickly and would find it hard to leave behind the unhelpful aspects of secular practice. But a change of mind-set will begin to make a difference, as many instances of reconciliation and conversion through prayerful love can demonstrate. At their best, congregations are already serving their parishes responsively and collaboratively, in ways that are designed to apply the Church's faith in the local community, following neither religious nor secular fashions. I suggest that God's call to do this arises most clearly in the context of the Church's worship, if that is not dominated by self-regarding motives (cf 1Cor 3). When in that unselfish way the Spirit is given control of the Eucharist he leads Christians to share in Christ's ministry to the wider community in empathy and intercession. The Spirit will encourage the congregation as a whole to reach the unity of vision and purpose needed to do God's will. They will come to understand that Christ's intercession 'at the Father's right hand' is not a matter of celestial geography but is intended to involve them. They will become more aware of God's holiness, and that he intends to work through them.

Wordless prayer and listening

We rightly teach people to pray as they can and not in ways that seem unnatural to them, but more than that the experience of spiritual growth shows increasingly that people do develop in stages. Christians of widely different temperaments are learning that all can enter into wordless prayer, because everyone has begun life with mother, relating pre-verbally person-to-person. This also applies to that part of listening prayer that leads to corporate decision-making and action. Not in the sense that God cannot lead at all when the Church uses other methods of administration, but that a contemplative approach in these areas can make our attention to God better than it is. If we expect Christ to make his will known even in detail, when we listen to him and to each other, benefits multiply on all sides. Many Christians today testify that this is so. In the teeth of the scepticism that has infected the Church progressively for some centuries, she is now able to recover the wisdom which takes seriously the 'knowledge' that is given in the Spirit.

Openness, courage and consent in leadership

In drawing the conclusion that I have done above, about the position of the apostles in relation to the whole community of disciples, I do not deny the authority the apostles and the ordained were held to have as leaders from the start of the Church's ministry. They were seen to have, and were expected to exercise in solidarity with the praying Church, the responsibility of acting on behalf of Christ, and in Christ on behalf of the Body. Yet the fact remains and has overriding significance: Christ intends to reign and act in and with the whole community of his Church. Evidently this can only develop through better teaching, and the practice of collaborative ministry at every level.

I have emphasised that we see on all sides that the Church is failing to communicate her faith adequately, in society at large but also within the congregations. I have been suggesting also that the reason for this lies in the over-defensive formation of the human person which is as damaging in the ordained as in other people. The way adults establish and manage their lives in this world has to be protective. None of us could cope without psychological defences, but typically people are too enclosed. The patterns in which we wrap ourselves are cultural as well as individual, as we have seen in chapter 2, and the general lines of defence are age-old. Because we are used to nothing else, we assume that the normality of human nature as we know it cannot be changed. What can now be perceived through psychological research, however, indicates that these patterns can and should be modified. We do not have to be at the mercy of the pressures which make us more defensive than we need to be. This I think is where wisdom is most needed in developing the potential of the Church as loving community, in recruiting Christian leadership for the future, and in working with others. In this respect the Church can be encouraged that psychiatrists are now realising what benefits contemplative practices have in patient care.

Mental health and an 'adult' Church
In Christian understanding mental health involves enabling children, adolescents and adults to grow in openness to each other, so that they develop healthier forms of personhood. Parish congregations have an integral part to play, because openness to God is critical in this process. Therefore lay and ordained leaders have a ministry to teach and facilitate others in learning to be aware of the spiritual needs all people have in relation to the Creator. One could say that Christian spirituality aims to bring to light humanity's intersubjective character so it becomes as familiar as the air we are given to breathe.

In his various discussions of judgement and acceptance, Rowan Williams shows how necessary it is for the Church to communicate that being secure in Christ enables believers to live in faithful awareness of God's judgement. To be passing through the fire is not to be destroyed but chastened and changed for the better. It is a process for those who are converted as well as for the unconverted world, for all are being remade and there is for believers much dismantling to be done. Conversion into Christ launches believers on a wild journey but with resources they did not have before. The 'proper proclamation of the Easter Gospel', writes Williams, represents a rejection of 'infantilism'. Explaining this, Higton continues that the call is to

> adulthood defined by gratitude and by openness to judge-ment – by God's acceptance and by God's disarming of our selfishness. It is not therefore, an adulthood that consists in ... possessing an identity that is complete ... that has left behind receiving or learning. (*Difficult Gospel* p.90)

In this section I have tried to give a broad sketch of the way the Spirit draws human beings to himself in congregations, coaxing them to recognise God's intentions and the resources they can exercise in Christ through the Spirit. We have seen that the emotional healing people need is released most markedly when God's presence with them has become intelligible and accessible through the suffering and risen Christ. So far I have considered only one of the two books named at the start of the chapter, and there remains one major aspect of Young's argument as yet only mentioned, concerning the confidence of faith. The next section will consider that and discuss it in the light of John Bowker's thesis in *The Sacred Neuron*.

B. Faith and extraordinary discoveries

The subtitle of Bowker's book is *Extraordinary New Discoveries linking Science and Religion*. It is concerned in a fresh and important way with the question of what we know of God through our engagement as human beings in the world of things.

> The recent explosion of work in the neurosciences and in neurophysiology throws much light on what happens in the human brain when it arrives at aesthetic and moral judgements. Taking that work into account, we can begin to see not only how we make the judgements that we do but also the reasons why they are related to facts independent of ourselves.... (p.37)

Bowker refers to Hume, pointing out that in his time 'it had long been assumed that rationality and emotions were divided from each other' and that 'it is the task of reason to bring the emotions or passions under control. Hume opposed this emphatically. He argued that the passions ... were indeed independent of reason, but in such a way that reason cannot enter into them, still less control them'. Bowker then comments that:

> this distinction between reason and emotion ... leads inevitably to the distinction between fact and value, between *is* and *ought*. But what has changed dramatically in recent years is our understanding of what Hume called ... 'the fabric and constitution of the human species'. The change will not lead us back to finding 'beauty' or 'goodness' as independent properties and observable facts which everyone who takes a look must see. However, it does lead in the direction of a rational and shareable understanding of the reasons why ... the vocabularies of beauty and goodness ... are not matters of subjective, or even of private, opinion only.... It is important to note that this new work ... shows that emotion and rationality are *combined* in making those judgements ... so it raises a huge question mark against the whole post-Humean, postmodernist, view that we simply add our own values on to initial perceptions in a way that must be entirely relativistic and subjective because *inter*-subjective rationality does not enter into it. (p.41)

Conducive properties

Bowker's discussion of 'Art in China and the West' conducts us into the recognition that although beauty lies in the eye of the beholder, 'a direct seeing of an object … evokes the language of satisfaction', and from that observation he then introduces the concept of 'conducive properties':

> so called because (from the underlying Latin, *duco,* I lead) they lead from the perceived object to one set of events within us rather than another, and they do this with a highly stable consistency…. (p.44)

Bowker explains how it is that, like animals, humans have the survival capacity to respond instantly to danger by a short-cut route of lower brain function, through the amygdala, while situations which call for reflection involve the thalamus and neocortex as well. Where the whole cognitive system is required

> [r]eason *and* emotion together review what is going on, so that human responses are formed from both, as we evaluate the signals from conducive properties in the objects of perception [p.46]. [E]motions don't just happen in the head: the whole body gets involved because emotions have to do with our most important moments – not just with matters of life and death, but with all the profound satisfactions and revulsions that make us human. Thus it is *people* who experience emotions, not brains, however true it is that the brains humans have are the necessary condition for humans experiencing anything. (p.48)

Importantly for religion, for art and for ethics the research and analysis that Bowker writes about seem to establish these further points that are relevant to my argument.

1. Bowker's expressions 'somatic exploration' and 'somatic exegesis' indicate that like other social aspects of human life the area of spirituality and religion involves the whole embodied life of people.

> At the level of the neurophysiology involved [conducive properties] are independent of any particular culture or tradition though … the opportunity offered by the … properties leads to vast cultural and individual differences. (pp.49-50)

2. Although these 'properties … invade the kind of creature that we are in very distinct ways'

we are not simply passive recipients ... as when a young
bird cowers at the cardboard silhouette of a hawk. We both
search for them and deliberately create them in the many
different kinds of human creativity.... (p.53)

3. What is true in the perception of value in art is also the case with
morality.

[T]he recognition of conducive properties leading to judgements of approval or disapproval is fundamental in the kind
of bodies humans have – so much so that the recognition
of what counts as good in relation to human good can be as
direct as the recognition of what counts as good in the case
of a stone wall or a fork. (p.88)

4. This means that we properly build 'bridges' between fact and
value, though not without making mistakes.

To be human ... is, in the moral respect, to be among those
who have interior knowledge of their ability to distinguish
right from wrong, better from worse, good from evil, and
who can act and judge on that basis. (p.91)

5. Drawing out the significance of this Bowker notes the kind of responsibility people have, and from this we are reminded how critical
is the care of people and community within which the Church has a
particular vocation. As we see very widely, Christians are prominent
in exercising and fostering social responsibility.

[E]ven though moral and aesthetic statements turn out to be,
like other ordinary statements, capable of being true or false
in relation to what they purport to be about, there will be no
such statements if people are not here to make them.... In
this sense, values/norms are not part of the furniture of the
world in the way trees, rivers and volcanoes are'. (pp.91-92)

About the recognition of conducive properties leading to rational and
emotional responses, Bowker makes the point that although some
people 'refuse or cannot make the connection', our involvement as
persons in moral judgement and action belongs to the natural constitution of humanity.

Moral facts are products of the will, or at least of agency ... they can be seen directly. But that does not require that
the recognition, and the evaluation of them must have the
same coercive constancy as the recognition of colour. What

is required is that there be reliability and consistency in the community of judgements (as there is), while accepting that this kind of human recognising and judging is less certain than the recognising of colour, and is thus more open to contest and change … [i]f you want to see a moral fact, look at a moral action or even a moral life, bearing in mind that no life is perfect. (p.93)

Where then is assurance?

The message of Bowker's book stands in marked contrast to Young's because it takes up such a different position with respect to confidence in God. The subtitle of *The Cost of Certainty* is 'How Religious Conviction Betrays the Human Psyche', whereas the message of *The Sacred Neuron* is that neuro-scientific advance is showing that the traditional biblical conviction has been right in its assurance that the way the human psyche works actually provides evidence of the Creator's purpose and character. Human nature in its integration of heart, mind and will is able to respond to the Creator and recognise that he is One who looks with favour on his creatures, and promises to bring them to a state of wellbeing that belongs to his own nature. The two arguments thus differ radically about what God is doing and giving in his dealings with human beings. Young's thesis denies that the Christian can have the assurance or certitude, that is certainty in the experiential sense, which according to the Church's tradition belongs to faith in God the Trinity. That faith does involve this kind of assurance because the believer experiences the Spirit enabling her to relate trustfully to the Father. As Young sees it, certainty is only sought by those not 'able to cope with the disturbing psychological effects of doubt' (p.147). He writes as if it would be wrong to hold that confidence in God is needed for wellbeing, and proper to our condition as created persons. He holds this view because

we are aware that all our convictions may be erroneous, that we know nothing for certain, and that at any time we may discover our beliefs dissolving. (p.146)

In contrast Bowker's argument demonstrates that

what is universal is the human ability to make evaluative judgements of character on the basis of conducive properties, and that is not affected by the fact that we may be mistaken (p.102). Erazim Kohak wrote … 'Were it not for humans who are able to see it, to grieve for it, and to cherish

> it, the goodness, beauty and truth of creation would remain
> wholly absorbed in the passage of time and pass with it. It is
> our calling to inscribe it into eternity'. Thus God enters into
> ethics ... as the source of value ... and ... as a real presence in
> the encounters of life. (pp.104-105)

If the Church is to come to a common mind about her mission, we have to choose which is true: is confidence in God's goodness something that belongs to our nature as persons because it is given in his presence and in the data of human experience? Or must we conclude such confidence to be either symptomatic of a psychological weakness or of an epistemological mistake? Young leaves the answer to these questions blurred, which is something an orthodox Christian cannot do.

In fact, Young's position is not as absolute as his proposals declare; he allows some ambiguity because he too wants to be able to 'show how God speaks to us through the Bible' (p.135). The only way he can conceive of this happening, however, leaves the believer isolated in private subjectivity, expressed in statements such as this.

> True knowledge of God is experiential knowledge: it is
> not attained by intellectual reflection, but only through the
> union of the soul with God through faith, hope and love....
> Even if the Bible is objectively the revealed Word of God,
> none of us can be certain that we know what the definitive
> meaning of the revelation is! (p.139-140)

This sense of resignation before inevitable uncertainty shows itself to be just as damaging as the tendencies towards fundamentalism or misplaced confidence of similar kinds. It leaves the would-be believer isolated from other persons, and with a markedly non-biblical notion of faith. In this state he may either be committed to his own privately chosen values, or be taken in by a collectively chosen ideology of what is valuable and right. Although so different, these are two positions of intellectual isolation, and fail to see that the consciousness of the human subject, when it is healed, is the reliable medium in which truth can be discerned – provided that the individual's subjectivity is not considered apart from the intersubjective arena in which it is set, and where its opinions can be tested.

A reliable theology of certitude
It is important, I am suggesting, that the Church comes to recognise corporately that fundamentalism and postmodernism are both dualistic

and individualistic, rooted in a common mistake, and motivated by a single fear – the fear of not knowing, or rather the fear that there is nothing ethical to know in the world as it is. That natural fear belongs to the subject-self who may cling like a toddler to a comfort-object because he feels alone. The biblical fundamentalist and the doctrinal traditionalist cling compulsively to a set of texts, while the postmodern believer keeps an equal hold on his own experiential isolation. There is a strong corporate component to each of these positions because those who adopt them are reinforced by others who share the same defence mechanism. But it is noticeable that their motivating drive remains private and subjective, and therefore not truly intersubjective. Instead Bowker points out that through behaviour and demeanour a person's character can gradually be perceived in community, and so we can say that the venture of faith in the Trinity is similarly open to a shared scrutiny and testing which is both rational and emotional.

It will be seen that Bowker's argument shows the relevance of a psychodynamic understanding of human nature with its emphasis on sensitivity and vulnerability. This sensitivity for inter-personal relationships and for growth towards maturity-in-community can be built on the foundation of basic trust, as people learn to contribute from their humanity in a corporately disciplined way. In this manner they discern and test what is objectively good, beautiful and true. Such inter-personal trust remains from conception to old age the foundation of wellbeing and growth; its sustenance and deepening is needed throughout psychological development. Thus Christian faith calls for a theology of certitude on which the certainties as well as the proper boundaries of faith can be understood. The stress Jesus put on faith, the characteristics of his own faith in the Father, and the way he looked for that kind of trust in those to whom he spoke, can show us what we still need today – a rational trusting that can lead to real assurance that God is actively and reliably at work.

While Young's proposal stops short of mere relativism, it is not clear about faith and so undermines the possibility of living in the way that the scriptures display and the Church has always sought to uphold. I end this section with the note that once again it is varieties of fear and disappointment in relation to personal life which disturb wellbeing, and only this emotional disturbance makes a spirituality of uncertainty seem plausible.

C. Gender theology and conversion

Elizabeth Johnson's *She Who Is*[8] enables me to put the argument I
have presented into sharper perspective at the points where it relates
to feminist theology in general. I support Johnson in advocating a
theology which starts 'not with … the "first person" of the Trinity,
but with Spirit, God's livingness subtly and powerfully abroad in
the world', and also her recognition that Christian experience begins
with the awareness of God's closeness and gentleness, although it is
somewhat disturbing to read that she introduces the word 'hostile' as
if we have reason to be suspicious of Father and Son being identified
in scripture (see her page 123).

Certainly the Church has very often presented both Father and
Son in ways that are open to grievous misunderstanding and this
has justified feminist theology in repudiating patriarchal habits, but
it is unfortunate that Johnson has not escaped from the conventional
treatment of the divine 'persons' as if they were different agents. Her
attention to the Spirit, however, has the great advantage that it takes
a step towards affirming that God's trinitarian action in the world is
the One Person's self-giving. The role of the Spirit in created persons
has to be stressed, for by his presence in the believer the Spirit is
effecting both God's parental embrace and participation in his filial
response, that these may shape the substance of the believer's life.
We have to be frank about it: God's cohesion as Trinity has never
yet been made clear enough. Moltmann stressed that God's distinct
character requires the Church to explain the three hypostaseis to be
of different 'shapes', but he did not acknowledge that they constitute
together one single personhood. Here too psychological scrutiny of
what the doctrine says makes the matter clearer. When we say that
God is Father, Son and Spirit we are acknowledging the activity of
his Spirit as his touch impinges on us in heart, mind and will in these
three different but complementary ways, for the purpose of enabling
us to live in God's Trinity. In trusting the Trinity we are allowing
the Spirit to fashion us, little by little, in the likeness of the Father's
Son, who gives himself to his Bride, the believing community, in the
koinonia of the Spirit.

A trinitarian psychology of human nature
Trinitarian doctrine as it arises from its NT roots has a two-fold
value as revelation. It reveals the character of God who is Love;
that is to say it states what is particular about God in his own eternal

and infinite being. But it is equally indispensable in enabling us to understand our own nature and the way God relates himself to us and gradually deepens our union with himself. This gift of life in God *involves human participation in God's activity* as people make response to initiatives of the Trinity, albeit in a strictly creaturely way. We can easily be misled by the notion that the Spirit binds together the Father and the Son, or *is* their relationship. Because of this it is understandable that little progress has been made in developing a coherent doctrine of the third hypostasis. The way to get out of that confusion is to be more attentive to the reality that all three hypostaseis are One God who always acts as One. What we seek to understand is not three distinct sets of relations but one complex of three eternal modes of being One divine Spirit – an understanding that is not 'modalism'. Certainly we cannot make sense of the Holy Spirit at all accurately if we treat him as some special sort of 'thing', a force, a power, even an influence. None of those words is good enough for the purpose of understanding how God works within us to make us members of Christ.

In thinking of the psychological development whereby human persons participate in God's mysterious life the emphasis is on the extraordinary exaltation of humanity made known through the incarnation. The whole cosmic process has its beginning and end in the divine Son/Daughter, the One who becomes flesh in the historic Christ Jesus, and then takes human nature into a much greater depth of communality as the corporate Christ. Inevitably Paul and his contemporaries could only see the Christ in masculine terms, but we can now see that the revelation points us beyond that limitation. It is the initially passive and inherently receptive (or feminine) nature of humanity which God has entered by the Spirit's gentle incursion of Mary's body. From that initiative of God's Spirit the life of Jesus becomes God's embodiment so that Jesus may be 'the image of the invisible God, the firstborn of all creation' in whom 'all things hold together' and also 'the head of the body, the Church' (Col.1. 15,17,18).

As a result of being able to discern God's life in Jesus, human beings are also able to recognise the three forms of God's presence – within which they themselves have the strange privilege of sharing. This human participation in God begins unconsciously but it is launched into consciousness through new birth as the person is enabled to respond with some awareness that God is present in his three-fold being.

Humanity created to be receptive

I see the most substantial value of Johnson's book to lie in the extensive way in which she identifies the many features of revelation in which divine femininity appears alongside the masculinity, and not in any mere additional or secondary sense. Not only do I support this aspect of her thesis but want to put even greater stress on the central point that God revealed in Christ requires a theology which affirms that there is nothing at all of God's sovereignty that is not entirely shaped by his mercy, his long-suffering, and his redemptive self-sacrifice. This is where her interpretation of female imagery in the scriptures and in the Church's tradition is so valuable.

There is, however, a matter of potential confusion to be cleared up at this point concerning the Spirit. If I have been right to identify divine masculinity with the Spirit why was it that in the biblical tradition God's wisdom was perceived to be female? The explanation, I think, clarifies and safeguards God's transcendence because he upholds the created order by acting entirely in it. In doing so the Spirit not only upholds but also sanctifies people from within their humanity. What Johnson describes is comprehensive: there is the responsive and vicarious life of God's Child (the 'Son'); the penetrating and enabling activities of the Holy Spirit; and the Father's embracing and upholding of his children. She also makes reference to the penetration of humankind in connection with the *Veni creator Spiritus,* in which, as I see it, the masculine Spirit is serving the feminine work of facilitating the development of interpersonal relationships through which humanity is able to serve the Kingdom in being the Body of Christ.

In penetrating the human order, God's Holy Spirit supports God's feminine activities, reflecting his Fatherly and Motherly gentleness. Because God's action is always unitary there can be no proper separation between the masculine and feminine features of his presence in the world. We are able to distinguish in our humanity what participates in God's masculinity and what in his femininity, while at the same time we see that life as a whole is structured on the Trinity. We can also say, however, that because God is love, the creation of humanity culminates in *a complexity of union which gives the feminine continual precedence over the masculine,* because the masculine serves the feminine. So I take the view that human personhood and spirituality should be regarded as in a real sense fundamentally feminine, in that people are created with the predominant capacity for receptivity that they may find their own fulfilment within God's life. Accordingly we can say that Father and Son share both gender characteristics directed in this particular way.

Thus it is on the ground of his character, marked by that feminine bias, that God gives his creatures a real participation in his own life, the life of Father and Son together as One Spirit, who is the transforming gentleness of Love. This means that the temporal impetus of human nature, showing itself day by day in its unredeemed dimensions as competitive, aggressive and self-advertising, is being disciplined and transfigured for eternity.

Standing against domination

Johnson speaks of feminist theology's critical task being to unmask the 'ruling-male-centred partiality' in Christian history. I agree this must be dismantled if the truth of the gospel is to be communicated, yet venture to doubt whether Johnson's positive approach is adequate. Like other feminist theologians she has in view 'the flourishing of all creatures', but writes as if the celebration of difference and the participation of all were a sufficient model of the divine purpose. It seems to me significant that this view has little sense of human life in God. If, as I have argued, every creature's dependence on the presence of the One who is Other than all creatures is the outstanding feature of the cosmos, and of human beings in particular, our account of ourselves has to envisage more than each one being true to his own nature. We can then recognise that the developmental process of creation has its climax in a human community of persons which can adequately embody and display the character of the triune Creator, who chooses to be at the heart of it himself.

What I have written earlier qualifies the patristic position and proposes that what the Fathers saw in terms of the several relations between the three hypostaseis may be better expressed as one of a multiple relationship in which the three encompass each other, because in their cohesion they constitute the divine being which is Love. This, I think, is where the proper significance of the co-inherence and perichoresis doctrines lie.

The human-divine relationship perceived in Christ

Besides drawing attention to the very necessary critique of patriarchy, Johnson also indicates why femininity must not be left out of our account of human nature in the way it has been for most of Christian history. Her stress on 'an intrinsic connectedness' in women's personhood is important, for she is identifying a schizoid individualism which is often characteristic of men but also of many people of both sexes in today's world. This outlook is certainly to be condemned as incompatible with the biblical faith and stands in

marked contrast to what was already being clarified in the earliest
days of the Church's life. In considerable degree the New Testament
and early Church testimony to God's non-dominating ways was
betrayed as her life and mission developed in an uncongenial world.
Feminism's protest has therefore been well justified, although perhaps not always well conducted. Building on the work of feminist
theologians and historians before her, Johnson summarises how in
later Christian history 'women were relegated to secondary status
in nature and grace', and even thought of as 'representative of evil
tendencies in the sin-prone part of the male self' (p.70). But while
I agree with her against defining leadership in narrowly masculine
terms, the way she sees women standing within the process of spiritual
growth seems to me to be significantly inaccurate and misleading. The
critical question is, *how is human identity in relation to God actually
affirmed?* In respect of women, Johnson's answer is emphatically
by self-assertion. In distinction from men, they have been realising
their identity by rejecting 'the sexism of inherited constructions of
female identity' (p.62). Misgiving about this is strengthened when her
account continues under the subtitle of *conversion.* It is not that the
political and moral struggle against sexism is not necessary. Certainly
women's courage, hope and determination is slowly accomplishing
a change 'in attitude and practice', but this is not conversion. She
acknowledges that she uses the word in a different sense, but her
distinction between ruling males and humiliated females in respect of
conversion is far from satisfactory. She supposes that the 'language
of conversion as loss of self, turning from *amor sui*' robs people
of power, and subordinates them 'to the benefit of those who rule'
(p.64). This argument, I suggest, is based on a misunderstanding of
Christianity and of the psychological barriers to real conversion.
The theological task here is to uncover the fact that if the distinctive
character of conversion is missed, a self-concern is encouraged which
can be just as damaging to human wellbeing as male sexism. Instead
NT Christianity exposes the unfashionable truth that humanity's
fulfilment is reached by way of dispossession. Accordingly there
are three aspects of conversion to be considered.

Conversion a matter of grace
First it must be acknowledged that no one can be converted except
from a position of some personal strength. We cannot surrender our
independence and give our allegiance to God, so as to be possessed
by him, unless our self-confidence is sufficiently real for it to be
surrendered. We cannot love God more than ourselves and care for

other people as we love ourselves, unless we are already secure in the knowledge of being loved. Feminists are rightly aware of their own disadvantaged position for they campaign not just from their disadvantage but from a properly strong sense of their humanity. The enslaved Israelites in Egypt could only respond to Moses' leading because of their inner assurance of being a people who ought not to have been oppressed. The word conversion does not apply to any group of people simply in being convinced that they have a just cause and deserve to be vindicated. Conversion in the Christian sense is revolutionary for all, in being concerned with the process of dispossession, whereby people learn to look away from themselves so that they may no longer centre their lives on themselves but on God. Thus conversion is something that God initiates by his self-gift, thereby facilitating repentance on the foundation of new birth. It is not something that we do for ourselves, nor is it initiated simply by our own choice. This radical movement into the converted state on God's initiatives distinguishes the non-religious Christianity towards which Bonhoeffer was being drawn. I do not mean to deny that all religions are in some measure responses to God's presence; I believe they are, but rather to point out that churches as institutions, whether on the small scale or the large, are characteristically self-driven, and to that extent hystero-schizoid and unfaithful. To the extent that this is the case, Christianity as we often find it has ceased to be the response to divine grace leading to dispossession, which is its distinctive character.

When resistances melt
A second aspect of conversion concerns the hostility that stands in its way. The divine gift in conversion builds on an already existing but largely buried sense of being loved, which will have been overlaid with negative emotions and the withdrawal of attention to the Creator's goodness. Since God never fails to respect the personal integrity of his children we can be sure that he will not convert people without their consent. So before conversion can take place God has to do something to restore the people concerned to some sense of his loving presence. What we call faith is reliance on his presence first given in each one's origin. According to the Fourth Gospel and 1 Peter, Jesus calls this restoration of access into the relationship of faith being born of the Spirit, born from above, or new birth. Being prior to conversion this new birth occurs on the initiative of the Spirit. Although it will not happen to anyone who is not already in a frame of mind to welcome this inner change, new birth is

often unrecognised as an event. In this people become conscious
that they are now inwardly free to believe; hence Jesus' answer to
puzzled Nicodemus, 'you must be born again'. Being born of the
Spirit re-starts a process of growing awareness of God.[9] With faith
enabled afresh through new birth, conversion becomes possible,
for without faith conversion has no meaning. Whether in a man
or a woman conversion is submission to God. However startling
it may or may not be it is always a matter of degree, for believers
go through many moments of conversion in the process of spiritual
growth. After one's initial conversion, however, repentance can
begin to be increasingly real, whereas without conversion it can
only be shallow, more a matter of remorse than the God-directed
change of heart that is repentance. These distinctions between
new birth, conversion and repentance, their relation to faith, and
the order in which they come, are of great importance if we are
to understand God's work of sanctification. *Experience* of God's
personhood becomes conscious when we have been born anew, and
then converted. From that point we can acknowledge who God is,
and amend our wills accordingly. The grace of God that is being
released in us reactivates the sense of divine love that once was
given but in the meanwhile has been partly or totally obscured. The
fresh experience of grace often appears unexpectedly, even with
no sense at all that it has a precedent, but my account of the baby's
personal origin (in chapter 1) explains why in reality the experience
is not entirely new.

Here we should face the question: if conversion is a divine activity
why does it appear to be relatively rare, partial, and delayed even in
those people who seem naturally disposed to believe? The answer is
in the very strong unconscious resistances, the disturbance of which
opens up our vulnerability. Resistances come from two directions; on
the one hand the pressure from buried or feared memories of pain,
and on the other the preference to hold on to forms of lifestyle shared
in community with others. Those defensive patterns of behaviour and
thought, sometimes markedly contrary to the way of Christ, are often
taken to be consistent with Christian living, and so may be tolerated
in the Church. But to live in Christ on God's terms, the human person
is invited to move on, beyond what she already knows of God's
beauty, into a maturity of relationship which can appear alarmingly
threatening to her present understanding of the faith.

It is here that the dispossessive character of Christian living comes
into view, and the need to remember the sequence of spiritual growth.
The newly born-again person, awakened to faith, will characteristically

begin to enjoy a blessedness of joy and security, and this is seen for example in the many traditional and recent hymns and worship songs that are me-centred. For many Christians this is typical of the first stage of their life in the Church, and it is likely to be long-lasting. In being led towards a deeper conversion the person will need, during that period, to be convinced that the 'loss of self' will be real but not harmful, in the sense that the person no longer has to hold on to her own independence. She does not need to claim ownership of her own life nor be particularly concerned to assert her rights. When the claim to own oneself is given up, there is the beginning of a service which is perfect freedom. Consequently there is no call for the individual to grasp her own 'power' because she has been given share in a power which belongs to the One to whom she has surrendered. It is crucial for the Church to recognise that conversion at sufficient depth does enable the believer to let go his defensive possessiveness, but it is an on-going task, involving gradual healing.

Being released from animosity

Thirdly in respect of conversion the questions arise, what is the nature of the good-enough sense of identity, of personal being, that is a sufficient base from which to respond to God? How are we to understand the way in which the marginalized and oppressed can be converted, despite being materially dispossessed and emotionally humiliated? Evidently it is difficult to answer precisely, since in the nature of the case God gives his grace in ways we cannot prescribe. But we can say from observation that poverty and deprivation do not always prevent people being open to grow in holiness. Indeed awareness of need, if it is not compulsively tied to a sense of grievance and self-pity, seems to be the proper ground on which to live in openness and receptivity towards God. Therefore conversion does not mean a repudiation of *amor sui* despite its goal in dispossession. What makes it distinctive and liberating is that the change of heart towards God will include the recognition that the Creator himself has not been instrumental in making them victims. It seems that release from bitterness is a necessary part of the change that conversion effects. When those who perceive themselves to be victims are healed and converted, they recognise at the same time that God is on their side and always has been, having chosen to be a victim himself.

D. The significance of Bonhoeffer

It was encouraging for me to discover how thoroughly Bonhoeffer had pioneered the ground I was exploring concerning human personhood and its christological character. In this section I look at his views with the help of three authors: Heinrich Ott, Harold Lockley, and Charles Marsh. In *Reclaiming Dietrich Bonhoeffer*,[10] Marsh makes clear how much Bonhoeffer's theology had in common with Karl Barth's, but went beyond it. Bonhoeffer's early study of philosophy, however, directed him to those themes of Christ's historical life and suffering extended in community which were to become central to his thinking. In his opening chapter which discusses 'Barth and Bonhoeffer on the Worldliness of Revelation', Marsh refers to the massive influence on both of them of Emmanuel Kant, whose thinking has been so dominant over modern culture, in Protestantism as well as in secular thought.

> The decisive consequence of Kant's inquiry is that God is absent from the world of phenomenal reality. Since our epistemic faculties are delimited with respect to what is empirically real... Barth tries to resolve the quandary of God's absence in experience by thinking of God as the divine subject who creates the world through his own knowing... God must be the knowing subject itself. (p.11)

This might be a way of affirming God as Spirit, but Bonhoeffer saw that it could be thought to make revelation even more problematic, and so in order to overcome that difficulty he developed the concept of collective person and of revelation made explicit in 'Christ existing as community'. Bonhoeffer's criticism is that Barth is 'unable to conceive the new being of the person [the Christian believer] as continuous with the old [as he was without faith]'.

> As a result, not only individual subjectivity but genuine community... is forfeited. Barth's conception of the new being of the person in faith terminates in a final collapse of the whole or total I.

In fact Barth in his early career was explicit about this discontinuity; he saw the Christian as

> the dissolution of the man of this world in his totality....
> [By] faith we are what we are not.[11]

In response Bonhoeffer does not question the distinction (as I do) 'between God in his triune life ... and God as he comes to us in revelation'. For Barth, Marsh writes

> humanity never comes before and to God directly, but always 'clothed under the sign and veil of other objects diff-erent from Himself' [p.31]. [Observing] that conceptions of revelation [in the Barthian perspective]... short-circuit the full reality of the world and splinter selfhood and community into discrete events of divine decision.... [Bonhoeffer] cuts right to the heart of the matter in his own disarmingly simple proposal: 'In revelation it is a question less of God's freedom on the far side of us, i.e., his eternal isolation and aseity, than his stepping-out-of-himself in his *given* Word ... having freely bound himself to historical humanity'. The event of revelation does not coerce a distinction between God's iden-tity and God's presence; Christ as community demonstrates the refiguration of both. What it means for God to be God is that Jesus Christ is the source of life together.... God's aseity is interpreted by God's promeity ... God's freely binding himself to the world in concrete community ... (p.13)

Bonhoeffer escaped from the Kantian inheritance in a way Barth did not. Bonhoeffer's critique of Barth was needed because, as Marsh puts it,

> we see Barth struggling to get beyond the 19th century and all the while remaining within its firm grasp.... [H]e so greatly overstates his protest that in avoiding the assimilation of God into the world, the world turns out to be consumed by grace.... The world is made to lie still, and silently let God be God. (p.24)

What is needed is a concept that adequately represents the way God acts in and towards the world of people.

It is striking that all manner of people do in fact act from time to time in godly ways, under the leading of the Spirit. So we must ask: can we think of faith being partly unconscious? My answer is, most assuredly we must, a view which came to be held by Bonhoeffer as much as it was by Karl Rahner. Only so can the broad range of faith and virtue make sense. If the way we represent God's presence is to be refigured because God has bound himself to historical humanity, it must be explained as his immediacy both in the corporate life of the Church and also in the unbelieving world. Otherwise the problem of continuity throughout an individual's life has not been resolved. God is truly accessible to all humankind, those who are potential as well as actual believers. He must be present to unbelievers, so that his constant accessibility can eventually be acknowledged when they are born again of the Spirit. Thus God gives to all people the status of being dependent yet free, in their rebellion and also in their faithful relationships with him. In this they have the capacity for joint-agency with God when they respond to the initiatives of the Spirit.

God reveals himself by enabling humanity to live in Christ
In the later years of the twentieth century it became common for theologians to draw back from the Church's traditional belief that humanity is the peak of God's created order. As a reaction to the horrors of contemporary moral disorders, including human misuse of other creatures, that response was not surprising, and yet it remains irrational as well as inconsistent with biblical thinking. The traditional doctrine means that by being contained within God's Trinity as crea- ted persons, made in the divine image, human beings are put in an extra dimension of closeness, of accessibility and of belonging to the Creator. Because God himself is personal, they have a special kind of affinity with him. Yet we need to stress the singleness of God's acting in creation, revelation and redemption across the whole range of his activities in the world he has made. To benefit from the full impact of the insight into God's accessibility, theology needs to be free of the old habit of giving attention to God's revealing and redeeming as if they could be understood in distinction from his creating. This also means that we have to resist the tendency to consider revelation apart from God's constant enablement of all human life in its natural condition. Dispute over whether and in what sense 'natural theology' is a proper Christian discipline is invited if revelation is isolated from the rest of God's activity. In this regard a chapter on 'Farrer's Theodicy' in *Captured by the Crucified* by William McF. Wilson and Julian N. Hart draws attention to Austin Farrer's view of that debate.[12]

> When faced with the option between either being a rational (or natural) theologian or a revealed theologian, Farrer said that he was 'hearty' enough to be both.... [He] always felt that this distinction between knowing God by way of nature and knowing God by revelation was artificial and indeed so abstract that no common believer could possibly entertain it, let alone live by it. (p.115)

Therefore it is encouraging that although Bonhoeffer had stood within the characteristic Reformation positions he was nevertheless moving steadily away from some of them, and that his teaching affirmed the fundamental oneness of God's activity in which creation, revelation and redemption are inseparable. They are inseparable from a theological perspective because of God being Trinity, but from a more experiential and epistemological viewpoint they are inseparable because God can only be known in present time, where all his activities impinge on us as one whole. We only distinguish between them by abstracting each aspect of the whole and letting the others fall away from immediate attention.

One great value in Bonhoeffer's teaching was that he observed this important fact that knowledge of God has to be realised in the present. We can learn *about things* through the evidence of past times or calculations of future time, whether of history or scientific fact, but direct knowledge of *persons* is only possible in present time. Bonhoeffer implies this in the way he spoke of knowing Christ, particularly in his early Christology lectures, referred to here by Heinrich Ott.[13]

> [I]t is very characteristic of Bonhoeffer's thought that ... he draws his picture in two main parts, the present and the historical Christ, and that in this he deliberately treated first the present Christ. Jesus as historical ... must interest us because he is now present and real. But as such he is none other than the historical ... 'Present' is to be understood in a temporal and spatial sense, *hic et nunc.* So it is part of the definition of the person.... The present-historical Christ ... is the same person as the historical Jesus of Nazareth. Were this not so ... we should have to say with St. Paul that our faith is vain and an illusion.

Three facets of a Christian understanding of humanity

In the rest of this section I wish to identify three features of Bonhoeffer's thinking that are necessary for a Christian anthropology which is both theological and psychodynamic. I have stressed earlier that each of these need the Church's attention, but it is striking that all three featured significantly in Bonhoeffer's thought. I list them now so that as I discuss his angle on them, their interrelation may be as clear as possible. Elucidating these three observations in the context of Bonhoeffer's work will in some respects recapitulate points already made but will also bring into focus aspects that have not been given much attention so far, especially the ethical character of God and the way human good comprehends much more than people's individual dimensions and achievements.

(1) People are met and maintained by God

In the world's finite conditions humankind find themselves obliged, psychologically as much as economically, to struggle antagonistically to achieve and survive at each other's expense. Yet there is another and deeper kind of obligation at work which leads people together in ways that restrain their antagonism. In that respect they are drawn to co-operate rather than to compete, responding to each other in ways that promote community. This happens on the foundation of basic trust, making it possible for the sensitivity of the infant, and then the adult, to be nourished and led towards the fuller realisation of personal potential. Certainly that good prospect is continually under threat by the competitive drives but significantly it is never over-whelmed absolutely. However fiercely the pressures to live selfishly undermine the priorities of community, where basic trust can be restored, that natural disposition to reach out to others will make for growth towards individual and corporate wellbeing. This built-in tendency in the direction of healing and peace-making maintains the strangely benign character of the Creator's purpose in defiance of intensely provocative evil which threatens to invade everything that people do.

Like Donald Mackinnon, another theologian whose thinking needs fresh attention today, Bonhoeffer perceived human receptivity and vulnerability in relation to God's providential intentions for individuals and families, and in his sense that the Creator is the pilot of history. He wrote from prison to a friend just posted to the front on 23rd January 1944, about trusting God.

> Our greatest task during these coming weeks... will be to
> trust in those hands. Whatever weakness, self-reproach and
> guilt we contribute to these events, in the events themselves
> is God.

Similarly he sees God calling the Church to acknowledge that the world situation of human society now requires a new and different missionary strategy. The Church is to help people to realise that God is not present in a separated, religious way but in the midst of secular life.

Understanding God non-religiously

In the last stages of his theological development, the theme of non-religious interpretation became central because Bonhoeffer saw ever more clearly that Christianity is God working and making himself known in the world beyond as well as in the Church. He condemns 'metaphysical' and 'individualistic' interpretations of Christianity because he sees them to be ways of presenting the faith in other-worldly terms. In contrast, God is urging us to recognise the reality of the 'this-worldly Christ'. What made the thought of non-religious Christianity significant for him was his encounter with people living without religious faith who yet behaved 'in uprightness and freedom from prejudice' whom he met 'with a deep sympathy and solidarity'. 'I often ask myself why a Christian instinct frequently draws me more to the religionless than to the religious'. Whereas 'I often shrink with religious people from speaking of God ... because the Name somehow seems to me here not to ring true ... with people who have no religion I am able on occasion to speak of God quite openly and as it were naturally'.[14]

Bonhoeffer saw that religious thinking is often of a *Deus ex machina,* the efforts of anxious people 'seeking frantically to make room for God', but for him, writes Ott

> God is not lost in the 'reality' of the world.... He is con-cerned with the reality of *God himself,* the living God, the 'wholly Other', but ... not in some asserted 'beyond' but as palpably in this world. [Preaching the gospel non-religiously begins] neither from a metaphysical assertion nor from an individualistic question of salvation, but from the fact of the revelation and of the redemption of the *world* ... in Christ.... [The revelation] shows man that he does not in his venture go out into the void, but that he *finds* something, namely, that the this-worldly Christ waits for him and comes to meet him.

The wide extent of divine revelation
Bonhoeffer, following the habit of reformation thinking, preferred to use the language of revelation and the Word with little or no reference to the Holy Spirit, but he consistently presented the meaning of revelation and of Christ as Word in a much wider sense than that which had often prevailed. For him God's self-revelation is as wide as the whole of human history and implicit in creation itself. What the Church needs to realise in the new situation that Bonhoeffer envisaged is that the New Testament speaks of the very substance of the universal life process in which we find ourselves. That breadth of perception came out in his references to God work-ing secretly.

> Bonhoeffer can describe Christ as the concealed centre of human existence, of history and of nature! ... [T]he universal

reality of Christ has always overtaken man, even before the
event of the Word meets him as a concrete event of preaching. (Ott, chapter 3 on 'Non-Religious Interpretation')

Discerning God's presence among unbelievers
It was during his imprisonment that Bonhoeffer wrote of a 'natural
piety' and 'unconscious Christianity', saying that he was 'more and
more concerned' with this thinking. Ott interprets him as saying that
there are 'ways of encountering and experiencing Christ apart from
the encounter with the *kerygma*. All real and essential experience
becomes in this way the experience of Jesus Christ as *the* real'. But
I would prefer to say that the *kerygma* is just below the surface of
ordinary life and found at the centre of worldly situations which do
not appear religious. Is this not just what Jesus was revealing in his
own teaching? In no way was he repudiating Jewish expectation
or the long history through which God had prepared the Israelite
people for the Messiah, yet the good news of its fulfilment proved
to be something far beyond what the national religion had become.
For this Messiah was bringing to light *the close presence and immediate action of Israel's Lord in their midst.* He was helping them
to recognise the reality of their faith's meaning in a form that
appeared to be in sharp contrast to what they were being taught in
the synagogue.

In faithfulness to this Bonhoeffer was teaching us to discern
God's activity in maintaining *every* human person in dependence
on the trinitarian life, even when that person is unconscious of such
maintenance (acceptance and sustenance in Lake's terms). So Bonhoeffer's attention to the universality of God's action in Christ and
his verdict on Christian religiosity is important for the Church's
mission in this age of disillusionment about traditional Christianity.
To be faithful to Christ the Church must not allow herself to remain
confined in religious practices, with so many Christians largely
ignorant of the communitarian dimension of living in Christ. But
the extent to which the believing community can in practice be
free of traditional ways of 'being church' will vary and cannot be
as simple as the prison letters might suggest. There are in fact no
signs of religion dying out, and modern spiritualities can become
as rigid as any ancient faith. While Bonhoeffer saw that religion
can be perverse and manipulative, he also saw the deeper truth that
wherever human beings are, however they behave, and whatever
they think, God is actively engaged with them for their good.
Below the surface and in every situation people are being given

the opportunity to notice God's benign presence, even when it is disguised by unhelpful forms of religious practice. Bonhoeffer recognised that the tendency, even more prevalent today, to live with 'no religion at all' – or with none of its customary forms – was itself an opportunity to discern divine grace within the reality of the world. This passage in that same letter follows immediately on the often quoted questions: 'what *is* Christianity, and indeed what *is* Christ, for us today?'

> The time when men could be told everything by means of words, whether theological or simply pious, is over, and so is the time of inwardness and conscience, which is to say the time of religion as such. We are proceeding towards a time of no religion at all: men as they are now simply cannot be religious any more. Even those who honestly describe themselves as 'religious' do not in the least act up to it.[15]

The fact that Bonhoeffer writes here of people being told 'by means of words' is particularly significant. This he sees has been the prevailing character of modern European Christianity, that is, from the Reformation onwards in being excessively verbal, a feature of religion which has surely become more and more marked. It makes the faith especially vulnerable to agnostic and atheistic criticism, for if faith is thought to be primarily about ideas to which the individual, in his almost disembodied solitariness, is invited to give or withhold his assent, it is not surprising that so many decide that it has no meaning for them. To a large extent we have lost any existential awareness of God as personal, giving structure to human nature. This loss actually shows itself in church services across the denominations, where any sense of worshipping the living God who is present can seem less and less apparent. Wherever that experience has been lost it is no wonder that a religious allegiance is thought of as something which one adopts as a private choice and through being 'told … by means of words'. This verbal emphasis and failure to recognise God's personal presence in community results in a form of devotion marked by two unhealthy features. On the one hand worship and prayer appear to be narrowed down to a private relationship with Jesus that each believer possesses for himself; and on the other, in relation to the world outside the believer's own group, the attitude of these Christians can sometimes appear rigid and unfeeling, as if their only missionary concern is to confront outsiders with 'the Word' which requires obedience. Fortunately, however, this type of Christianity is also declining.

(2) The presence of Love invites and enables

The second facet of human nature that Bonhoeffer makes clear is
also relevant to today's theological revision, because in this as in
the first facet, he was helping us to recover something at the heart
of the gospel. It was something that had fallen out of sight, or had
been so severely distorted that for very many in the institutional
Church, and even more emphatically for the majority on the fringes
of church life the claim that God is good was no longer a confident
conviction. Frequently faith had been replaced by doubt and double-
mindedness, and where that situation prevails the Church as God-
centred community dries up. Human nature does remain resilient and
so religious customs can go on, but in a self-centred way, impelled
by motives towards human achievement or simply for comfort. In
contrast we are concerned here with the reality of God being the
Trinity of Love, who holds us to himself in all circumstances, even
when outwardly we are destroying ourselves.

At the time of his imprisonment Bonhoeffer regarded his unfinished *Ethics* as his major work and he held on to the hope of
bringing it to completion. He was working on it between 1940 and
1943, and already the thought of interpreting Christian faith non-
religiously was stirring in him, but so was the intention to expound
a christology of cosmic dimensions. He was experiencing, writes
Ott, 'a terrible tension' between Christ

> who speaks to us his demand and his promise and … [the
> world's] palpable reality which surrounds us and is in our-
> selves.… This tension it is the task of the Christian to endure
> and indeed to overcome… 'in prayer and in doing justly
> among men'.

Aware of this tension, Bonhoeffer's constant concern is to present the
faith in a way that the non-religious can understand. Having this great
concern for the gospel to be made intelligible, when modern people
despise the Christian religion and have no use for the hypothesis of
God's existence, he was presenting his hearers with a proposal that
appeared to be radically new and something his contemporaries were
likely to think was contrary to the tradition. Yet we can now see that
it was affirming the New Testament more faithfully than conventional
Church teaching has allowed.

> Whoever wishes to take up the problem of a Christian
> ethic … must from the outset discard as irrelevant the two
> questions … 'How can I be good?' and 'How can I do

good?' and instead of these he must ask ... 'What is the will
of God?' This requirement is so immensely far-reaching
because it presupposes a decision with regard to the ultimate
reality ... namely the reality of God, the Creator, Reconciler
and Redeemer. What is of ultimate importance is now no
longer that I should become good, or that the condition of
the world should be made better by my action, but that the
reality of God should show itself everywhere to be the ultimate reality.[16]

Surrender to the unsurpassable reality

At the heart of Bonhoeffer's ethical thinking is his faith that we can
trustfully play our part in the world with all its distressing burdens
and problems because God has taken them upon himself in Christ,
and thereby *reconciled* the world already. His exposition of godly
or holy action is in terms of living *responsibly*: this is an important
concept for the Church.

> The responsible man ... has no principle at his disposal
> which possesses absolute validity and which he has to
> put into effect fanatically, overcoming all the resistance
> which is offered to it by reality, but he sees in the given
> situation what is necessary and what is 'right' for him to
> grasp and do.... The man who acts ideologically sees him-
> self justified in his idea; the responsible man commits his
> action into the hands of God and lives by God's grace and
> favour.... Responsible action ... precisely because it is not
> its own master ... can be sustained by an ultimate joy and
> confidence....

Bonhoeffer here was pointing the modern Church back to the character
of the NT gospel with particular reference to the nature of personhood,
to personal relationship between God and his children, and to the
kind of responsive dependency to which Jesus calls them in being his
disciples.

God reveals himself as personal goodness

In order to see this in more detail I turn now to Harold Lockley's
study *Dietrich Bonhoeffer, his* Ethics *and its value for Christian Ethics
today*,[17] which helps us to focus on what we mean by God's goodness.
It suggests that all Christians share an urgent need to make a fresh
return to the New Testament, and to look for a far more fundamental
and unitive kind of reformation than the ones which occurred in the

sixteenth and seventeenth centuries, one that we can hope may be realised in the course of the twenty-first.

> From an early stage in his academic life Bonhoeffer was
> preoccupied with the problem of authority.... [As he came
> to ordination] the responsibility of speaking an authorita-
> tive word to his congregation ... occupied his attention....
> [He was facing the] perennial problem of how to bring both
> (church members and the 'real' people ... he met outside
> the church) into an encounter with God.

In the Barcelona address of 1928 he declared

> ethical decisions cannot derive from a set of abstract or time-
> less principles, not even from the principle of love; absolute
> moral laws make for legalism and casuistry, when applied to
> situations, and have the effect of restraining freedom. (This
> passage printed in *No Rusty Swords*)

And in addressing theological students in New York in 1931 he
explained the conviction, which he shares with Barth, that God himself is the authoritative source rather than human reason, conscience
or sense of justice.

> The revelation of God in Christ is not a revelation of a
> new morality, of new ethical values, a revelation of a new
> imperative, but a revelation of a new indicative. It is not a
> new 'you ought' but 'you are'. In other words the revelation
> of God is executed not in the realm of ideas, but in the realm
> of reality. (pp.99-101)

Responding to the divine Person

What makes Bonhoeffer's own ethical exploration so important is
that, more explicitly than reformation theologians who preceded him,
he sees the need to expound the divine commandment as a particular
and personal summons which can only be heard and obeyed *because
God himself is present* to the person hearing it. The authoritative
Word of God is intimately related to the particular situation in which
God speaks to people. What is happening is within the complex
intersubjective but worldly place, a network of relationships, where
God has put those people. Lockley points out that there is in this
an 'outright rejection of Kantian transcendentalism, as well as traditional moral teaching' (p.101); 'the ethical task is not to be seen
as the attempt to live according to certain timeless principles, but as

taking on the form of Jesus Christ. He is life itself, restoring to man his true manhood as he stands before God' (p.107). Here again the response God calls for is focused by believers in their unity at the Eucharist and then enacted in the world.

As we are realising under the pressure of highly emotional controversy about moral rules, this is of far-reaching importance for the Church today, not just in communicating the faith in its fully trinitarian dimensions, but also in moving towards the restoration of the Church's institutional unity and intellectual integrity. Bonhoeffer was emphatic that those who preach and teach "must take into account the contemporary situation when articulating the commandment so that [it] is relevant and applicable to those to whom it is addressed.... Only the Word of God is the word of authority, and 'only as a concrete saying is it the Word of God to me'" (p.102). The Trinity makes himself known as the living God within intersubjective experience in the present.

The Spirit's role not affirmed

Bonhoeffer's thought was so grounded in assumptions that dominate Reformation theology that the work of the Spirit is insufficiently acknowledged by him. This was unfortunate because the substance of his changing awareness in the immediate pre-war and wartime years was actually breaking free from the limitations of that tradition. The focus in Protestantism on the concept of the divine Word had all along made it difficult for the human mind to perceive the way God communicates. Despite the benefits of *Logos* theology in the early centuries, what happened in all the later periods of European history was that the notion of objective Word came to encourage an over-emphasis on propositional revelation and, in effect, on the brain functions of the left hemisphere. As Lake put,

> it is as if the 'enlightened' left-hemispherical rationality, arrogant rather than humble in its scientific elitist yet fashionable humanism, cannot submit to the possibility of a superior vision, or to wisdom being granted to some unlettered individual on the basis of an intuitive right-hemispherical vision.[18]

So the whole Church, catholic and protestant, has now to face with renewed humility the need to return with determination to the scriptural focus on revelation in the Spirit. Of course this can only be fruitful in mutual willingness to listen to all fellow believers with openhearted penitence for past intolerance and insensitivity. However precious and authoritative the canonical texts are, they are subordinate to Christ who is the Word, and to the Spirit who communicates the Word.

The preacher and the prophet in Christ can get it wrong because they are fraily human, but they are called to listen to and be directed by the Spirit and also to submit what they believe they hear to the consensus of fellow believers in the fellowship of the worshipping community. They are to declare what they hear with confidence that God is speaking, but also with self-criticism trusting that the Spirit will eventually make good any harm they may do. A man's 'work will be shown for what it is, because the Day will bring it to light. It will be revealed with fire ...' (1 Cor 3:13). Both the believing spea-ker and the believing hearers in this situation are to act *together* as the one Body, because the discipline of response to God in Christ requires believers to see that the world's reality provides the setting for 'responsible living'. 'Good is not a quality of life. It is 'life' itself. To be good is to 'live" (*Ethics*, p.221). Therefore Lockley comments

> students of *Letters and Papers from Prison* will be able to detect more than a hint of Bonhoeffer's later thinking about 'worldliness' and living life to the full in these references from *Ethics*. The discussion has taken us from Bonhoeffer's rejection of any form of ethical activity which involves abst-raction from life, to action which is concerned with looking deeply into life.... It is only a short step from here to the startling prison statements, 'God is in the facts themselves' and 'God meeting us no longer as 'Thou', but also disguised in the 'It'. (pp.107-108)

The gifts of the Spirit
What Bonhoeffer was saying in those prison statements is an insight we need to hold on to, absorb and develop in today's controversies within the Church and in communication beyond the Church. But clearly if we are to do so, it will only be in recognising what he imp-lies about the risen Christ and the Holy Spirit who move us to deeper dependence on the Trinity. Awareness of this need in a practical and direct way had not been a significant part of the Reformation message, and the same has been true of all the main Christian traditions, whe-ther Protestant or Catholic, up to but not including twentieth-century Pentecostalism. Consequently we need to take the Pentecostal and Charismatic movements with seriousness, because they have begun to act as God's corrective, bringing the Church back to a central element of his activity which historic Christianity has allowed to atrophy.

Although I believe this is the case, I am painfully aware that Pentecostalism has been contaminated by fundamentalist assumptions that are inconsistent with its main perception. It is not surprising that the Spirit's ministry in Christ does not appear explicitly in Bonhoeffer's awareness, yet what he was affirming about the worldliness of God's acting is equally corrective. In fact the two correctives are complementary and mutually dependent. Although Bonhoeffer writes so little about the Spirit, his personal sense of dependence on God became increasingly strong as his martyrdom was looming. That commitment of self to God marks his theology and spirituality with most practical relevance, and points us to our agenda for today.

One of the most striking and important of all Bonhoeffer's letters from prison is the one he wrote to Eberhard Bethge on 21st July 1944, expressing his thoughts about holiness.

> I discovered and am still discovering up to this very moment that it is only by living completely in this world that one learns to believe. One must abandon every attempt to make something of oneself.... It is in such a life that we throw ourselves utterly into the arms of God and participate in his sufferings in the world.... (*LPP* Fontana edn p. 125)

When God is allowed to direct
That letter leads me to refer again to the situation Anglicans (but also Christians of other traditions) find themselves in at the present time of doctrinal crisis. Over homosexuality and other areas of acute controversy, a gulf between church leaders now threatens to disrupt such unity as we have had hitherto. The good thing about this crisis is that we now have the opportunity to perceive and address the issue in depth, whereas in the past the easier and apparently safer course – that of avoiding confrontation and plastering over divisions – could sometimes be adopted. The hope is that we may now learn not just to tolerate one another, but actually take other believers seriously enough to listen to them and to God. Only so can *his* leadership of *his* Church be restored. It means deliberately setting aside the temptation to adopt easy answers to difficult questions, whether in terms of scripture or of tradition.

The crux of the matter concerns both personhood and the nature of God's morality. We have to face the question not just in terms of biblical texts but also as a matter of total interpretation. Has not biblical faith as an historical complex acquired presuppositions from the time of Moses onwards which encourage believers to trust the letter rather than the Spirit? The Bible interpreted by the Spirit makes it possible for believers to have 'the mind of Christ', to understand the will and truth of God. But Christians generally have not been prepared to let the Spirit lead them far in that interpretation of the gospel because it is alarming, as Christ warned it would be.

Conscience set free in Christ
Bonhoeffer was able to penetrate the intricacy of this problem in his discussion of conscience in its relation to the natural and potentially sinful drive to claim an improper degree of autonomy for the human individual. He discusses this in the important chapter VI of *Ethics* entitled 'History and Good'.

> The call of conscience in natural man is the attempt on the part of the ego to justify itself in its knowledge of good and evil before God, before men and before itself, and to secure its own continuance in this self-justification.... We can now understand that the great change takes place ... when the unity of human existence ceases to consist in its autonomy and is found, through the miracle of faith, beyond the man's own ego and its law, in Jesus Christ.... Jesus Christ has become my conscience.... I can now find unity with myself only in the surrender of my ego to God and to men. (p.243-4)

Bonhoeffer made it clear that what he calls 'natural conscience' is no ready ally on the road to God's holiness. It can foster 'the most ungodly self-justification'. The leading and discipline of the Spirit enable us to observe such defensive self-righteousness lying behind the animosity of much inter-Christian controversy. Just as much as any other human faculty, conscience needs redemption, and only in Christ crucified and risen can it be set free from idolatry.

(3) The communality of human life
This third facet of Bonhoeffer's thinking is again one that has been continually avoided by the Church in recent times. Significantly, the corporate dimension of personhood is difficult to perceive, except in a minor degree, because each one of us seeks wellbeing within our own individuality. The freedom to do so must be respected and the guarding of individual human rights is properly regarded as a matter of ethical priority. Yet the wisdom of Christianity has always pointed to the fact that the value of what we *are* together far exceeds what as individuals we can *have* within ourselves. From the biblical perspective human beings are created to exist with their attention

directed beyond themselves. Thus the salvation of human individuals should be understood as liberation from the various behaviours (sins) which follow when they cling to their individuality and establish their personhood as centred within themselves rather than within a God-given milieu of community relationships. Taking up John 1:4, Bonhoeffer wrote

> My life is outside myself, outside the range of my disposal; my life is another than myself; it is Jesus Christ. This is not intended figuratively, as conveying that my life would not be worth living without this other, or that Christ invests my life with a particular quality or … value while allowing it to retain its own independent existence, but my life itself is Jesus Christ. (*Ethics* p.218)

Holiness in the corporate Christ
The character of Christian living as a sharing in the gift of God's holiness and creativity is to be found in the context of this communality, but in the western traditions at least holiness has not survived well at all. Although the Hebrew sense of corporate personality has long been a matter of scholarly comment in OT studies it seems hardly to have impinged on the main traditions of Christian doctrine. Often modern scholarship appears to proceed on the assumption that theological diversity in the texts is simply evidence of pluralism in the first-century Church that can be seen in parallel to the great range of opinion among Christians today. But what if the various NT perspectives on Christ are not to be taken as alternative, even rival, versions, but rather necessary attempts to express one consistent whole, in which each has to be amplified and corrected by taking the others into account? If there were simply a series of alternative Christian ways in the early Church it would be difficult to justify the belief that the canon of the NT is authenticated by the Holy Spirit. For the canon implies not only authority but the faith as one coherent whole. In today's world of high mobility and individualism, by contrast, it is taken for granted that Christians should select the practice that appeals to their temperament from a broad range of options, in interpreting scripture as well as in other ways. The form of doctrine favoured may be a vaguely Pauline, Johannine or synoptic version of the faith, or more likely be just plainly reductionist. Thus a parish may offer either rigid biblicism or a kindly tolerant free-for-all which encourages believers to choose their own understanding of the historic faith. Both of these attitudes can be accompanied by a loose variety of worship forms

to express these alternative and restricted versions of Christianity. A not untypical consequence of this situation is a parish church's policy that advertises its comprehensive and 'moderate' character in providing 'services to suit every taste'.

In contrast to all that, it may be that there are signs of a new trend towards some consensus among scholars, and if so perhaps a firmer insistence on the part of the Church's leaders that the present pluralism of Christian thought is failing to commend the purpose for which the Church has been created. If so the hope is that more careful teaching will lead to a clearer sense of the Spirit who can lead the Church back to penitence, a real change of heart, a recognition that she has neglected the gospel itself. In *The Climax of the Covenant: Christians and the Law in Pauline Theology*,[19] Tom Wright was drawing out in great detail the universality of God's redemptive action in Christ, the way that Paul demonstrates the meaning of Jesus' own faith, and how the outpouring of the Spirit was proving effective in the first-century congregations. Wright expounds the theology of Galatians chapters 3 and 4, with the focus on 3:15-20 in particular. The 'Galatian church needs to hear' that its ex-pagan members 'do not need to 'judaize' in order to belong to the true people of God'.

> *All* those who believe in Jesus Christ and are baptized into him ... form one single family ... these are not, in Christ, [two] *different families*.... Paul's ... real fear, which emerges into the light in 4:1-11 [concerns the threat of] far more than two families. There will not only be Jew and Gentile, but Athenian and Roman ... and so on *ad infinitum.* Concede the Torah its permanent validity, and any gentiles who come to believe in Jesus will have no reason to abandon their ethnic loyalties. The *elemental spirits* [or heavenly bodies] will still rule the world.

So we have here Paul's key insight into the significance of Jesus as the Jewish Messiah, the 'one 'in whom' the people of God is summed up precisely *as* the people of God'.

> Many of Paul's frequent 'incorporative' expressions cluster together in (Gal 3 vv 26-9), in just that passage where the worldwide church is affirmed to be 'one' and therefore 'the seed of Abraham'. (pp.163-5)

The absolute universality of the gospel has to be affirmed again and again in the context of the Church's mission so that people in and outside the believing community may see that the Christian vision concerns creation's fundamental purpose. In this view people find their true satisfaction through a process of personal engagement with each other in God, being drawn by the Spirit into community where they participate in what the Creator is doing. If that is so, we can appreciate how faulty religious perspectives are prone to be, whether biblical or not, in that they tend to obscure the divine activity by overlaying it with human interpretations of what is going on. Accordingly it is not just Israel but all of us who are condemned when we are most religious. We are condemned in being denominational, sectarian Christians and in our inveterate desire to be acceptable in ourselves. We come then in the context of Christianity's mission to see how radically it builds on the communitarian nature of humanity.

Galatians 3 is an extended discussion of the covenant with Abraham, that concerns 'covenant judgement and covenant renewal' with particular reference to Deuteronomy 27-30 (p.140). This is far from being a theological picturing of the release of people from their 'individual transgressions' as many Christians constantly suggest. For Israel sin is the corporate condition of the nation as a whole, while for Christianity it refers to the entire range of psychological and moral disorder in which the race is imprisoned and engaged (cf Gal 3:22).

> God promised Abraham a worldwide family, characterized by faith. The promises were entrusted to Israel, the people whose life was lived [under law]. The Torah, however, held out ... the curse which had ... come true ... in ... the exile and its strange continuance.... How could the promises ... now reach their intended destination? (p.142)

Paul answers that the usual cycle of 'repentance, sacrifice and atonement', that is, of 'judgement followed by mercy' has ended. In its place the world as well as Israel now has

> the renewal of covenant by God's circumcising of the hearts of his people so that they love him and keep his Torah from the heart.... For Paul the death of Jesus, precisely on a Roman cross ... brought the exile to a climax. The King of the Jews took the brunt of the exile on himself. (p.146)

The import of this teaching for the world's wellbeing lies in the fact that 'Paul is thinking of Israel as a whole, and of the curse of Deuteronomy not in terms of the future *post mortem* damnation which hangs over the heads of sinners, but [of] ... Israel's ... subjugation at the hands of pagans' (p.148). Thus the NT faith is about God's work in Christ which makes possible the radical transformation of humanity when people choose to embrace the offered change of status, allowing themselves to be built into the *redeemed community life* now open to all peoples. Accepting this offer in Christ they can 'count' themselves 'dead to sin and alive to God in Christ Jesus' (Romans 6:11), and discover that they are being changed.

Glory unveiled in the Spirit
In the chapter that follows, Wright expounds 2 Corinthians 3 to show the remarkable fact that human nature transformed by the Spirit through the gospel begins to reveal God's glory. This aspect of Paul's witness, as much as the universal inclusiveness of the New Covenant, needs to be appreciated in the context of the Church's communality. Where the Church's life in congregations is not renewed in the Spirit, however, any mention of God's pentecostal intentions for his Church may only be an embarrassment. Christ's gift of being 'baptised in the Spirit' may well be ignored, especially in a time of evangelistic opportunity, because any claim that the Spirit reveals God's glory in the life of believers may seem both incredible and divisive. In these circumstances it will certainly be less persuasive for many traditional Christians than the tangible appeal of their familiar denominational religion. In the Corinthian Church Paul was confronted by Judaisers but he was able to point out that *in this respect*

> Moses is actually ... a *precursor* of the new covenant people in 3:18, since he, alone among the Israelites, is able to look at the divine glory with unveiled face.... Moses had to use the veil, because the hearts of the Israelites were hardened ... Paul's overall point is that his boldness correlates with the new covenant membership.... Christians are themselves the 'letter' written by the Spirit. (p.180)

What we often notice in church life is that those Christians who are now 'able to look upon the glory with unveiled face' are sometimes poor examples of the transforming Spirit. (This we gather was also the case in Corinth.) Commonly we do not understand what God is doing for us and in us, so we may have to confess that our hardness of heart is only melted on the surface. Accordingly, many Christians who are less enlightened by the Spirit may be suspicious or even contemptuous of what they observe. We have to admit that the situation is often ambiguous, but those who disparage 'happy-clappy' worship make more difficulty for themselves. Tiresome it can be, but not necessarily devoid of the Spirit's inspiration. Like the Judaisers, those who oppose the gifts of the Spirit cling to the old religious ways, being content with lesser degrees of glory.

Believers become 'mirrors' for one another

If we are alert to the psychology we shall not be surprised when renewal in the Spirit is abused. When we seek charismatic gifts with eagerness we have to be wary of our own possessiveness. Paul took up the account of Moses' face shining with God's glory to show that the experience of the congregation at Corinth was an instance, despite its shameful shortcomings, of what God intends the Church to be everywhere – a mirror of his glory. When he writes 'we ... all reflect the Lord's glory' (2 Cor 3:18), Paul means *each Christian does.* Referring to the dilemma of scholars in answering the question 'what is the mirror?', Wright explains

> the 'mirror' in which Christians see reflected the glory of the Lord is not, in this passage at any rate, the gospel itself, nor even Jesus Christ. *It is one another....* Paul ... makes ... the astonishing claim that those who belong to the new covenant are, by the Spirit, being changed into the glory of the Lord: when they come face to face with one another they are beholding, as in a mirror, the glory itself. (p.185)

Recognising the homely familiarity of God

Bonhoeffer can also help the Church in the twenty-first century to grasp how basic to human consciousness is God's presence even when he is not recognised. We do not know him until his self-revelation is identified, and then gradually understood, but he is always present to our existence. With regard to the scriptures Bonhoeffer favoured the more primitive of the two genesis myths. Commenting on Genesis 2:7 in *Creation and Fall*,[20] he pointed out that giving God the proper name Yahweh, rather than the generic term *elohim* as in Genesis 1, focuses attention on his immediacy and on the sense that he is familiar to human consciousness. The 'undisguised mythology' is actually an advantage. Its 'childlike anthropomorphism' can direct us away from over-confidence in the more sophisticated first creation narrative.

> [T]he fact that we simply cannot conceive of 'God in himself' is perhaps expressed much more plainly in clear anthropomorphism. The abstract concept is ... more anthropomorphic, just because it is not intended to be anthropomorphic. (p.43)

In the earlier account the Creator 'makes me [in] fatherliness ... [and in that experience of his fatherliness] I worship him.... Man's origin is in a piece of earth'. Referring to Michelangelo's portrayal in the Sistine Chapel of Adam being created 'resting on the ground' Bonhoeffer wrote that

> man experiences life through bodily contact with the finger
> of God.... Man as man does not live without God's Spirit,
> [but] as body in Spirit. (pp.44-45)

But what that picture could not express so vividly is that humankind is made one flesh, in the union of a deeper and broader communality. This too was affirmed in Bonhoeffer's theology. Since the unsurpassable reality God cannot be domesticated, keeping the integrity of Christian faithfulness in these respects presents the Church with her most urgent pastoral and evangelistic challenge.

A theology of human community without pretence
Under the title 'The communion of Saints', Ott's chapter 5 traces Bonhoeffer's consciousness of the Church as being Christ 'existing as community' in the world, and of 'the collective person' being a 'structural component of his picture of humanity'. As in Paul's reference to being condemned by God's love in Christ, Bonhoeffer declares that being conformed to Christ crucified makes us real people, it exposes us as we are and that means as 'sentenced by God'. Ethical action, in Bonhoeffer's view, involves identifying oneself with Christ as he was in the world, and thus on the cross.

> To be conformed with the Incarnate is to have the right to be
> the man one really is. Now there is no more pretence ... no
> more compulsion to be something other, better and more
> ideal than what one is. God loves the real man.... Humbly
> [the Christian] bears the scars on his body and soul, the
> marks of the wounds which sin inflicts on him. He cannot
> raise himself up above any other man.... (*Ethics* p.81)

But at the same time, in being conformed to Christ crucified, the Christian believer is being 'conformed with the Risen One' (p.82). This provides the background against which to understand what Bonhoeffer teaches about the Church which is "nothing but a section of humanity in which Christ has really taken form". The intimate and immediate sense Bonhoeffer had of the communality of personal life appears in a letter to his parents, referring to air raids on Berlin

It is remarkable how we think at such times about those we should not like to live without, and forget all about ourselves. It makes one realise how closely our lives are bound up with other people's, and in fact how our centre is outside of ourselves and how little we are individuals.[21]

Collective substance, responsibility and guilt

Bonhoeffer grasped this corporate reality, writes Ott, not just in christocentric terms, but as the real nature of humanity.

Human life, the reality of the individual man's being, reaches out beyond individual existence and does so in a completely real way that is not at all to be understood metaphorically or secondarily.... I am not only associated with others and co-operating with them ... I am unified with them in a much more original way. They are part of myself.

It was evident also that Bonhoeffer only came to this realisation because of his Christian experience, and his strong interest in the Old Testament concept of the people of God.

The call is to the collective person, and not to the individual. It is the people that is to do penance as the people of God.... God does not only have eyes for the nation; he has a purpose for every smallest community, for every friendship, every marriage, every family.... It is not only individual Germans and individual Christians who are guilty; Germany and the church are guilty too. Here the condition and justification of individuals is of no avail; Germany and the church must themselves repent and be justified.... It is clear this can happen only 'in' the individual. Only thus can the hearing of the call be concretely comprehended and yet it is not the individuals, but the collective person who, in the individuals, hears, repents and believes. The centre of action lies in the collective person.

It will be seen how closely this view of the collective person complements what I have written earlier about intersubjective personhood and how relevant it is in pointing towards the needed revision of the Church's spirituality and mission. The task of the next section will be to see that by existing in the intersubjective dimension of personhood everybody can share in what God seeks to do in the world with and through people.

E. God's agency and desire enable our own

In drawing my account into a coherent whole I come now to discuss 'joint-agency' more precisely than I did earlier and to relate it
to the Augustinian theme of desire. I look first to Diogenes Allen and
Edward Hugh Henderson writing on Austin Farrer in *Captured by the
Crucified.*[22] The heading of Henderson's contribution, 'The God who
Undertakes Us', is a phrase of Farrer's which affirms the precedence
of God's initiatives while giving his human creatures freedom and
responsibility to act with him. That responsibility is to contribute
to the creative process within the conditions of the world's history,
which Jesus describes in terms of God's Kingdom growing through
time. Because human freedom is limited by those conditions, its limits
point to an eventual end of human attempts to undermine what God
is doing. Therefore Christians can be confident that God will bring
the process of the universe as a whole to the conclusion that satisfies him. At the start of his chapter Henderson has a quotation from
Farrer that includes this advice. 'Go with the truth you have, and let
it carry you into collision with the hard rocks of fact, and then you'll
learn something'. Similarly Diogenes Allen, in writing about Farrer's
spirituality, takes this quotation to emphasise Farrer's belief 'that … a
pressing need existed to rethink orthodox Christianity … and … to
share with others, both academically and pastorally, the results of his
investigations'. (p.47)

> Faith perishes if it is walled in, or confined. If it is anywhere,
> it must be everywhere, like God himself: if God is in your
> life, he is in all things, for he is God. You must be able to
> spread the area of your recognition for him, and the basis of
> your conviction about him, as widely as your thought will
> range.[23]

This is the outlook also of clinical theology in using psychological
observation to elucidate the experience of believers in relation to all
human living. Farrer also recognised that the world's circumstances
impose a forceful discipline on people for their good, out of which
they can learn how to be partners with God.

> Farrer did not fear that our efforts and improvement would
> inevitably become acts of self-righteousness.… [He] stressed,
> 'we do not learn what dependence on God is, except by
> having our self-dependence broken' … [and] was all too
> aware of, and constantly preached on, our utter dependence

on God's grace for our very breath at every moment, and for our powers and talents.... Even in his sermons, Farrer ... reminded his hearers of divine and human agency as a 'double agency'... for example, in his sermon 'Thinking the Trinity':[24] *God gave the world room to be itself. He would not so inhabit it as to make it the passive reflection of his own ideas; or like the machine which does no more than embody the design of its constructor, and perform the wishes of its manipulator. God ... did not just make [the world]; he made it make itself. He released a half chaos of brimless forces as alien from his own being as anything could well be; and they blinded away, not in the paths of a godlike wisdom, but according to the very limited principles of action implanted in each. Nevertheless ... by an invisible art, and by a secret attraction, he has brought out of a blind interplay of forces many organized intricacies and much sentient life.... God made the world in unlikeness to himself; we look there in vain for the lineaments of his face. He made man in his own similitude, and it is in the face of man that we must look for the countenance of God.... We can achieve nothing truly human which is not also in a manner divine.* (pp.53-54)

Learning to think this way

If the Church, with an increasingly corporate commitment, can start developing her teaching programmes in a way that helps ordinary Christians to understand what Farrer was saying in that paragraph, she will be able to recover her proper confidence. Thinking this way about the world and our human place in it will strengthen Christians to live the Christian faith and commend it to others. The whole thrust of Farrer's philosophical theology was to demonstrate that as believers we should always be ready to submit our convictions to critical examination and that when we do so we are able to understand more clearly *how* God does what we already believe he does. We are then in a position to commend our faith with reason, not on the basis of mere assertion. In Farrer's own words, quoted by Henderson, the personal relationship of faith is one of will, of our free consent and desire to acknowledge him:

God does not stand alongside us or on a level with us, nor do we become aware of him through any external collision, mutual impingement or interaction between his activity and ours. How could we? He is related to us in quite another

way: as the will which underlies our existence, gives rise
to our action and directs our aim.... How can we have experimental knowledge of the will behind our will? Only by
opening our will to it, or sinking our will in it; there is
no other conceivable way. We cannot touch God except by
willing the will of God. Then his will takes effect in ours,
and we know it, not that we manipulate him, but that he
possesses us.[25]

Allen points out that it can seem contradictory to speak of double
agency, but only if God and creation are treated as if they were
members of one mathematical 'set', as if God were a being among
beings.[26]

Every agent or being that acts is simultaneously an action of
God's creative and providential power. Although we cannot
specify the divine agency apart from creatures (and then
only because of the insufficiency of creatures to account for
their own existence and order), we can nonetheless show that
double agency is the correct way to think of the Christian
doctrines of creation and providence, so that creatures are
not reduced to utter passivity. (p.54)

If we compare Farrer's theology and spirituality with Bonhoeffer's
we can see they had a great deal in common. Farrer's emphasis on
prayer parallels Bonhoeffer's, and both of them see that theological
study will only remain soundly Christian if it is resourced in devotion
to the living God. Like Bonhoeffer, Farrer was acutely aware of the
unbelieving world's power to corrupt or at least isolate the Church's
witness.

I believe in Jesus Christ, born, suffering, risen; yet I may
leave the desk for the table, and find in my fellow diners the
objects of my rivalry or the sources of my amusement, but
never see the Christ in their hearts, or acknowledge in mine
the Christ who goes out to meet them.[27]

It is encouraging also, to notice how both these theologians active
in the mid-twentieth century were leaving behind one aspect of their
roots to the extent of being open to the need for the Church to take
experience seriously. Henderson writes that for Farrer the mystery

of how God's action takes effect does not mean that
we do not experience double agency any more than the
mystery of how our decisions take effect means that we do

not experience our intentional control over our own bodily movement. Indeed, St Paul said of the whole life of faith: 'not I but Christ lives in me' and 'for me to live is Christ'…. Farrer points out that 'the whole mystery of practical religion comes down to that familiar phrase of our daily prayer, 'whose service is perfect freedom''. Therefore, believers say that they experience the action of God in the actions of their own lives and that the experience is not the experience of being coerced against the grain of their own natures, of being diminished as persons, of losing their freedom, or of ceasing to be finite human beings; rather, it is the experience of being enhanced and fulfilled as the very persons they are. (pp.86-87)

Reflecting on Farrer's account of double agency we may say that God enables the three elements of our self-experience to be strengthened together. The intellectual element and the emotional are nourished by the Holy Spirit in a way which consolidates thinking and desire into the formation of settled will. This third element embraces the other two, thereby constituting the created spirit of the person which, as Farrer evidently thought, is the area of the self in which the human person may allow himself to grow in conformity with Christ.

The conflict over want and desire

In this context I refer to Nick Earle's book *Does God make sense?*, which he says is for 'absolute beginners' and is not 'about religion'.[28] In it he discusses how the word 'God' can be used properly, that is, in a way which is logically coherent. In the chapter headed, 'Can I choose what I believe?' he argues that

> to believe that what ought to be will be – the choice of faith
> – must begin, in principle at least, with a resolution of that
> conflict within myself in favour of what I ought.

This proposition is in parallel with the argument of this book which points to the nature of the inner conflict. Earle focuses chiefly on the straight conflict between two wants.

> Choice is always between things we want to do, more or
> less. And the act of choosing ends when, after whatever
> deliberation is possible to us, we do what we most want to
> do. Not what you most want in the short-term necessarily.
> (p.73)

Thus the conflict is represented in the way Paul did in Romans 7, 'between what I want and what I ought' (p.72). But Earle also makes the point that

> 'ought' brings its own 'want' with it. It may be a very feeble want. But if I do not want to do as I ought *at all* then I simply do not understand the word. The choice between what I want, regardless of what I ought, and what I ought regardless of what I want, is only resolved when one out-weighs the other to the extent of leaving it powerless. Only then am I completely at ease with myself in making the choice to believe or not to believe. When and only when 'I want' becomes 'I ought' or *vice versa* can I be said to choose freely or, which comes to the same thing, not to choose at all. (p.73)

What is of interest here is why and in what way does 'ought' bring its own 'want', because understanding the answer to those questions helps resolve 'the conflict within myself', enabling people to make 'the choice of faith'.

On the previous page Earle has pointed to a difference between wanting and wishing because 'wishing may have nothing to do with need'. On the other hand

> [w]ant implies a lack so that wanting to do something is, at least in part, *needing* to do it. We do what we want to do in order to obtain some satisfaction, emotional or phy-sical, intellectual or moral, short – or long-term. I want to do something in order to be better for having done it. If I didn't want anything, not even my next breath, I should be dead.

Consistent with this, my proposal begins from the recognition that every 'ought' springs from God the giver of life. For this reason I use the words want and desire to distinguish between the wanting that is self-centred and the desire that develops out of a gift of love already experienced in personal relationships. I suggest that distinction is fun-damental because it is the latter kind of wanting – for which I use the word 'desire' – that characterises the deepest wellbeing. It concerns the love that God gives in giving himself to the creatures who are made to be his children. The satisfaction they enjoy in receiving that love in the depth of their being evokes their desire, which is to share in God's outward loving. God expresses his love in creating people in his 'image', enabling them to be creative with him in and through their lives.

So in distinction from the wish that may have nothing to do with need, I am using the word desire to mean the kind of want that springs from the need of persons to belong together as members of a community of love, the love that God is, and which he has given each one to share. That kind of need, the need to live within God's loving community, explains why 'ought' brings with it its own distinctive 'want' or desire. The moral obligation which the word 'ought' indicates in relation to people is characteristic of being persons created by God in his image. The satisfaction people seek in their personhood is a continuing plenitude of what they have already been given in a foretaste. About spiritual growth Earle writes 'our future wants will include wanting to become something other than we are'. What we have to 'amend is not so much what we *did* as what we *were* – what it was that made us do it' (p.74). All this helps to underscore the Christian realisation that human ideas of morality (and all religious codes of behaviour) are severely judged, as Bonhoeffer was showing. They stand in need of revision from the standpoint of the New Testament as much as the Church's doctrines do.

Human history being God's school
What then are we to understand about Christian discipleship in resolving 'that conflict within myself in favour of what I ought'? Here again I follow Lash's preference for representing the process of spiritual development in terms of the Creator's schooling of his human creatures, and his emphasis on the point that the fulfilment of human nature lies in the formation 'of a common humanity shared by *all* members of the species'... including 'those who have died'.[29] In this perspective we are able to see that human beings are created with a spiritual appetite to share the intersubjective life of the Trinity. This desiring must develop within a community that is learning to be self-critical and sensitive to the otherness of persons. Such a community will have three distinctive features.

The first is that the spiritual desire proves to be a *divine desiring* given to human persons, through which they find themselves not just loving God in some measure but being a channel for a love which they realise gradually is not their own but his. Secondly, such mediation of divine love in creatures only happens because the community is made up of *needy people*. It is the neediness or lack of sufficiency which makes possible the reception of divine loving, and this discovery points us to why God has to make such a world as this. Thirdly, the character of human need and the way to meet it within community *must be understood* if people are to respond to what God is initiating in their lives.

Divine love flows into humanity in so far as people's deepest needs are being acknowledged, and as we have seen this involves emotional healing and the nurturing of a life which is holy or attentive to God. In that setting people's lives can blossom because through healing they become more open to enjoy and give love. Yet opposing that purpose a world culture and climate of unbelief combines with every malign influence to confuse, mislead, and then corrupt God's gift. For this reason it is only the community of Christ's Body, properly disciplined in the Spirit through the cross that can provide for wellbeing.

F. Recovering confidence in the gospel

At the end of the previous section I implied that human beings are needy in two respects: in wanting immediate satisfaction in the circumstances of their present stage of life, and in having a comprehensive, ongoing appetite for a long-term fulfilment in spirit which they sense will somehow complete their being. Their condition shows in various ways that they are unfinished creatures, and are consciously or unconsciously yearning for changes which will lead to their fulfilment. I conclude the chapter by relating my argument to the thought of a particular school in contemporary theology. Radical Orthodoxy tries to solve the dilemmas of doubt and uncertainty for those who are growing in faith as Christians, although in a thoroughly postmodern way. Secular postmodernism treats religion as an area of private speculation and practice, with which the thinking person will be wise to remain uncontaminated. It thinks the public commitments that citizens should share together for the common good, nationally and internationally, are best met when there is an agreement to keep politics and morals free of religious loyalty and prejudice. In contrast, however, these theologians advocate a church-centred approach that aims, on a narrative theology basis, to win the debate in the public realm. Their project was launched by John Milbank with his work *Theology and Social Theory: Beyond Secular Reason*[30] and taken further in *Radical Orthodoxy: A New Theology*,[31] in order to confront prevailing secularism in a most forthright but relativist way. Although opposed to its major premise that Christianity cannot be justified rationally, I share with these theologians the conviction that the Church must reassert her historic faith without compromise, yet by accepting the scepticism of the postmodern position Radical Orthodoxy has, I think, no discipline by which to avoid the dangers of religion. Thus Christianity is presented via the belief that 'narrative is our primary mode of inhabiting the world'. 'Objects and subjects are, as they are narrated in a story'.[32] These phrases are quoted in *Radical Orthodoxy: A Critical Introduction* by Steven Shakespeare,[33] to whom I am indebted in the following paragraphs. The response to the problem of doubt is limited by the view these writers have adopted.

> There are no rational foundations, [and] Christianity will be seen by many as just one story among others. [Accordingly Radical Orthodoxy stands] on 'the plain unfounded narrative of Christianity which is the only 'universal' for those who situate themselves within it' (*Theology and Social Theory*

p.173). Secular reason 'cannot be refuted, but only out-
narrated, if we can *persuade* people – for reasons of 'literary
taste' – that Christianity offers a much better story' (p.330)....
The claim is this: Christianity must seek to master ... all other
stories, because it is the only story which is able to renounce
mastery and domination ... those who tell the Christian story
participate in the mind of God. (p.57)

It will be seen that the theological anthropology I have offered does
not rest on these assumptions. Instead the dilemmas of thinking
people can be resolved in a more traditional Christian way through
the recognition that God has created humanity with the capacity to
discern personal presence. The Christian world-view relies on the
gift of that discernment, but it does share with Radical Orthodoxy
a number of important affirmations that are integral to orthodoxy.
The way I see the two positions being related is drawn out in the
following summary of my thesis.

Fields of shared consciousness and God's presence

Human awareness of God is not mediated through language, nor is
it a matter of inference, because consciousness is prior to conceptual
thought. In consciousness the human being has an intuitive knowledge of persons in distinction from things. Although a society
dominated by the physical sciences gives little attention to this, the
existence of every individual with other people does constitute the
milieu within which all are open to the reality of the Creator, simply
by virtue of being created spirit, that is, persons. The point of this
openness is that there is two-way access in which God's initiatives
are pre-eminent. As participators in a field of shared consciousness
people can grow in intellect and emotion, gradually learning to communicate largely on the basis of language, but before this, the in-built
dependence of persons on God the Trinity has made it possible for
them to communicate in spirit as well as in mind. It is true that there
are significant differences between the 'stories' which characterise
human cultures, but all are grounded in the one personal humanity.
This commonality shows that universal communication and a single
community of communities is possible and is intended. Here lies the
prospect of reconciliation and the resolution of conflicts. Languages
and cultures are open to translation and mutual enhancement. The
universality of God's presence makes the Church's mission viable.
Radical Orthodoxy's *exclusive* focus on telling and enacting the
Christian story undermines the mission by failing to see that God

facilitates real interfaith dialogue and secular co-operation as the following three points underline.

(1) The priority of healing the world from within

One of the strong points in Radical Orthodoxy is that it makes a decisive counter-cultural stand. I can see that Milbank may well be justified in his criticism of Karl Rahner in that the latter may not have been critical enough of secular accounts of society's concepts and institutions. Milbank states Rahner's view (which I accept), that 'there is no such thing as a state of 'pure nature': rather every person has already been worked upon by grace', but he rejects this, calling it naturalising the supernatural, wanting to make Christianity yet more religious than it is at present. [34] He does not sufficiently acknowledge that God's incarnation in Jesus is the centrepiece of what he has always been doing in humanity as a whole.

In my view the way Christianity confronts the civil institutions that 'are fatally infected by capitalism and secularism' is by ensuring that the Church, which lives in the world and whose members are involved in its institutions, continues to work for the healing of individuals *and* communities. The institutions themselves cannot be taken over or replaced by the Church, but they can be transformed from within through the influence of the risen Christ upon his members.

(2) The risen Christ acting through Church and society

The post-Easter presence of Christ in the world is not at all prominent in Radical Orthodoxy, but there are some pointers towards it. In his second chapter on 'Community: the all-consuming Church', Shakespeare discusses the way Milbank has modified his position in response to his critics. Whereas he had seemed to insist that the Church had to be perfect if it is to communicate Jesus' perfection, he admits that recognising the truth will depend on 'a sifting from the many human "imperfections" in the ecclesial transmission process'. [35] And in the second edition of *Theology and Social Theory* (2006) he wrote:

> while 'positively' I recommend Catholic Christianity as the one final and universal truth, I quite clearly envisage Catholicism in 'liberal' terms… [meaning] generous, open-ended and all-inclusive. [36]

He then agrees that the Church is an 'other governed' community which 'must never mistake itself for God'. It is 'a lived project of universal reconciliation' but it ... 'only exists through ... the "mess" of institutional debate and conflict' (Shakespeare pp.107-108).

While this is a step in the right direction, I have pressed the case that the Church must see herself as the subservient partner in a Christ-centred movement in which the Spirit is active in all communities, seeking response to the living Jesus. Where that response is sustained, the Spirit is bringing the Church into existence, but I acknowledge that my argument here cannot be upheld without giving much more attention to the atonement than has been possible in this book; something of this is, however, expressed in the next chapter.

(3) Suffering related to disorder in creation

The largest contrast between my account of Christian orthodoxy and Milbank's concerns death and suffering. Radical Orthodoxy is based on a concept of God's goodness which does not allow that creation could include the necessity of death. It simply says that 'sin 'invents' death just as it invents the contrast between good and evil'. In my view this position ignores the finite world's reality and the character of its development. Milbank believes that it is

> quite simply impossible to be a Christian and to suppose that death and suffering belong to God's original plan, or that the struggle of natural selection (which one doubts is even proven as a full account of evolution) is how creation *as creation* rather than thwarted creation genuinely comes about. To do so is to embrace a sickly masochistic faith, against the explicit words of scripture (and one notes here the co-belonging of kenotic and evolutionary Christologies).[37]

This fundamental point of difference denies the central substance of my position for it declines to take seriously God's work of healing broken lives and their transformation through the uncovering of suffering. As I see it, the rejection of kenotic theology, which Milbank shares with many other contemporary theologians, is highly significant in today's climate of anxiety. The nub of the matter concerns God's respect for the freedom of his created children. Does not his love for them oblige him to create them within a world that involves sin, suffering and death?

This consideration does not mean that Radical Orthodoxy is closed to developments beyond its initial concepts. Shakespeare shows in his chapter 'Desire: what we really want' that these writers are working on the issues of openness to the world where the Spirit constantly takes Christians beyond the entrenched perceptions in understanding Christ the Word. In relation to *The Word Made Strange*, Shakespeare asks 'is the Church so identified with the divine Spirit, that its interpretation of the Word is always faultless? (p. 143) Here as elsewhere our understanding of God's truth is being disturbed that we may be grasped more comprehensively by Christ and the Spirit to understand and to serve. Shakespeare notes that Gerard Loughlin and Graham Ward warn against supposing that

> we have got the relationship between God and the world all mapped out.... [T]he Church is inherently open and in flux. [I]t must risk going beyond its boundaries, and even suspend judgement on other faiths. (p.142)

On the subject of the Eucharist, we need to disregard Catherine Pickstock's preference for the Latin Mass while accepting what she and Milbank have to say in some other respects, for 'trust in the Eucharist points us back towards a trust in everything, and especially the ordinary and everyday'.[38] This is because the risen Jesus is active everywhere. I agree that in a sense the Eucharist 'makes' the Church but only because the Spirit inspires believers to root themselves corporately in the historically embodied life of Christ (his 'flesh' and 'blood'). For that reason we can also discount the romantic notion that by transubstantiation 'the split between words and things ... is completely overcome (pp.146, 69). As Steven Shakespeare puts it, that doctrine 'actually empties ... material reality of (its) substance' because of 'God's unearthly presence' (pp.167-168). Instead his presence is always earthly or immanent in the everyday despite his Otherness.

The Eucharist directed to the world's salvation

I have drawn attention to the very strong emphasis that Radical Orthodoxy places on the Eucharist because surely the Supper directs every Christian to the suffering and dying Jesus. But this school of thought also seems to remain focused on Christ present to nourish his members rather than to change the world. In this it is remarkable that in modern times some Catholic and many Protestant versions of Christianity have tended to converge in failing to see the significance of the Church's intercession in relation to God's agency. Accordingly I cannot but accept some of Shakespeare's assessment when he writes

> Radical Orthodoxy wants so much to avoid dualism and to give value to this created world; and yet to achieve this it

> pushes its claim for the perfection of the Church and the
> Eucharist so far that they are taken out of this world....
> [Ironically] this position ... ends up by condemning the world
> outside a few Christian enclaves.... [T]he desire for God is so
> identified with ... the immediate connection provided by the
> Eucharist, that it turns into a desperate parody of capitalist
> desire. The Eucharist becomes the object to end all objects,
> the ultimate commodity to satisfy our lack. It becomes an
> addiction. (p.127)

Even if this criticism were too harsh it is true that a focus on union
with God through the Eucharist can push the actual purpose of sacramental communion out of sight. Baptism has incorporated believers
into union with the risen Christ, but it is the passion of Jesus that
is shared at the Supper. Non-sacramental Christians have always
known that God gives himself to them, but, I have argued, Jesus'
prayer at the Supper concerns the Church's mission (John 17:20, 21)
and confirms that our corporate union in Christ's self-giving is for
the world's salvation. The sacrament is given to Christians that they
may pray as members of the Body and then go as his ambassadors,
equipped with his resources, as members of the Vine which reaches
out to bear fruit throughout the unbelieving world.

In contrast to the thinking of Radical Orthodoxy, original orthodoxy affirms that the Eucharist is instrumental in relation to the
unredeemed. Its unique role in Christianity is that it constitutes the
necessary gathering of God's people who focus on the corporate task
to which they have been called. Certainly the Supper is a worldly
participation in God's joy, a foretaste of heaven *in via,* and in this
transitory condition it provides for believers the strongest possible
nourishment – but it does so as they face the world's need.

It is also vital to remember the present context of this action. Far
from being principally an eschatological moment withdrawn from
the world's business, the Eucharist is where our marching orders are
renewed. At each celebration, the strategy and the tactical particulars of the congregation's engagement with life are being unfolded
by the risen Christ who stands in the midst. This is not a simplistic
communication of instructions, which would preclude the hard intellectual and co-operative work that mission entails. Rather the risen
Christ is leading his people to allow the Spirit to bend their many
wills away from themselves to what the Trinity intends them to see,
to pray and to do.

Conclusion

This chapter can finish as it began, in facing doubt and uncertainty. Doubt will serve faith, if it encourages believers to meet their unbelieving neighbours, but even more valuably if it enables them to rethink their own settled opinions. In this God goes on challenging people to listen and allow themselves to be changed. It is the process I have called the Spirit's coaxing, whereby those who accept God's invitation into the relationship of faith are induced into listening to him in what often appears to be silence. Growth in holiness comes by learning to 'hear' God who speaks distinctively by being present, so that by trusting the inspiration of the Spirit believers may understand the meaning of sacred scripture. In present practice church worship is often interspersed so much with words directed to keeping the congregation cheerful, with their anxieties allayed, that the words succeed only in being a distraction from this listening. It is listening, however, that is key to learning to recognise God's invisible presence and his whispered guidance in the midst of the gathered Church.

Chapter Four
The witness of corporate holiness

In the Christian view, the world is designed to bring God's humanity into existence, and so to embody himself in his creation. It follows that he is using the world-process as a whole to explain himself. In this closing chapter I begin by drawing out the Christian understanding of human destiny as it has begun to appear through the earlier discussions. Little by little the 'new' creation in Christ will be *more and more expressive of God himself* (2 Corinthians 5.15-17). To do so I focus on five aspects of the orthodox faith that are particularly important for the Church's witness and mission. If congregations and individual members are to be fruitful in today's culture they need to be equipped to grasp the theology behind these major points, so that it comes to shape the Church's life and outreach. This will mean stressing the Christian's responsibility to witness to what God does through the Church, in deliberate contrast to the fact that in present circumstances Christians are often avoiding God's call and forcing the Church into preoccupation with domestic controversy. I begin by recalling the starting point of Christian faith – the resurrection of Jesus – that authenticates the truth of these five aspects.

The risen Jesus effecting change in people
The changed situation after the resurrection is brought out in an outstanding book by Arthur Vogel, *Radical Christianity and the Flesh of Jesus.*[1]

> Jesus' life changed the lives of the disciples because the activity of his life changed the activity of their lives. Jesus did not come to suggest a new way we might think about things.... [T]he full power of his life showed more fully in the lives of others after his death than during his life before his death.... The unique thing about the resurrection is that, after Jesus died, his life was not remembered for what it was; it was newly experienced for what it is.... (pp.80-81)

Daniel Hardy also affirmed this in a sermon to be found in *Finding the Church*,[2] where he contrasts our conventional, modern understanding of the world at a 'distance from' God with the way the first disciples found him to be with them after the resurrection.

> As Jesus shows ... God is always very close to us, closer than we are to ourselves, loving us to true holiness from within us.... [W]e see the two – God and us – deeply interwoven.... [But] like the disciples who tried to keep children away from Jesus we 'externalize' [his goodness] – to set it at a distance – to keep it from touching us as deeply as it needs to. Some of this goes back to a long-standing tendency (since the seventeenth century at least) to remove God from regular active involvement with the world, because God just doesn't fit with the reliability we find in the world. Modern suppositions that the world is autonomous and that human beings should be self-governing are traceable to that.... Some of it is also traceable to a primary distrust that God is genuinely and reliably good in loving us. (p.227)

To recover that early Christian experience we need to relearn the discernment, especially evident in the psalms, of God relating to us as particular people.

> To refer to God is not another way of talking about a generality, some 'ultimate state of affairs' into which we are to fit somehow, but ... to One who is personal in very particular ways that match us as we are. (p.228)

This is where the Church's witness has now to be concentrated even more than in the past, taking into account the psychological conditions that I have been tracing. Asking how 'we are to understand this strange process, where we are touched at such tender, uncomfortable spots and yet offered transformation?' Hardy instances his friend John Hull who, after becoming blind in middle age, became Professor of Religious Education in Birmingham (p.229). At first alienated by the Bible when unable to read it as he had before, Hull discovered that what 'the Bible says to me has changed since I lost my sight' (p.229).

> God is the one who broods over blindness, calling it out of shapelessness and confusion, giving it a place of beauty and order in the fullness of creation. God blesses blindness and hallows it.[3]

The sacraments as God's focus on our changing

In his study of the atonement, Tom Smail writes that the gospel sacraments proclaim our being 'included in his dying and living which are present and potent realities that are there waiting – or rather reaching out – for us' (p.144). They direct us to live in Christ, acting in dependence on what he did then, and allowing him to make us fellow-agents in what he does now. This is how Christians witness to God's holiness.

> [W]hen and because we are in him by our baptism, he can be in us in the giving and receiving of the Eucharist.... We are to participate in the new humanity that has been offered in sacrifice on our behalf in the midst of the old crucifying humanity, so that the one may overcome the other in us.[4]

This fits with the insight of the Orthodox Church that Christians are baptised in order to participate in the Eucharist. I don't mean, however, to commend the other-worldly sense that eastern Christianity has encouraged. Arthur Vogel brings out the this-worldly character of the sacramental action. Jesus, he says, newly created the Eucharist to be

> a means by which the action of his life enters the action of our lives, so that his re-creation of the world could continue in our lives. [This] ... is the one thing Jesus told his disciples to do ... 'to recall me'. (pp.93-94)

Through this eucharistic celebration the triune God trains us to act together as the corporate Christ. Vogel goes on to underline the poverty of our liturgical practice and the tendency to reduce 'ritual meaning to words'. With reference to John's Gospel chapter 6 he draws out the contrast between Christ's gift and the manna the forefathers ate in the wilderness, which was taken to be a symbol of the Torah (on the basis of Deuteronomy 8:2, 3). Jesus identifies himself with that divine gift only to go on to declare that what he gives is very different from verbal teaching.

> The new bread from heaven ... the only thing that truly lasts ... is Jesus' life as proven by the resurrection. 'Teaching' exists only in the mind of a living person.... Words are just words.... Only life can nourish life.... (pp.105-106)

This profound but simple perception needs a lot of exploration and explanation if the Church generally is to act on it, because our minds have been trained to give priority to ideas and our own action, while distrusting the immediacy of God and the activity of his personal goodness. Dislodging people from that bias, which our society prizes so deeply, is hard. Yet if we start afresh on the path of self-examination and look to the Spirit it is possible to escape from this self-made predicament.

The substance of this chapter is now devoted to the five closely connected aspects of Christian faith as they bear on the Church's witness and holiness. The first concerns that 'mixed' animal and spirit-bearing constitution comprehended by the word *flesh;* the second involves the continuity and healing of personal life from its origins to its heavenly destiny; the third focuses on eucharistic living and mission in relation to the book's argument as a whole; the fourth considers unbelief among Christians, the practice of ministry and the nature of the Church; and the fifth area looks at Christian community being made holy through penitence as believers are healed and enabled to grow in the Spirit.

A. The significance of 'flesh' in Jesus and in ourselves

Vogel's attention to the scriptural meaning of this word is valuable, encouraging the hope that the Church will grow away from its presently aggressive controversies towards a real unity of heart. First he emphasises that we belong to the world; we are not saved from the world but with the world. Starting from the preface to John's gospel (1:14) he writes

> the word 'flesh' is...a synonym for Jesus having 'lived among us'. The flesh we receive in the eucharist *is* Jesus' life in the world. In biblical usage, 'flesh' refers not so much to *what* lives as to *how* a person lives. In our use of the terms, 'body' is an abstract noun indicating a common feature of human existence; 'flesh' on the other hand, has a concrete, singular meaning for us. We use the term 'body' collectively to refer to a body [group] of people, but we never speak of a 'flesh of people'.... [B]ecause of the change of connotation...we miss the very essence of what Jesus was saying if we use the word 'body' instead of 'flesh' to describe Jesus' presence in the eucharist. (pp.98-99)

Vogel then draws from John 6 a lesson which is also resisted by our current ways of thinking, when it is assumed that giving our allegiance to God inwardly and in spoken words is all that he calls for. He quotes the NT scholar Raymond Brown concerning verses 51-58.

> 'No longer are we told that eternal life is the result of believing in Jesus; it comes from feeding on his flesh and drinking his blood (54).... Even though the verses 51-58 are remarkably like those of 35-50, a new vocabulary runs through them: 'eat', 'feed', 'drink', 'flesh', 'blood" (*The Gospel According to John, 1-12* Anchor Bible 1966). The new truth to which Jesus now leads his listeners is that they (we) can have right *belief* only by *doing* something. (p.98)

Because we are so prone to live in withdrawn ways, keeping much of our personhood uncommunicated, we can fail to live as engaged members of the communities for which we are made. It is clear from all the gospels that *acted faith* is what Jesus constantly commended.

Vogel discusses the two senses in which Paul uses the word flesh, the one meaning humanity in health and wholeness, the other unhealthy and sinful. Lustful living is withdrawn, possessive, self-centred, and it has nothing of the generous, participating life of fully personal relationships. From this perspective we can and should make an attempt to defuse the explosive and polarised controversy in the Church that has come to a head in our time over all matters of sexuality. But no progress can be made without willingness on all sides to acknowledge that the fear of sexual power and the desire to use it for socio-political ends have always played a major part in human *religions*. As a result, from its beginning in early Israel the benign character of biblical faith was damaged with notions that are contrary to God's purposes. Using historical and psychological insights we can now see more clearly how harmful misogynistic and other gender-based abuses have been through the centuries. Not a few traditional attitudes and opinions, long assumed to be orthodox, do not belong to the integrity of Christian faith – for example that, because the apostles were male, the ordination of women to the priesthood is contrary to God's will. Increasingly Christians are realising that such views only became part of the Church's understanding because of long-standing social custom and that, especially in the light of all we can now see of human nature, they have no place in what God has actually revealed. Rather they are themselves symptoms of the disorder from which God has redeemed us in Christ.

Whatever changes of heart and mind are needed at this time it is clear that Christians have to witness that the moral order which God seeks to establish is one based on the recognition that we are created sexual beings not only for procreation but equally to ensure the groundwork of desire on which to build intimate, loving and mutually responsible relationships. Such relationships of care and respect for each other can be fostered well if people's emotionality is nourished, and healed when it is hurt. Rules and customs that inhibit such personal growth, and prevent respect for and empathy with people who are different, are alien to Christianity. What the world needs from the Church and other agencies are initiatives which open people's eyes to the tenderness of children at the earliest stages of life, for that is where our sexual formation is grounded and needs to be protected.

Here I refer to David Edwards' book *Yes: A Positive Faith*.[5] Being sensitive to the large number of Christians world-wide who 'continue to believe deeply that [certain] practices are wrong', includes the recognition that 'traditional teaching was related to traditional soc-ieties' and that the NT shows how Christians have an obligation to relate God's will to the realities of the society in which believers are called to live. Patience is needed for new perceptions to be understood.

Ensuring justice for minorities is important, but is only one priority if unity and everyone's nurture is to be secured 'in the bond of peace' (Col 3:14). Throughout earlier history women 'were usually married' and while 'many children died in their early years, it was hoped many would be born'. Yet even in those circumstances the practice of divorce in Jewish and Christian practice was far from being outlawed. Since

> the law of ancient Israel allowed a husband to choose [divorce]
> if he found 'something objectionable in her' (Deuteronomy
> 24:1-3).... Divorced wives must have been numerous among
> the prostitutes whose friend Jesus was. (p.33)

Against that background we can see the significance of Jesus' friendship with Mary Magdalene, and be encouraged to adopt Edwards' balanced assessment of how to move forward from the divisions and uncertainties in which Christians now stand. Again, in respect of homosexuality, it is not true that liberal Christian proposals always surrender to secular hedonism. Where the practice is not deliberately chosen but deeply rooted in the person's makeup we are obliged to acknowledge that this condition is now shown to be the result of constitutional changes in the middle stages of a person's foetal life. Recognising such advances in knowledge, both Church and society need to see the limitations of rule-bound moralities, without encouraging social practice to degenerate into ways that fail to protect the vulnerable, and the stability of responsible shared life.

> If self-fulfilment through practices which many people still
> do not think of as 'natural' is given publicity as if it pre-
> sented no problem at all, hostility is often provoked. So
> sensitivity is needed when, for example, it is claimed that
> homosexuals in actively sexual relationships have equal
> rights to be church leaders. (pp.34-35)

B. Faith and the continuity of each person

Jesus talks of God as Father, Abba, not only because of his own uniquely close relation to the Father but because he wants all people to know themselves related to God as *their* Father. Daniel Hardy notes that in addressing him as Father or Mother, Christians are 'identifying God more clearly as the person who is not only the origin of, but also always involved with, a son or daughter' (p.222). That sort of intimate involvement is the personal relationship with our Creator for which all people have been made. It is a corporate and inclusive relationship that the Creator himself actualises and energises, in a quiet, matter of fact way through our response to the risen Christ and the in-breathing of the Spirit.

This perception of relations with God is a reminder that in his life of atonement on our behalf Jesus formed in himself a new way of relating to God which makes it possible for our humanity to mature to its proper fulfilment in God. In this second theological area we are back therefore with the doctrine of God's Trinity and with human nature being corporate in the image of God. Since God is creating a community of transformed communities we must keep in mind that every family lives on from generation to generation and each individual is not just genetically united with fellow members of the race, but also personally connected with her particular ancestors. It is evident, from many tantalisingly intangible indications, that the lives of individuals survive after physical death in an incomplete, disembodied form, awaiting a proper fulfilment. That fulfilment Christians call the 'resurrection of the body', that is, life renewed in that different form which was discerned but not wholly exposed to view when the first disciples encountered the risen Jesus.

Because believers have been given new birth in the Spirit they can 'know' the personal being of God, and in that assurance they are able to trust that the resurrection of Christ reveals God's intention for everyone. In the perspective of the *koinonia* which life in Christ gives us we can be confident that the state for which we are being prepared will be even more socially sustained than earthly life is. Even more significantly we realise that it will be centred in God in a more manifest way; and this we expect will develop gradually as those who have died are enabled to adjust to the new conditions. However, if this understanding of people's further development after death is broadly correct, the process of adjustment will surely be somewhat protracted, since the work of emotional healing and spiritual change will certainly be considerable. We know that spiritual growth through psychodynamic healing *in this life* brings much benefit but that few are able to make that kind of progress, and that it is in any case limited. Consequently the great majority die burdened and far from whole. So much detail of this prospect is hidden from us, but we have enough insight not only from scripture but also through therapy and the history of spirituality to be confident that God will complete through some kind of process what he begins here and now. Although everyone is likely to resist the need for personal change, we find that people do change as life goes on, for the better or the worse. Sometimes the turn into a godly direction can be remarkable, but Jesus himself makes it plain that all spiritual growth occurs on two conditions. On the one hand experience of suffering and disadvantage will be involved, and on the other the person whose character is changing must choose to go along in the direction to which he is being drawn.

Death as Jesus experienced it
A further strand in this sketch of the continuity between life now and life after physical death can be seen by considering Jesus' own experience of death and resurrection, and the inferences we should draw from the textual evidence. In this connection Tom Smail expresses a widespread interpretation that I suggest points beyond itself to a rather different conclusion. He writes that at the cross the 'mutuality of the Father-Son relationship is broken but the unifying and sustaining gift of the Spirit by the Father to the Son remains',[6] whereas I contend that if the relationship is secure between Son and Spirit so it must be between the Son and the Father directly. It distorts the nature of God's Trinity to argue that the Spirit, as the bond between Father and Son, mediates the Father's goodwill while the Father himself had actually withdrawn from Christ! Jesus certainly felt bewildered and 'god-forsaken' in undergoing his execution, but that layer of conscious experience did not expunge the undergirding and upholding presence of the Father himself. I agree his presence is submerged, but the awareness would have remained that he, the man Jesus, belongs to and is inseparable from the Fatherly being of God. Smail in effect acknowledges this because in dismissing what Fiddes had argued he stands firmly for the truth that Jesus' endurance was not purely human.

> Jesus in the patient endurance of the Spirit maintained and affirmed his eternal relationship with the Father. It was this that enabled him to give himself to the Father on the cross. (pp.135-136)

So in this connection I am only disagreeing with Smail in respect of the inferences he draws on the ground of what I take to be a mis-representation of the trinity doctrine. This view of trinitarian roles has become current in the Church because the hypostaseis have been understood to be persons in too easy a parallel with the human individual. Instead we must continue to affirm that no divine action in the world, whether of God the Son or of God the Spirit occurs without the presence of the Father. These 'persons' of the Trinity always act as One.

In the light of this fundamental truth we should not draw the wrong conclusion from Jesus' cry of dereliction expressed in the opening verse of Psalm 22. I find it misleading therefore to say that this cry is 'the prayer of one who is still trusting when every ground of trust has been removed', because, as Smail puts it himself, 'when it seems that God has abandoned him' the Spirit is

> there in a way that does not destroy his identification with us but that enables him to cope with it ... not as the ecsta-tic Spirit of Pentecost but as the reticent Spirit of patient endurance. (p.135)

It only *seemed* to Jesus' consciousness that the Father had abandoned the Son. How are we to be sure of this, and why do I see it to be important that Christians declare the assurance? The answer begins with realising that human consciousness is multi-layered. Accord-ingly we should not be surprised to notice that at times we fail to keep in mind something we know to be real but which, because of the emotional stress of a certain situation, we no longer take into account. Our own experiences help us to understand something of what Jesus went through. If it were really true that the Father had abandoned Jesus it would not have been possible for Jesus to have continued trusting him. An actual abandonment of Christ on the cross would also make nonsense of the incarnation and atonement. Since the Father-Son relationship is eternal and constitutive of God's being, there can be no sense in suggesting, as Smail appears to do, that Jesus as man maintains his relationship with the Father with the aid of the Spirit without the Father's participation. He seems to imply that for a period the Father's attention has to be withdrawn from the relationship so that Jesus may endure the human condition. In contrast we must affirm that the eternal union of Father and Son is inseparably active in the self-giving which not only constitutes the incarnation but also undergirds a relationship between God and every human person. That people do not recognise and enjoy this relationship is because of prevailing unbelief. It is thus of great practical importance both for explaining Christian doctrine with accuracy, and for pastoral ministry in enabling people to understand their own emotional and intellectual difficulties, to be clear that there never is any situation in which it is true to say 'every ground of trust has been removed', for God is always present. Moreover, Christians are obliged to declare that it is the triune God who took flesh, who suffered and died in Jesus, for such is God's fundamental unity. No device of dividing the roles of the persons can enable us to avoid the truth that the Father is involved in the cross. *In no way did God withdraw,* leaving the human Jesus to suffer, as if the Spirit were detached to sustain him in the absence of the Father.

Our own death and continuity

Turning, however, from Christ to ourselves, what are we to say of the created person's continuity and the nature of his death? Whether or not there has been a positive response to the Gospel there will be at death a sudden end to this life's physical powers. In that condition whatever the departed person knows, is aware of, will not be via the brain which is dead. It can only be in some way dependent on God's Spirit, who sustains the created spirit of the person concerned. But does Smail's view require me to change my mind? I see nothing in scripture, in reason or in the evidences of experience to justify the absolute ending of personal life by the death of the body that he proposes.

> When we die all our relationships with God and with people are severed and we are carried from being to non-being.... Death is the collapse of all relationships into unresponsiveness. (pp.138-139)

I have agreed that the dead are more helpless but not that they are cut off from God. Indeed what Smail himself writes in his next chapter, entitled 'For the Whole World', finely expresses the hope of Christocentric universalism, but that is hardly compatible with the sentences quoted above. What can be the explanation? The answer, I believe, may be surprising for many Christians but it concerns the very nature of the redeemed life. It is a life which begins in the earth and takes into account every circumstance of earthly development, so that a sinless world is eventually created from so humble a base. It is worth remembering that the author of Hebrews is specific on this point – death does not separate from God but the fear of death holds people in slavery. The diabolic power to deceive God's children has to be destroyed (Heb 2:9-11,14,15,17; cf John 8:44). The 'atonement for the sins of the people' which Jesus made involved him in enduring all that humankind suffers. He was tasting 'death for everyone' that they may become holy. Through the perfection of his obedience death becomes what it is intended to be and has its proper fulfilment in healing, reconciliation and glory. This fits profoundly with the psychological realities of the human condition.

Consequently the best way to understand our continuity after physical death is in parallel with what happened in the death of Jesus himself, and in the interval that we keep as Holy Saturday, awaiting Easter morning. Despite the difference between him and ourselves, the condition of the earthly body and of every individual's dependence on the personal life of the Trinity mean that the process of change must be similar, although for Jesus resurrection came at once. But Smail sees it quite differently.

> The Son of God is dead; his death is our death. It is an evil undoing of the work of the Creator which looks like the final triumph of all the powers of darkness that have brought him to the cross. He is dead and unresponsive to his friends and he is dead and unresponsive to his Father. This is the ultimate disruptive attack on the unity of Father and Son, this is the permitted intrusion of death into the Trinitarian life of God.

Why does Smail write this, when he goes on in the very next paragraph to qualify it by declaring 'what we said ... about the desolation holds true even here ... the dead Son is still in profound unity with the Father'? (p.139). As we have seen, he argues that '*the Holy Spirit who is distinct from both* (Father and Son) *holds them both together....* And ... when the Son is dead the Spirit lives and goes on relating him to the Father even in his deadness' (p.140). Not only does this distort the doctrine of God but it also misrepresents what Jesus had achieved through his dying in confronting the human origins of evil. Smail's thought seems to rest on the assumption that to die is to be overcome by evil, yet is it not true that death is leading to greater life through the new covenant in Christ's blood? He recognises that it is not God but we who must be changed (p.88), and rejects the notion that 'Christ was punished in our stead' (p.98). But he seems unable to get away from the idea that atonement is fundamentally a transaction within the Godhead. Jesus, he says, 'deals with sinners by dealing with his Father' (p.90). It is a view that fails to put foremost emphasis on reconciliation as the passionate aim of the One triune God (2 Cor. 5:18,19). Smail quoted Colin Gunton to the effect that the cross initiates a process of transformation in which the reconciliation of persons enables the acknowledged evil of the past to become the basis for present and future good.[7]

Even the grossest perpetrator of evil can be transformed. This is not followed up, however, because in Smail's account only the endurance of God's wrathful judgement on sinners is taken to be the meaning of Good Friday and only 'on Easter morning' is God's 'Yes' given expression. Can this be the NT message? Bearing the death of all the victims and perpetrators seems to be taken as a matter of fulfilling Christ's loving obedience to the Father rather than the extension of God's converting love to the people who need to be reconciled and changed. In contrast I hold that the atonement doctrine expresses the gospel that through Jesus' sin-bearing on the cross, God entered into the suffering of sinners for their reconciliation and liberation from evil as it grips human wills. He made a new way of life for humankind to share. His death was not to satisfy some principle which is thought to be inherent in the righteous transaction between the Son and the Father. The Son's gift of loving obedience undoubtedly saves the world, but it is the life of God's Trinity in human flesh, breaking evil's grip, and drawing rebellious creatures into union with himself which constitutes that obedience. Thus the resurrection is the evidence of what God did on Good Friday.

Starting from the same New Testament conviction that 'his death is our death', I agree with Smail in reference to Romans 6:10 that Christ died *to* sin rather than for sin. By accepting that God put us to death with himself, we too can die to sin. By his death for humanity's sake, Jesus achieved God's purpose which is to condemn sin and save sinners. Smail, however, argues that the past is

> destroyed: Christ takes the sinful humanity that belongs to that past down with him to death so that it does not disrupt our relationship to God any more. (p.118)

In my view this does not allow an adequate account of what spiritual dying involves. It is the death of the sinful will that matters. In terms of my distinction between subject and person, it is the sinful acts and disposition that are put to death by the subject-self's new choice (cf Col. 3:5-10). This dying does not destroy the whole personhood and its history in which sin has been dominant, but it does change its direction and character, and makes the transition from the death of sin to the life of righteousness in God's spirit. In consequence the redeemed individual is still the person he was before conversion, but in character he may be barely recognisable so great can the change be. He now sees his personal history of sin in a completely different light. The dreadful marks of rebellion are noticeable, just as the marks of Christ's wounds are still upon his body.

Accordingly, I would say that it is not the past but sin which is 'abolished' and 'destroyed'. By accepting Christ's dying for us we die with him so we can be rid of sin's attraction and its harmful effects. In this way sin is destroyed and believers are given increasing freedom to trust God's promise that our entire lives may be transformed rather than be replaced. Replacing our past would in effect make us different people. Stressing that Christ died for the ungodly, while we were still sinners, Paul was declaring that the cross exposes both the judgement of sinners and the will of God to change them at the same time. God's love is victorious in human suffering and degradation, for that is the place where his love is accessible to us. The cross is where God nailed our condemnation in order to make us alive in the risen Christ (Col 2:13-15 and 3:3), and for that reason the crucified Saviour will forever display the glory of God's Trinity.

Beyond death, the glory to come
In being raised and ascended Jesus was revealing a new view of the universe which contradicts the Judaic perception. Second-Temple Judaism saw death only as 'an enemy to be defeated' but that was because the Jewish hope was focused too narrowly on the world under its present familiar conditions. In the words of Tom Wright

> [m]ainline Jews were not hoping to escape from the present universe.... [W]hen the kingdom came ... they would need new bodies to enjoy the very much this-worldly *shalom*, peace and prosperity that was in store.[8]

For the Jews death was an 'intruder... that had invaded the created order at its heart and corrupted human beings themselves' whereas Christians 'believed that Israel's god had acted in him (Jesus as 'son of god') to fulfil the covenant promises by dealing at last with the problem of evil' This he had done through death itself, and the result was that the fear of death was broken (cf Hebrews 2:14,15). Death could now be seen in its true light. Wright goes on to say that in the NT 'the resurrection was never a *redescription* of death, but always its *defeat*'. To this I suggest we have to add that death is defeated because the resurrection made evident *the defeat of sin on the cross* and its apparent power to abolish humanity forever. Death can no longer reign as it seemed to do before, by bringing human life to a terminus in the grave and leaving people without ultimate hope (cf Eph. 2:15). This is evident in Paul's letters, especially Romans 8:18-25 and 34-39. As 'a life-giving act of the covenant god', the resurrection of Jesus was the completion of a process, not a mere reversal. In consequence the Church was obliged to see death in an entirely different light. We can understand that the conceptual implications took time to sink in and to be applied to all that was said about death. The way I understand Wright's words is that the resurrection builds on, but takes humanity beyond death's disciplinary function and restores its life-giving purpose. As Paul puts it, death, like suffering, is to be seen in the context of creation, comparable to 'the pains of childbirth' (Rom 8:22). Christians were convinced that the '*eschaton* had arrived' and 'the long narrative of Israel's history had reached its climax'.[9] That truth had within it a further staggering implication – that death had never been an entirely negative ending, as had been assumed. Death was corrective in God's purpose, and a stage in transformation. It did not need to be reversed, but restored to its proper transitional role. Beyond its punitive and regulative functions death serves primarily to be the means through which God's purpose for the life of persons can be fulfilled in the age of resurrection. This would be one of the 'many things' the Spirit was to uncover as the Church's experience expanded. Persecution and the faithfulness of the martyrs would have strengthened that changing awareness. Thus Christians were discovering that death in Christ leads to the promised glory.

When this has been clarified the whole redemptive purpose of God can be seen in its true proportions. The Saviour is not 'primarily dealing with his Father' but with those he comes to save. Accordingly the Christian position is that the Father is with Jesus and the Spirit from start to finish. There is no transaction to be enacted invisibly within the Godhead. Rather the atonement action in Christ, which is the life of Jesus himself extended by the Spirit's ministry in transforming other people, is an integrated activity of God's Trinity directed to rebellious humanity. He comes to seek and to save the lost. Jesus is not lifted up on the cross that the Father may see his Son's righteousness, but he is lifted up to draw all people to himself; it is they who are to see and respond. In this man, crucified and risen, there is their own life already glorified.

So I come to consider the condition of Jesus when his body is taken down from the cross that it may be laid in the tomb. I believe that when Jesus uttered the words, 'It is finished', and then gave himself up to the Father, he knew that what he had to do in suffering and dying was complete. What had to follow was that time of earthly appearances over the 'forty days' which we can understand was much needed for the frightened disciples to become adjusted. No doubt also the tradition is correct that 'he descended into hell', for he must go on doing that as part of his everlasting priesthood until the world as we know it ends in the triumph of his Kingdom. But what is exposed in that descent, and must continually be exposed through the Church's ministry, is his love fulfilled on the Cross. At the moment of his release from living in his embodied condition, Jesus would be acutely aware of what the Spirit had enabled him to do. There would be for him no more waiting for the Father to act. So we have, I think, no alternative but to affirm that the mystery of his resurrection came into existence the instant Jesus died. His appearance to the disciples, however, was gradual, as the realisation of what had happened dawned. The 'three days' delay before the event first became evident was needed for them, not for him. It is important for the Church to be clear about this continuity of personal life. In being spiritual we are not immortal in the sense of having something about our created being that cannot die. But as personal creatures we have two kinds of dependence on the Trinity; one as material beings and one as spiritual. As created spirits we can die eventually in the ultimate sense, but that is because we have the freedom to cut ourselves off from the personal life of God until we cease to exist. If that does happen in the case of any person it will only be made final at 'the Last Day'.

The significance of this difference in dependence is that the created person in this present 'age' is unfinished and potentially unstable. Being weak and fragile physically, emotionally and intellectually, the person needs to grow and to be healed, so that the new life of spiritual dependence on God can be taken further. Inevitably the process can be long and painful, and can only take place with the person's active participation; it will involve the whole range of that person's experience. The goal is not just individual sanctification but the development of a corporate maturity for which the continuity and the inter-relations of individuals' lives within their family history provide the raw material. In adjusting contemporary Christian thinking along these lines, it is helpful to notice Wright's discussion in *Surprised by Hope*.[10] Referring to 1 Corinthians 15:20 he writes: 'Paul doesn't mean that physicality will be abolished.... The contrast is between *corruptible physicality* on the one hand and *non-corruptible physicality* on the other' (p.168).

> One of the greatest problems of the western church, ever since the Reformation at least, is that it hasn't really known

what the gospels were there for. Imagining that the point of
Christianity was to enable people to 'go to heaven', most
western Christians have [misread Paul as well as the gos-
pels]. This long tradition has screened out the possibility
that when Jesus spoke of 'God's kingdom' he wasn't talking
about a 'heaven' for which he was preparing his followers,
but about something … happening in and on this earth,
through his work, then through his death and resurrection,
and then through the Spirit-led work to which they would
be called. (p.215)

Christina Rees in her book *The Divine Embrace: Discovering the
Reality of God's Love* records a remarkable message about God's
suffering with us, that a relative of hers, Jennifer Rees Larcombe,
was given.

She had been in hospital for several months, very ill and
in severe pain. At one point she remembers the pain being
so great that she shouted silently at Jesus that his intense
suffering on the cross had only lasted six hours, but hers
seemed to go on for ever. The answer she heard within
astounded her. 'My suffering will go on until the last of
my children are safely home, because I live in each cell of
your physical bodies. I feel all your pain as you feel it, I
also feel the pain of your broken hearts and the distress of
your deranged minds. Please don't think I have separated
myself from you.[11]

Those words which reassured Jennifer confirm the Christian conviction that God is intent on converting and transforming people's
lives, but not in some spiritual arena withdrawn from the world's life.
The changes of heart and mind to which he leads all who will trust
him are directly related to the events of their lives, much of which
they share with others. It is out of the terrible depravity, the proud
self-concern and the neglect of responsibility in human behaviour as
well as every form of suffering in which people are involved that God
remakes the world to his glory in Christ and so enables humankind
to enter into his joy. Therefore the forgiveness and healing that God
brings does not, as many Christians believe, involve a forgetting.
That notion arose from the Old Testament belief that God's holiness
requires sin to be put out of mind, but the New Testament reverses
that ancient conviction through Christ's passion. The memories of
sin and suffering are retained after redemption and healing. Because

their vicious character has been eliminated through the cross these memories are transformed but not obliterated.

The problem of spiritual blindness

I include Smail's book in this study because he gives specific attention to the tension which became pronounced in the second half of the twentieth century between traditional approaches to the atonement and what he calls theodicy-type theology of the cross, a category in which Lake's thinking may be thought to fall. Smail takes into account all the views of atonement and relates them to the biblical material. In relation to that sense of tension he presents a comprehensive evangelical view that takes seriously Christ's identification with human suffering as well as with sin. Neglecting the full significance of suffering has been a deficit in all the different theologies that the Church has produced so far. The atonement involves God's remarkable entry into human pain in order to change the way his children respond to suffering as well as to selfishness. In this perspective, theodicy-type theology in the twentieth century added something which the earlier atonement thinking had been unable to explore. The latter was so preoccupied with sin itself and with the anxiety that can surround death, that the redemptive function of Christ's suffering was too narrowly restricted. If we attend to the consequences of sin more broadly we can discern that God's suffering does more than destroy sin. He reaches out to all people before they sin, and touches all the circumstances of their mortal existence. An understanding of the human predicament too narrowly confined to deliberate sinfulness has led the Church to give the world the impression that once the means of restoring relationship with God has been established in Christ's life, the Spirit has only to enable believers to appropriate his forgiveness. If we draw attention directly to God identifying himself with suffering humanity, we are prompted to look beyond the problem of sin to what one might call the problem of blindness. This is consequence as well as cause of sin in all its forms, and reminds us why unbelief is the great barrier (John 6:29 et al).

It is relevant to compare the secularly inspired fashion in late-twentieth-century thinkers to protest against theodicy as an irrational and almost immoral pursuit, with the position of conservative theologians. Although the latter come to very different conclusions, these bible-centred thinkers can be influenced by a similar motivation when they attribute suffering and disorder *entirely* to the deliberate and culpable sin of individuals. What I think is shared by the two groups is the notion, incoherently conceived as it usually is, that if the propensity of individuals towards criminality, self-centredness, and abhorrent evils of all kinds is dealt with, then human life as we know it would be all right. If there is some truth in this observation we should think again about Christ's suffering and its meaning in God's purpose. I believe that the central message of the Bible as a whole and the NT especially is that God identifies himself with the suffering of his children for a purpose that is much broader than his condemnation and reconciliation of individual sinners. The constructive centre of that purpose *is to release true life by breaking the power of communal self-deceit* for that is what entices people into sin. Because this power deceives and traps people in isolation from himself, God's judgement is primarily of shared complacency, only secondarily of individuals. This feature of biblical faith may not have been noticed sufficiently in Christian theology. We have to keep in mind that Judaism inherited and was greatly affected by the widespread pagan notion that suffering was evidence of guilt. Although that doctrine was opposed by Jesus, it is not surprising that the undercurrents of its prejudice would come to influence the development of Christian doctrine adversely as time went on. It is significant that Jesus teaches his disciples not to judge and that the whole emphasis of the gospels is on compassion as Jesus deals with people and tells his parables. It is striking that the first letter of John sums up the Christian message in the words: 'God is light, and in him is no darkness at all' (1:5). How can the world eventually come to recognise this? The answer is emphatic: because Jesus suffered and died the death of a common victim (Heb 4:15-5:5, 13:12). Once this has been realised, Christians should not be afraid to acknowledge that the creation of embodied persons involves their being victimised. God allows humankind to be victims of their precarious condition for only so can his creative purpose be fulfilled, in a community of freely loving communities. For this to succeed he himself must become one of his creatures and so be victimised.

In perceiving this, modern theodicy-type theology, although insufficient in itself, has made a needed contribution to the development of a reliable doctrine. With this in mind I draw attention to the way Smail keeps theodicy and atonement together (p.57). He is anxious that theodicy theologies of the cross can relativise 'the sin problem over against the suffering problem', which is true, but he affirms that the gospel presents

> the crucified Jesus as *both* the one who died for sinners *and* the
> oppressed victim who suffered in a way he had done nothing

> to deserve. We might even say that in a central atonement
> verse like 2 Corinthians 5:21, Christ is presented to us as at
> the same time vicarious sinner and vicarious victim. (p.49)

Smail acknowledges that Moltmann 'has helped us to see that this kind
of theodicy is an authentic aspect of any full Christian understanding
of the work of Jesus' (p.51). In fact it appears that Moltmann's views
have had a considerable influence on Smail – to the Church's advantage. Recalling Paul's reflection on himself in Romans 7, Smail refers
to Jesus praying for his executioners as those who are also the

> victims of their own sinning and have to be regarded less with
> condemnation than with compassion.... Even as responsible
> sinners, we are helpless victims.... This dialectic relationship
> between the sin we commit and the sin that has victimised
> us is at the heart of the much-neglected doctrine of original
> sin.... We are ... victims of a sinful situation far beyond our
> own making and yet at the same time *willing* victims, who
> have made common cause with the race in its rebellion....
> We must not, as in the modern tendency, allow the realisation
> that we are victims to exculpate us from responsibility for our
> actions: equally we must not allow the reality of our respon-
> sibility to obscure the reality of our victimisation and our
> helplessness. (p.55-56)

Smail's recognition that 'the two approaches ... need to be rein-
tegrated' helps us to see that a truthful statement of redemption from
sin depends on the perception that Jesus died as victim. Jesus' love
invites us to die with him and through him to all the sin that sets us
against God, our own and that of others. By his initiatives God enters
into the mental pain that the perpetrators of evil will eventually suffer
for themselves, when they want to respond to him. The proximity and
sequence of physical and mental pain in the world makes it possible
for God to work in this way, redeeming us by facilitating, through the
cross, our conversion, healing, repentance and transformation. Smail
writes, with reference to 1 Peter 2:24, 'The wounds inflicted on him
as victim become the means by which he accomplishes our healing
as Saviour'. (p.52)

In the world of human interaction, spiritual and intellectual blindness can be as harmful in its long-term effects as deliberate sin. This
means that everyone contributes to the human problem including those
who are doing much to overcome it. For this reason God's redemptive
action has to achieve more than the eradication of sin in its deliberate

forms. He must awaken humankind to the indispensable priority of his own gracious life, and the extraordinary nature of the destiny to which he is leading his 'children'. In a word, we are having to learn how to respond to his holiness, and the call to unity which it involves. It is perhaps this aspect of atonement doctrine, and Christian obedience in consequence, that will require the greatest change of direction in the Church's life over the years ahead.

C. The individual's commitment to the Church's mission

The third of these aspects of Christianity that needs especial attention extends what I have written earlier on the involvement of believers in what God is doing, through their gathered life together as Church. By returning to these themes I draw together several strands that have occupied previous chapters so as to focus on the Eucharist, not just as the centre for reformation of the Church's life, although this has been widely ignored, but as the spearhead of her mission as well. Thus in both respects one of the main conclusions of this book is that Christians have to return to eucharistic living in a far more radical way than has yet been perceived even in any of the Church's ancient traditions. The need is to rediscover that Christianity is the religion of God's table, and that this marks out the Church in the Abrahamic family as the branch which does not see its significance simply with reference to the precepts of a book. Certainly biblical scripture must not be sidelined. In Christianity the documents of the two covenants remain determinative, yet even the new Testament is subordinate to Christ for it is the personal status of Jesus Christ revealed in his resurrection that clarifies the meaning of those scriptures.

The Risen Jesus with his people at table

I refer to this by looking at the experience of the two disciples at Emmaus. It was not of course that they simply recognised the characteristic gestures of his action, as they had seen them so often through all the times they had eaten with him. What came to them so forcibly that evening was the meaning of his words and actions at the Last Supper. That was the decisive eucharistic occasion because in it Jesus had signalled that his coming suffering and death would be the place of God's victory. 'This is my body, which is for you. This cup is the new covenant in my blood'. Nothing in Paul's letters witnesses more significantly to the early Church's faith and practice than the fact that he takes up, from the earliest tradition of the Lord's life, this one item that he 'received from the Lord (and) passed on to you'. Here is the very heart of the community's life in its allegiance to Jesus (1 Cor 11:23-25). Yet its full significance has not been seen very clearly at any stage of Christian history. On the one hand the story of Catholicism and Orthodoxy tells how Christians allowed alien thinking to interpret the dominical action and words, so that for centuries almost the entire focus of devotion and ministry was on the discrete sacramental elements in some distinction from the living presence of Jesus as he had lived in the days of his flesh. On the other hand, this diminishment of the Eucharist's significance was not corrected significantly by Protestantism. The period following the Reformation has been marked by similar forms of unfaithfulness. The modern liturgical movement has made an improvement, but its influence has remained weak just because the depth of the earlier misunderstanding has not been uncovered sufficiently.

There is now some real readiness to learn new and flexible ways of being Church, although much of it assumes that it is better human action that is important. Is it not rather that more *attentive passivity* is needed, in the sense of greater reliance on letting God lead the way in the Church's mission? I believe we have to ask ourselves afresh: why did Jesus institute this symbolic ritual? Evidently his intention was to build into the fabric of the Church's interpersonal life a practical way of shared personal dependence on God's nourishing, in the Holy Spirit, through which he himself would continue to be the leader of his disciples. But this intention was quickly subverted, not only by treating the bread and the wine as if they were semi-literally body and blood, but also in the ministry of the presiding priest. By thinking of the elements being changed into supernatural items through ministerial agency, the clergy appropriated to themselves a role which diminished the liturgy of the whole membership. The sheer paradox of this was that by treating the sacrament as a pair of objective gifts the very purpose of the Supper had been avoided. All this corrosion of Christian thinking took place long ago, and so it is not surprising that the damage done is largely absent from our consciousness. The fact that from early days the Church's intellectual development was dominated by Greek philosophy meant that very soon the Church's thinkers were in no position to see what had gone wrong, even when they were attending to the scriptures. What followed was only further confusion.

Christopher Cocksworth quotes the Scottish Presbyterian Robert Bruce who asserted in 1589 that

> [i]t is certainly true that we get ... no other thing in the Sacrament than we got in the Word .... Why then is the Sacrament appointed? Not that you may get any new thing but that you may get the same thing better than you had in the Word.... [12]

However understandable this idea was in view of the earlier misreading, we need to see how perverse we are if we continue to think that way. Christian believers have always understood, more or less, what is going on when they listen to preaching and teaching or read the biblical texts themselves. But modern Christians, like those of the reformation period, have largely lost any clear idea that the sacrament provides something that goes beyond the scriptures and the spoken Word. In fact it gives us a twofold benefit. Firstly, the Supper is God's way of sharpening our attention to Christ's presence with us in the community of faith. The intention is to embrace into unity and mission all who are gathered round the table in prayer week by week, and to do so in a way that minimises superfluous talk which may only draw people's attention back to themselves. And secondly, although it provides the Christian's staple diet, the Eucharist is not given to us in separation from the world. We receive for ourselves, but do so in prayerful solidarity with all humankind. We celebrate this meal as the baptised who put themselves alongside the Crucified, the One who has identified himself with the world. So the character of Christian prayer as predominantly vicarious is most evident in the Eucharist, since it is the prayer of Christ in his Body as he continues to give himself for all. The prayer of individual believers is always to be understood in that context. Their service throughout the day is one with their corporate liturgy in the Eucharistic assembly. We join the Saviour put to death outside the city gates, not only that we may share his holiness for ourselves but to be with those who are yet to fix their eyes on Jesus (Heb. 12:2,10).

If, then, the Eucharist is the chief occasion for Christians to engage in the corporate task of intercession and witness, the difference between the two parts of the service needs emphasis, and every opportunity should be taken to restore the perception that in respect of the meal itself words can only be a subsidiary aid. Many Christians in modern times have been brought up to assume that the Eucharist is entirely for the benefit of communicants. Certainly, nourishing is involved in the ministries of both Word and Sacrament, but in being together listening to scripture, and waiting on the Spirit's declaration of God's Word, the Church *sits* in receptive mode in order to be strengthened in mind and heart. Then comes a radical change to more active engagement, for in being round the table in celebration of Easter and Pentecost, the Church *stands* in Christ to share in his priestly intercession and witness. In this case the spiritual work properly precedes the nourishing. Does this undermine justification and the priority of grace? Not at all, because the Eucharist has no meaning unless it follows on the reality of conversion and baptism. This then is the something different that is happening in the eucharistic meal. At the table there is a plainness of activity that requires us to look to God actively present in the immediacy of today. It is a time to stop talking and pay attention to God. Some liturgical words are necessary but they are disciplined to guard against language taking precedence over the action of the meal, and over the remembered action and passion of the risen Jesus. In the Eucharist our attention is not withdrawn from today's world, but we aim to see the communities to whom we are sent in the light of Jesus crucified and risen, relying on the Holy Spirit to unite us in the Father's mission. Christ activates our empathy with his, as he turns us daily towards the world in compassion, and so to suppose, as many Christians do, that frequency of attendance in church is a matter for private decision is to misunderstand the very heart of what it is to become a member of Christ.

The mission of God's table-people

This trinitarian emphasis in understanding the Eucharist is funda-mental, directing us to God's action. Our active role is not primary but it is there in our subordination to the Spirit. Through this human activity God acts towards the unconverted, not towards us as if we had been drawn out of the world to be favoured. Brought together as a community to serve Christ, we become channels of his intercession and his self-giving. (John 6:51). Unless clergy and congregations are helped to wake up to the full dimensions of the sacramental meal, and the kind of attention it should be given, the Church will continue to flounder as I believe it does at present.

We should be asking ourselves not just the question that the scho-lars have answered: what does the word *anamnesis* mean? Rather the simpler question is the more important: what about himself did Jesus intend to make present through our act of remembrance? Gregory Dix assumed, and even those who have not received his other opinions with favour have, I think, also assumed that the command to remember him (Luke 22:19 and 1 Cor 11:25) was about

> re-calling before God ... the one sacrifice of Christ in all its accomplished and effectual fullness so that it is here and now operative by its effects in the souls of the redeemed.[13]

In the meal, the Spirit certainly releases the benefits of God's one per-fect self-giving, its overcoming of evil and its fruitfulness in human sanctification, but we are not healed in isolation. We are among those who share in declaring the gospel for the conversion of 'the many', therefore our worship should always be marked by that intention. The aim is not so much to set forth the wondrous cross before the baptised but the unbaptised. The shape of Paul's sentence makes the point emphatically:

every time you eat this loaf and drink the cup you are publicly
proclaiming the Lord's death until he comes again.[14]

It has been shallow thinking not to recognise that the command
to repeat this sacramental event whenever Christians meet at their
Lord's table is for a double purpose; both that they themselves may
be renewed in Christ, and also that the Spirit may act mysteriously
to open the eyes of the unconverted. Awareness of this was lost at
some early date, so to recover the full intention of Jesus' command
at the Last Supper we must go back to the gospels, especially those
of Luke and John. As I do this in the next paragraph it becomes evident, I think, that the function of the Eucharist stands out far more
clearly than current assumptions about it allow.

Harnessing his members to the yoke
Even if we take the abbreviated text of Luke's account of the supper,
with the words 'This is my body' standing without the rest of verse
19, that statement is enough, in the context of Passover, to declare
that his impending execution will establish the new covenant. With
verse 20 omitted, verses 21-27 follow immediately to assert that the
execution will happen through betrayal by one of his own closest
followers. Whether they were actually quarrelling on this occasion
over which of them was to have precedence, Luke thinks it the appropriate moment to record the teaching that calmed the dispute. Such a
desire to exercise power over others is incompatible with the service
to which he calls them. They are to be ones who serve (Luke 22:27),
yet in the verses that follow he affirms that having 'stood by (him) in
his trials' he confers on them a kingdom which is his own. In spite of
the paradox they are to 'sit on thrones, judging the twelve tribes of
Israel'. Jesus' teaching makes it plain: the instruction to be servants is
radical; it means that God has made people to live not for themselves
but for him. When Jesus sends out seventy-two evangelists their vulnerability is stressed (like lambs among wolves), but they are given
his power to offer peace and healing (Luke 10:1-24). Jesus models
the way they are to act. Everything he does is directed by the Father
and enabled by him (John 6:37-65). The pattern, style and direction
of the Christian's life is to be for the welfare of others as prefigured in
Christ's life (John 12:24-26). This way of living is corporate as well
as dependent on God (John 15:1-16). In companionship with fellow
Christians, it requires the constant practice of asking in order to
receive from God. Sent by Christ they will be made holy because he
has 'sanctified himself' for their sake (John 16:23,24; 17:18,19). The

Christian disciple alongside his Lord finds foremost satisfaction in meeting the needs of others and in sharing corporately the Creator's good gifts (cf John 4:34; 1Cor 9:18). We can fairly deduce that Jesus' command to 'remember me' is fulfilled by a repeated celebration of this meal, when it is directed not to the well-being only of those who enjoy its nourishment now and the fellowship of their companions at the table, but to the well-being of those not yet gathered to join the feast. Perhaps the verse which most graphically displays this missionary intention is John 12:32: 'I, when I am lifted up from the earth, will draw all people to myself'. Just because Christ has included believers in himself by his atoning work on the cross, the Church has become the chief sign of his presence everywhere and the agent of his universal intercession. Through the Holy Spirit Christian communities across the world provide the scaffold on which he can be lifted up for those who may be touched by him in their hearts. The people Christians pray for do not need to be present physically, but wherever the Church has gathered to remember Christ in united faith, the meal becomes a potent channel of his love.

If maintained by the right teaching the Eucharist becomes more effective because it is more comprehensive than any other kind of prayer meeting. It points away from what each member is or does on his own, to what all members do together in serving the One who has called them to be with him and in him. The action with bread and wine is designed to direct attention to what God is continually doing in the world to restore human *unity* in himself. Failure to act on that outward, missionary direction of the meal is even more tragic in its local consequences since it has deprived parishes of the repeated opportunity to demonstrate and live out the faith in a way even children can understand and share in actively. But it is easy for the Church to get God's message wrong as so often in the past. The word Eucharist, meaning the blessing of God for his goodness, can be turned round to convey the more comfortable notion that we celebrate God's blessing of ourselves. Therefore we must return repeatedly to the Godward direction of what we are commanded to do.

D. The ministry of Christ's Body

Divine presence, human communality, and the corporate Christ have been recurring themes throughout my argument. Yet it is apparent that at present these fundamentals of Christian faith do not feature prominently in the Church's mission and message: how can they be restored to their proper centrality? Ronald Rolheiser wrote in *The Shattered Lantern*[15] that our society is set 'apart from past generations' in that 'the problem of faith today is especially that of unbelief among believers' (p.15).

> We still have some experience of God, though rarely is it a vital one wherein we actually drink, first-hand from living waters. Most often, in so far as God does enter our every-day experience, God is not experienced as a living person to whom we talk, person to person, from whom we seek final consolation and comfort, and to whom we relate friend to friend, lover to lover, child to parent. Rather God is experien-ced and related to as a religion, a church, a moral philosophy, a guide for private virtue, an imperative for justice.... (p.16)

The unbelief in the Church is there, I have suggested, because of deep-seated fears which have developed in part through our own individual histories but are also ingrained in the social culture, much of which Christians have absorbed. By this culture we are largely obliged to live, even when in some measure we choose to rebel against it. Whether we respond to it positively or negatively the culture's influence on us may be largely hidden.

In another of his sermons Daniel Hardy said, with reference to John 14:6,

> that before the last 200 years, referring to 'I' or 'me' meant something different. Before, it was assumed that an 'I' was always interwoven with 'we', and 'me' with 'us'. The 'I' was simply not divided off, but was an extension of the 'we'.

Although in some respects we are more alert to psychological rea-lities today, in this instance the earlier tradition was right. Hardy then points to the pre-modern view of our relation to God.

> [T]here was no sharp division between God and the world as we now assume. Then, the world was vivid with God, so that its order, purpose and energy were always to some degree symptomatic of God's own life. For a prophet to speak from

God was only a concentrated version of what was possible
for anyone. By that account, God is really stirring in the
world, and in your mind and heart at this very moment.[16]

From the start I have been pressing this awareness of God's presence,
and believe we have to recover and explain precisely this perception
of his immediacy. The double focus of ministry, within and beyond
the Church, calls for renewed attention because the effectiveness of
a congregation's ministry depends on the quality of its shared understanding and devotion. When the interior life of worship is right the
gospel tumbles out in mission wherever Christians go.

The nature of Christ's new embodiment

This happens because the infection of God's Spirit that Christians
carry can encourage other people who are already being touched by
him; and that encouragement can be significantly advanced according to the depth of missionary commitment which congregations
bring to their celebration of the Eucharist. We can be assured that
this springs from Jesus' atoning work on the cross because he is now
active everywhere in the outcome of his resurrection and ascension.
In Christopher Cocksworth's perspective, however, Jesus does not
seem to be directly engaged in the Church's mission. Instead Jesus
'lives in us by the Father's Spirit' (Eph 3:16)… that we may 'put on
the New Man that has been created on God's principles' (Eph 4:24).
He is being emphatic, as I have been, that

> a real participation in the permanent humanity of Christ
> is the beginning, middle and end of the salvation which
> God… gives to our receiving faith. (p.202)

Yet he implies that we can be in Christ without having the immediacy
of his presence. Cocksworth takes up his position because he feels
obliged to suppose that there is a 'dimensional' presence of Jesus
'seated at the right hand of the Father in heaven (Eph 1:20)'. Christ's
'dimensional presence cannot be diffused into an omnipresence without compromising the authentically human characteristic of the risen
Christ', because if that were the case there would be 'a new being' not
having the 'distinguishing features of what it means to be human'.[17]
It will be apparent from chapter 1 that this view fails to appreciate
the intersubjective character of human nature and its grounding in
God's Trinity. The confidence of NT Christians that as members of
the Body of Christ, they already share in the dimensional presence
of the risen Christ at the Father's right hand is most clearly stated by

Paul in Colossians 3:1-4. Christians are not in two places at once; our lives being 'now hidden with Christ in God' does not mean that we are absent, for our share in the order of heaven has begun here and now. Since the 'things above' are already accessible to believers, a distinction between Christ in heaven and Christ alongside the world's people is no longer plausible for those who were promised: 'I am with you always'. Christians believe that their experience of the risen Christ who is now invisible and intangible will become evident to all at 'the end of the age'.

The interpersonal nature of the ascended Christ, made evident in the Church, does not mean that the individuality of Jesus disappears at the ascension. He continues as the historical personage who lives forever, relating now to everyone, as he did on earth to the relatively few he could meet and be with in those circumstances. Every personal creature therefore can enjoy his own relationship with him, as every believer already realises. But all these relationships are within his greater reality as the corporate Christ. That reality is 'the new creation' of human existence, redeemed and restored through the concerted work of the Trinity, to be the intersubjective realm, or *koinonia*, for which humanity has been created. As I understand the doctrine, we have no reason to say that the Holy Spirit alone mediates the presence of the risen Jesus in the conditions of this life. The Spirit is indeed at work *in believers* to enable each one to respond to Jesus, but he, the Son, is himself present (as is the Father) to everyone directly. Consequently the risen Christ *is* omnipresent, and the Christian's participation in the Body involves Jesus the individual being with him. This must be part of being incorporate in Christ, the new Adam. There is, therefore, a constant mediation between the risen Jesus and Christ incorporate in the believing community with which Christians are familiar, even if it is not often referred to. This is what is expounded in John 14:6-23; 15:1-8; 17:22-24 and also in Ephesians 2:1-10; 3:8-19; Colossians 1:25-9.

The risen Jesus and parish ministry

Again the femininity of human nature as receptive is relevant here, as Sarah Coakley shows in the book referred to earlier.[18] The women's testimony to Jesus' resurrection on Easter Day led Thomas Aquinas to comment on women's 'greater capacity for love' (p.149). Coakley refers to the spiritual senses tradition of the Song of Songs as expounded by Origen to point out that human knowledge of God develops through spiritual growth as the faculties are 'progressively purified' (p.136). Rather more accurately than Origen, Gregory of

Nyssa recognised that a '*transformation* of normal sense perception becomes the requisite for resurrection belief'. (p.152) In Gregory there is a '*continuity* or development from the physical to the spiritual in the spectrum of purgation of the senses' (pp.137-8) as Frank Lake was to observe in psychological detail.

> [O]n Nyssa's view the toehold for spiritual perception is precisely in the physical ... when suitably prepared for the nuptial embrace of the Bridegroom [the Bride] becomes the supreme knower and recognizer of Christ. (p.138)

Thus Coakley concludes 'only the "feminised" soul ... can fully respond to the embraces of the Bridegroom, the exalted and heavenly Christ' (p.149).

How then are we to see the relevance of this perception to the spirituality that needs to develop in the parish congregation? If the life of heaven is truly anticipated in the Church's life and worship what teaching and facilitation is required to enable believers to grow in that heavenly dimension? Heaven, the Christian must surely affirm, is not a place in which God exists but that condition of life, beginning now, where God develops his creation into a closer relationship with himself. It is wherever we are sharing Christ's resurrection life. In that condition we may gain some inkling of what the Body of Christ becomes eventually, and even what our own spiritual existence will be like after death. As Paul's words suggest, to make sense of what it is to be members of the corporate Christ means thinking of extra dimensions of God's creation (1 Cor 15:36, 37, 42-49).

When the worship is right, I wrote, the gospel tumbles out in mission. This is because such worship springs from a group who share the discernment of Christ's presence, although some members may not know that he is the source of what is happening.[19] Gradually it becomes clear that the Church's mission is not an operation of individual ministers and members but rather a task for which God commissions the community as a whole. The Church as a community is named the Body of Christ because the risen Jesus is directly involved in union with all members. He wants to act through the corporate whole for the purpose of extending his mission under ascension circumstances. This *priority* of living in the presence of Jesus risen has been lost in modern versions of the Church's life. I am putting such emphasis on Christ's direct involvement in the congregation's life because I believe clear teaching on this will do much to make the mission more fruitful. It will help Christians understand what sharing in God's holiness means in two practical respects. First, holiness becomes recognisable when believers make themselves available for Christ to act through them. Secondly, it begins to appear that holiness has its best flowering in the corporate life of communities rather than in Christians individually. Christian leaders, however, have to take account of the fact that whereas faults and weaknesses in an individual can be confronted, forgiven and healed comparatively easily if his will has been moved accordingly, when they become general in group behaviour they can be disguised as normal and tolerable. In the latter situation holiness is corporately resisted in the Church as much as outside her bounds. Thus to ensure the good practice of Christian ministry the Church needs to be reformed so that her members and especially the ordained can experience what it is to be members of the Body and live under the inspiration of the Spirit. Only the Christian's experience of the Church functioning in a God-centred way as a community of prayer prepares him or her to minister well for the benefit of other members. Learning to be self-critical is the starting point. Assumptions and attitudes that belong to the world's unconverted cultures have been absorbed by Christians over generations and allowed to distort the way the Church's life is conducted. When leaders are ready to question their customary ways, however, it becomes easier for Christian communities to adopt reforms that will make for holiness and effective mission. If we follow this path we will show that we are serious about Christ and the resurrection, that we are willing to let him be Lord of his Church.

But is such a prospect feasible? Is there any possibility that British Christians for example, as they are today in this postmodern time, could so combine across the denominations and work together to loosen the defensive way in which the Church usually works? Such God-given changes can and do happen when believers are sufficiently desperate to rely on him. Like Frank Lake, Ronald Rolheiser sees the teaching of John of the Cross to be relevant to the malaise of our time, but the mystical tradition took for granted a sense of God in the broader community which no longer exists in the comprehensive way it did in pre-modern times. So in a culture as deeply alienated as today's, one of the questions we have to ask is how may the Church build non-monastic congregations who are aware that God is in their midst. Rolheiser expresses something of the awakening that this involves.

> Only after passing through this dark night (of the senses)
> do we move somewhat beyond manipulation to empathy,
> beyond reduced vision to wonder, and beyond projection
> to actually seeing. (p.74)

What, I suggest, the modern Church has to do is to develop and discipline congregational life so that this sanctifying process becomes normal growth for the many and not just the relatively few.

The nature of existing Christian division

A practical way of moving forward in that direction is needed so that the Church's present strands of inspired energy, being exercised in wide variety, can contribute in partnership and share a common vision. This is surely possible in so far as there is both willingness and courage to acknowledge where the Church is failing at present. It is relevant to notice that as Christianity declines in westernised cultures two separate tendencies become more visible within the Churches, both being heavily influenced by agnostic thinking. In the one case eagerness to recover lost ground drives Christians to strengthen their hold on what is familiar and traditional. In the other case, believers choose to concentrate on what they feel to be the core of ethical value inherent in Christian belief, so as to take best advantage of any positive elements in contemporary culture. Each is essentially conservative, in that they are psychologically defensive and overcautious, and can be intensively focused on human agency with little practical reliance on God or even on genuine cooperation with fellow Christians. Similar emotional pressures are at work in both groups, even though they are moving in opposition to each other.

If this is fair comment it lends plausibility to the notion that the Church's present crisis is one of internal conflict, in which two or more power-blocks are trying to gain control, or at least maintain their influence, over their fellow believers, over the institutional Church and, less consciously, over what is going on inside individual Christians themselves. If we do not allow the tension of present disharmony to depress our expectations, we can help to expose the power-wielding spirit at work on all sides. From a therapeutic perspective much of the Church's current life displays the signs of anxiety-depression, and this is not surprising since public opinion portrays the Church contemptuously. The media is mainly hostile, often promoting the view that Christianity has long been discredited, and disseminating a picture of the Church as one religious sideshow among others. This disparagement may have been largely provoked by the Church's intellectual and leadership failures in the course of the 20th and earlier centuries (failures that we should frankly admit), but today's Christians bear responsibility for perpetuating the damage. The wise course is to meet the situation with honesty and openness, not attempting to hide the pathology into which church communities have fallen. One striking similarity in traditional and in more adventurous parishes is that both can be strongly motivated by the fear of losing members, or not attracting new ones.

Spiritual growth for congregations

By openly acknowledging weaknesses and recognising that to live in Christ is to share human vulnerability as Christ did himself, individual Christians and congregations are able to live in true dependence on the Trinity. I have tried to show Frank Lake's contribution has been the pioneering of an approach that can be applied within the Church at every level, from the congregation to the episcopate. Yet the psychological way is not likely to bear spiritual fruit if it is not pursued in the context of Christian discipleship, for its potential goes further than the release of individuals from the disadvantages of neurotic forms of defence. The emotional growth and healing that Lake expounded enable us to know ourselves in psychological depth and thereby make it easier to be open to God. By seeking this benefit, in a way appropriate to each particular community, congregations can gain greater freedom to let the Holy Spirit take them into closer union with the Father in Christ. This does not mean that the traditional language of faith is not relevant, nor does it imply that the congregation is the appropriate place for therapy in the narrow sense. What it does mean is that God's work of salvation can be welcomed more wholeheartedly when people understand that psychological barriers may be making their growth in faith more difficult if not impossible.

Both personal affirmation and self-criticism

The greater concentration on spiritual growth and repentance within congregations that my argument has been pressing for is clearly felt by many to be more demanding than our contemporaries can be expected to accept. In consequence energy is devoted to evangelism on the supposition that if the gospel is being proclaimed with love and imagination, and combined with some moral rule-keeping, the inner discipline of the heart can be left to the Holy Spirit. Only a little reflection and honest observation is needed to show that this prescription ignores the reality of God's ways and of human need. For God begins with the heart and never ceases to call his people to their own renewal and change. I believe that the gospels and the NT letters clearly imply that the disciplined life of Christians will benefit society generally, for the conversion of others is often bound up with the godliness of the Church. Witness before the world springs out of the inner truthfulness of those who bear the testimony.

This is the main reason why the spiritual condition of the ordained leaders is the most critical factor making for or against the wellbeing of the Church. The pastor's own process of sanctification is needed to facilitate what the congregation is being called to experience and to do. Much congregational life is under unnecessary strain, its vigour draining away year by year, when clergy cling intransigently to habits that have become endemic. They may insist on keeping everything over which they preside under their own control, or they may be unable to teach and lead worship with sufficient competence to make services stimulating and rewarding enough for all who come. But behind all such weaknesses there is usually the emotional condition of not being familiar with one's own neediness and therefore of being unwilling to seek that fresh inspiration and growth that everyone needs. This rigid state of affairs can quickly change for the better when a breakthrough to growth occurs. Through our own spiritual progress we can be free in heart and mind to be self-critical as pastors and to encourage the same reflectiveness in church members, without spreading discouragement in the process. The pastoral and evangelistic policy that bears long-lasting fruit is one that begins in the congregation, so that the church community becomes a place where people's deepest needs are being met, week by week. The Church can best serve the local community at large by becoming the setting where people of all ages are able to find the resources that are not available elsewhere. In their ministry the leaders supported by the members generally will be affirming everyone in their faithful participation, for all need such unstinting support, while at the same time reminding them of the Christian commitment to continual repentance and change. The reassuring message will be that the Church is doing what needs to be done, but not doing it with sufficient clarity, penetration and whole-heartedness. Christians must be encouraged to be comfortable, not just in confessing private sins to God, but also in rehearsing together the sins and failures of church and society for which we share responsibility, so that they become material for intercession. The congregation itself can be at home with the unfamiliar notion that Christians are not under obligation to pretend piously that the Church as of now is 'fit for purpose', and that the present structures of her life should be perpetuated without development. They will then be free to acknowledge that too often what happens on Sunday and during the week is found to be boring, inconsistent, unconvincing, though thankfully this kind of severe criticism is far from being valid everywhere. Yet when all the positive points, that must be affirmed warmly and rightly, have been made we come back to the recognition that all is not well. The Church's spiritual condition remains disturbingly superficial. Tested against her message of gospel and Kingdom she appears disempowered, and one conclusion has to be that the Church has disabled herself by leaving Christians in uncertainty about the risen Christ.

Holiness is not a quality we can actively acquire or exercise, but it is a characteristic of living which can show itself in people when they cease to think that they belong to themselves, and find themselves part of what God is doing. When the Spirit makes and keeps people open and adaptable to the divine creativity their lives become holy with his holiness. As the Church models the community for which humanity has been created, so out of the ferment of new life in a particular Church or group of congregations there can flow, by personal contact, the communication of divine love. When this happens in a non-possessive and non-triumphant way the Church's revival challenges existing disorder and complacency and may awaken a sense of need for God that secular cultures are likely to obscure or misdirect. People are touched intellectually and their hearts are exposed to a deeper sense of life's shared meaning.

Episcopal ministries under the risen Christ

But such spiritual recovery will not necessarily mature. The history of revivals shows that remarkable beginnings regularly subside and often congeal into fleshly forms that can do as much harm as good. For this reason the disciplines of supervision for pastoral carers is critical. In this the wisdom of unity, mutual submission and communal openness to the Spirit encourages the corporately centred spirituality which sustains Christian discipleship in its missionary character; (cf I Cor 14:26; Acts 15:22,24-28; 4:27-31; Eph 3:5,6). As westernised Christians of the twenty-first century we cannot avoid being influenced by the culture of suspicion in which people *fear* to make a close personal commitment to God's presence in the world. Understanding how this fear operates we can help others to be alert to the way it prevents the development of faith and encourages Christians to withdraw into sectional living of one kind or another. When they are freely acknowledged, problems and fears in discerning the presence of the risen Christ can be addressed constructively.

As we saw earlier, it is relatively easy and beguiling to conclude from the synoptic gospels that following the ascension Jesus is in heaven, and that thereafter only the Holy Spirit acts to enable the Church to have fellowship with and in Christ. For example we have a contemporary song, 'There is a Redeemer' in which the chorus contains the lines: 'And leaving your Spirit till the work on earth is done'. But such a thought overlooks clear statements to the contrary in Matthew 28:20 and 18:20; and is also contradicted by a wide variety of statements in the epistles and in Acts which express the Christian experience of living in Christ day by day and of being guided by him. Particularly notable is Acts 23:11 because Luke records it as Paul's experience in the course of his narrative. It is a clear expression of how the early Christians sensed their relationship with the risen Jesus. If we hold to this perception we can do much to overcome our unbelief, although it will need nothing less than a re-training in discipleship and in the corporate spirituality discussed above. To move in this direction ministers and lay leaders can help each other to face and work through their doubts and fears. While it is comparatively easy for believers to know the assurance of the Spirit's leading, it requires greater sensitivity to know that the risen Christ is with them. Developing that discrimination matters if we are to understand what God is doing, and how he wishes us to give Christ precedence in all that we do individually and corporately. To illustrate what this means I turn to a monograph by John Foskett, *The Gossip of God's Siblings*.[20] It gives an account of the European Pastoral Care and Counselling Movement from its inception in 1972 through to 2005, and is dedicated to the late Irene Bloomfield, the psychotherapist who founded the Jewish Counselling Service in London and did a great deal to sustain the European movement. Since the development he traces traversed several crises as members learnt to trust and work with each other, it provides an instructive and encouraging example of interfaith enterprise, in working ecumenically and across the boundaries made by 'party' allegiances within the churches. Foskett writes about the movement and its conferences held in different countries.

> In an ever-changing Europe, we confronted our fear of the different; and this has given space to risk more than we could at home, where status and livelihood depend upon preserving accustomed ways of working. Exposed to awe-inspiring engagement with the worst of Europe's history in places like Mydaneck, we have grown a new identity, and with it the will to practise our ministries with new authority.... We need to learn how to overcome corporate anxiety and resistance. Knowing that we ought to behave in a less frightened and more just and equitable way will never be enough to make us change. The defences against fear ... have to be unmasked.... (pp.34-35)

The experience he describes points to the kind of struggle in the face of fear that Christians who want the Church to become effectively united and Christ-centred find themselves in. But the strongest impression I get from Foskett's piece is that the most difficult moment comes when leaders and community members are challenged to admit that what they already do and think is not bearing the kind of fruit that is needed, partly at least because of a narrow reliance on the ministry of leaders. So for example at the 1997 conference at Ripon there was a recognition that 'the congregation [is] the primary source of pastoral care' and 'the specialists – pastoral counsellors and practical theologians – [are] servants of the parish'. I have been arguing that the resources needed are given through God's Spirit and in Christ's own incarnate presence, and that these are characteristically made available hiddenly. What God gives in the Spirit is behind and within all the natural resources we need. We should acknowledge therefore that God does not want all these areas where we serve human wellbeing to be treated 'religiously'. That procedure only increases the fragmentation of an already over-polarised age, and fosters the illusion that the sacred is once again marked out from the secular. As Bonhoeffer was beginning to teach us, we have to recognise the divine activity as it works anonymously in the world. If we speak of it too stridently and possessively in religious terms, we may falsely separate it from its position in the entirety of nature and disguise its universality. We are to be obedient to the divine presence, however, in order to protect ourselves, believers and un-believers alike, from the various dire consequences of supposing that the dignity of human personhood is a matter of each one's private right to self-determination and self-fulfilment. That creed of individualism can be used defensively to prevent individual freedom developing, and to weaken growth in community living.

A godly Church at home in the secular
I speak of God acting anonymously to underline the way in which every divine activity is wrapped within the world's normal reality. Throughout its history Christianity has widely failed to observe and imitate Christ's lead in this respect. Christians have often supposed that to testify to God's presence they must dress or undress his activity in ways that objectify his self-gift so that it is taken into institutional control. I say this not to encourage iconoclasm but rather to see art-istic and communicative skills for what they are, within the worldly arena where God makes himself known. The best route for Christian ministry to follow is to let Christ take the lead in every situation, recognising that his acting is necessarily out of sight and that he does not always call on us to announce his presence. That we pray and what we pray is of the utmost significance, but whether in any

particular situation we make it publicly known that we are praying is a different matter and requires its own disciplined decisions. We pray to and through the triune God because he is already in action, and so we seek to respond to his initiatives. Invoking God to act further is a second stage and perhaps more a matter of declaring that we want our wills to be one with his, asking that what we do may become part of what he is doing. In this perspective we see how critical and prior is the communal worship of the Eucharist with enough teaching being given to enable the whole gathering to share intelligently in the prayer that is involved. Each celebration of the Lord's Supper has in mind the totality of Christ's creative and redemptive work, but relates it to the local situation as he gives himself afresh to and through those members at that particular date. In that setting God meets the needs of their situation and calling.

Appropriate line-management for clergy

The subject of ministerial supervision is usefully compressed in Jane Leach's article, 'Pastoral supervision: a Review of the Literature'.[21] Reflecting on Frances Ward's *Lifelong Learning*,[22] she notes that for Ward the client's 'deep learning' from experience should be facilitated through the process of supervision, viewed not simply 'as a tool for training but as part of ongoing discipleship'. The words quoted are Leach's, but Ward wrote that being

> a disciple is to follow a path of life that calls for openness to
> change and a willingness to be transformed by the presence of
> a living God whose grace breaks through in the world. It is to
> see signs of the living God ... to foster those signs so that others
> are empowered to flourish and build up the common life.[23]

Although 'Ward deliberately distances herself from the 'watching over' metaphors associated with the term 'oversight'', says Leach, she does deal with supervision in situations of ministerial development. When Ward has referred to a curate whose training incumbent is unwilling to hold regular staff meetings, Leach notes that 'lack of structure undermines the possibility for relationship'. She observes about the literature generally that 'the lack of direct reflection on the relationship between supervision and oversight reflects the gulf which still exists ... despite the fact that the two words are synonyms ... in ordinary language'.

> Stephen Croft argues that those placed in ecclesial over-
> sight must have 'the ability to keep watch' both over

communities and over the work of their lay and ordained colleagues in ministry.

Yet the 'dialogue is embryonic' between the specific focus of supervision as understood in psychotherapy and counselling and its usual lack of precision in relation to *episcope*. My argument is that the two disciplines ought to be partners so that the skills and insights of the former are brought to the correction and development of the latter. The Church would benefit immensely in that way, but as yet very little improvement has appeared.

> Croft identifies some of the reluctance of the clergy to engage with these key tasks of leadership as originating in a concern about being taken over by secular models. [Some] ... are resistant to seeing themselves as managers of organisations and people. Likewise, there is resistance to the notion of being in supervision, grounded in a suspicion that this is therapy by the back door.[24]

She comments that 'much of the fear may be more primal than these rationalisations suggest', and so the fear needs to be faced in the Church at every level not only as a matter of policy but also in personal support. Again we have to affirm that in any case therapy for change is what we all need; it is a mistake to assume there are exceptions. I have tried to show that it *sometimes* happens spontaneously as God deals with us in the settings of church life – where they provide appropriate support for all members. In relation to the clergy and other leaders this is where group work is so valuable, although everyone can benefit in groups.

Although it is not a substitute for the one-to-one supervision that is needed, a system of obligatory groups for all clergy in ministry can provide support and facilitate self-understanding. This has been argued again in the recent article by Mary Travis.[25] Under the title 'Supporting Clergy in Postmodern Ministry', she gives an account and evaluation of a group set up for Bristol Diocese by herself and Peter Barwell in 2004-5. Such groups have to be empathetically led, as these were, by psychodynamically trained people. But where they are led in that way there may be even greater benefit, as a supplement to supervision, if clergy share in groups with professionals in other fields of caring ministry.

Made capable ministers of a new covenant
These considerations are relevant not only to the care, support and development of clergy in post but also in the selection and training

for ordination of people who will be able to meet the Church's need. Where ordained ministers of whatever denomination insensitively exercise power to influence or control a congregation's life we may get the kind of constriction of spiritual life that is often described as the cork-in-the-bottle syndrome. Especially when working alone, many clergy are reluctant to face their own personal weaknesses. It does not take a great emotional disorder to keep this kind of reluctance in place. Just the blinkered vision, to be found in any or all of us, is enough to prevent an ordained person from recognising that some weakness holds him or her back from working well as a priest. I am not referring to those who are working devotedly under stress, and whose ministry has come to suffer from illness or external hardships of one kind or another, but rather to those who should not have been selected for ordination because their dominant motivation or the direction of their personality is incompatible with the responsibilities they are going to be given. Where that kind of appointment has been made, the situation is often difficult to detect, since from outside the congregation one may see little more than that the work of the parish is being maintained but not advanced.

One result can be that people come to a congregation expecting to find a lake where many can both receive and take part, but find instead only a pool. Everything that goes on is being drawn down to the pool because the congregation's life revolves round the minister, and perhaps a small group colluding with him, often out of loyalty. I do not mean to portray an obsessively narcissistic personality who performs selfishly for his own satisfaction, but rather a person who is so desperately concerned to assert his competence that he keeps others in subordinate positions in order to gain a sense of his own status. If his wellbeing is largely dependent on this endeavour, his willingness to delegate and share ministry will be negligible, since he must assure himself that he is in control of everything and does not need to learn from others. He is not to be blamed for this, because he has no freedom to do otherwise without a major healing process for which he has not been prepared.

It is the Church that has made the mistake and been unkind to that person, as well as to the congregations who suffer in trying to be faithful under his leadership. Healing is always possible, preferably before, but also after ordination; and to be most fruitful this is likely to be through the sustained ministry of a supportive group under experienced leadership. Through the group's empathetic listening an individual's underlying mental pain, of which he may be as yet totally unaware can receive attention, as the roots of his self-preoccupation gradually appear. God's presence may then start to become real to the person's awareness in an area of past experience where previously it was not appreciated. The whole tenor of the person's life and ministry can change remarkably as a result. The prayerful caring by others will need to go on and other opportunities for exploring past hurts may be needed, for the healing process must not be left behind too soon, but a beginning will have been made. Hopefully that person will increasingly be able to benefit from the company of other believers and gain the ability to minister to others the care and insights he has received for himself. This is a fundamental stage for anyone to reach, but especially for someone called to ordination. Until a person is open to the Spirit at that depth he will not be able to treat the congregation properly, and thus he will not be a person who with safety can be given such a measure of pastoral responsibility.

The dangers of being 'in charge'
An Anglican 'incumbent' or any other minister in pastoral charge of a congregation is given the awesome burden of having to make a potentially formative or deformative impact on the spirituality of a community and its members. Although every one of us is likely to look back with painful awareness on slowness to recognise areas of fault in our own ministry, our selection for ordination should have included the assessment that we were capable of growing in wisdom and insight because we showed signs of being able and willing to repent and amend our lives. Without that investigation being satisfied appointments are dangerous. The need is to distinguish between the person who can be partially blind to his faults and occasionally subject to weaknesses of obstinacy and self-concern, and the person whose make-up displays settled determination to deny faults and to resist every notion of personal change being needed.

Because the work of ordained ministers, being essentially *episcope*, is extremely complex, delicate and demanding, a closed and rigid personhood may prevent good-enough service. In serving the welfare of Christ's people in the three areas of personhood: heart, mind and will, the task of priest and pastor in caring for people is to encourage their intellectual capacities and the directional energies of their wills towards the understanding and developments of their capacity to love. The Church's recovery in Britain and elsewhere surely depends very largely on raising higher our awareness of this task. A congregation suffering under the kind of leadership described may become debilitated and its members' potential to go on growing in the fruits and gifts of the Spirit can dwindle. The vivacity of worship declines, not only because members are not being stretched mentally but also because their response to the Lord in joy is also diminishing. The congregation's successes can also contribute to spiritual weakness if they are dwelt on too much. For this reason the work of preaching is best shared and developed to meet the congregation's need for emotional sustenance while at the same time members need to be disturbed into sharing in God's discontent with things as they are. The aim will be not only to do both these things, but to do so in a way that strengthens the cohesion of the congregation as an interdependent community. The experience of unity through listening to each other and learning God's will together is critical for the Church's wellbeing at every level. To this end group-work, in house groups for example, becomes increasingly important so that members learn to receive God's inspiration through each other as readily as in listening to the minister. The danger of falling back into wrong kinds of dependency is always lurking, so the minister must be constantly directing attention away from himself to God. A particularly helpful way of building up the right climate of mutuality in church life is to ensure that in being trained both ordained and lay Christians have been ministered to for themselves before they offer teaching, guidance, counselling or prayer for others. In one of her vivid insights Julian of Norwich saw the Lord presiding in the fellowship of his people from no fixed point, in a way that gave his presence to each member, for God's humanity exists in the corporate unity of inter-relationship and mutual exchange with all. There is today an unfortunate tendency in congregations to conduct worship in the manner of a TV chat-show, where the whole focus is on the presenter and a few other individuals as foils to him or her. This style of gathering is damaging in being contrary to the true character of the Church and of corporate worship. Not only does it make for excessive wordiness and distract attention from God but it strongly reinforces an individualised concept of the relationship between believers and God. Undermining the communality of the corporate Christ, it makes nonsense of 'the Body'. For this reason the physical focus of the congregational gathering should always be the Table and not the president at the table.

My last observation in this section returns to the Church which embodies the *koinonia* of the Spirit into which God wants to draw all people. The Body of Christ here on earth has to be localised in inclusive congregations which are commissioned by the risen Jesus to exercise the ministry in which all his members share. Here we can see how accurate is Rolheiser's perception that today's problem of faith is not primarily out in the non-Christian world but in the

congregations of the Church and in the minds of her ordained ministers. It is true there has been an awakening to this insight in recent
years through the charismatic movement, but it has not always been
deep enough in recognising how necessary it is for the effects of
buried mental pain to be healed, so that the gifts of wisdom and self-
awareness can be received. It is these gifts of the Spirit which enable
the Christian to minister safely to others, whether as a priest or a
lay member. Therefore we cannot say that the position has changed
radically as yet. Too many ministers and congregations appear to
have no clear sense of how, because of his resurrection, Jesus continues to be present in order to be the foundation of the new age of the
Kingdom, of which he taught so much and for which he was born
(cf 1 Cor 3:1-7). The ministry that is properly Christian will all the
time be submitted to the living and present Christ. The resources
of the Trinity (Ephesians 1:17-23) are present to it, yet unless the
obstacles which make us blind to them are neutralised, Christians
remain unable to access that power.

The spiritual body is the corporate Christ
God has reconciled the cosmos to himself and on this Christians are
united. But they are not all united in perceiving that through his resurrection and ascension Jesus now reigns in the midst of his people
as they engage in conflict with evil. The Churches seem almost to
have forgotten that God's purpose in including us in Christ is as
much *to stay with us in that engagement* as to prepare us for heaven.
It must be remembered that the two intentions involve each other.
If that were truly kept in mind, the Churches would surely not be as
complacent about disunity as they are. In light of this, I turn now
from the ordained ministry to the Church herself. In this we have
to note the most remarkable and mysterious truth that the spiritual
body of resurrection, to be given to each one of us, is part of that
very same Body which is God's Church. Therefore in some sense
we have been given our resurrection bodies already because we now
live through the risen Jesus who is the corporate Christ. From this it
follows that our own resurrection bodies, which we cannot inhabit
properly while we are in the natural flesh, will be both individual
and corporate in character. Evidently in the heavenly order, which
Paul was reflecting on in 2 Corinthians 5:1-10, we shall participate
in Christ in a way which will include our own individuality within
the corporate 'dimensions' of Christ's Body. How to conceive of all
this with any accuracy is beyond our present thinking, but we can see
a little of what our resurrection will be like. Because we are already

clothed with power from on high (Luke 24:49), we are already citizens of heaven (Col 3:3,4; Eph 2:19-22); and to that extent we can sense 'our heavenly dwelling'. The 'eternal house in heaven' of which Paul wrote (2 Cor 5:1) may already be palpable to believers here and now. Renewing today's Church in this understanding is of great importance. As they grow in holiness, congregations will be learning that this is part of what we celebrate. By participating in the prayer of heaven, as the spiritual Body of the ascended Christ, we intercede in him and with him for the conversion of the world. With this purpose in mind we remember that our humanity in the Body of Christ is being recreated as a direct outcome of the passion, death and resurrection of Christ. Thus in describing the Church as the Body of Christ orthodox Christians are declaring that the deep reality which gives significance to the institutional aspects of the Church is that God intends to possess the Body of Christ more fully than he possesses the rest of creation. The Trinity enlivens these institutions to the degree that Christ's believing members give their active consent to his purpose.

Trusting the Trinity

This way of understanding the status of the Church is radically christo-logical and trinitarian, and it recognises the importance of human faith – meaning simply the believer's trusting relationship in the Trinity. Faith is what God uses to build and extend his Church. Here again it is the universal presence of the risen Christ who is to be acknowledged – not the Holy Spirit only. Re-born in the Spirit the believer is able to respond to the risen Christ because his original awareness of God's fatherly love has been reawakened, and thus he is ready to become active in the corporate Christ. So it is through the simple avenue of faith as trust that God builds and holds his Church, possessing the institutional organs of her existence, disordered though they are in many respects.

We do not believe the Trinity to be in the world because he is active in the Church. It is because he is active in the world that he has created the Church in Christ. The new humanity in Christ is being brought into effective action in the Church, but God's initiatives start in the world at large, not in the Church apart from the world. For the incarnation is an action of God in the world, from which the Church is brought into existence. This is not to deny that God roots the Church in the old Israel by being incarnate as a son of David, but this place in Abraham's family only identifies the location of that particular action which is in Adam's stock. Through his incarnation in Jesus now risen, God the Trinity brings his creative process to a climax, that from the ascension humankind may be incorporated into Christ. The Church is not only a restored Israel, but is primarily a restored humanity, in the risen Jesus. The Church is made out of the offspring of Adam, that the community of the new Adam may develop. This is the universal spiritual Body into whom all people can be drawn through the cross.

E. Our penitence elicits God's further action

Real and consistent repentance is extremely difficult for human beings; hence the necessity of Christ's dying and the work of the Spirit incorporating them into him. Without a deepening penitence made possible in the Spirit there is no growth in holiness, or in continuing mission. For this reason the prevailing state of the Church in many places remains one of division and enfeeblement. Conversion to Christ is critical, making possible the reconciliation of believers with each other and of believers with unbelievers. As people experience this reconciliation their discipleship deepens. Human defensiveness is such, however, that this experience may only come very gradually, if at all. Our fears and self-regarding motives work to project on to others the sins of which we are guilty ourselves, and this avoidance of responsibility sets the scene. For this reason the scapegoat idea was attractive in ancient times, and is expressive of the background think-ing within which the death of Christ came to be interpreted. This being so it was natural that as time went on the Church concentrated more on what the Saviour's suffering accomplished on behalf of all, and gave less attention to the magnitude of the change which has to take place in the sinful and troubled person, yet the two sides of God's action need equal emphasis. The imbalance between them has been preventing the clear recognition of what God continues to do after Easter and Pen-tecost; and this situation brings us back to Frank Lake's insights.

By exposing neurosis repentance can be released

In those closing weeks of his life Lake restated his understanding of the gospel, setting the new perceptions of his foetal research in Christological perspective, as was his usual practice. The following excerpts from *Mutual Caring* relate to a person's capacity to repent.

> I have a growing conviction, strengthened by Sebastian Moore's *The Crucified Jesus is no Stranger* and now by Rowan Williams' *Resurrection*, that one of the central dynamic functions of the spotless innocence of Christ, the Lamb of God ... is to make it possible for the millions of people who are paralyzed in the conviction of their own innocence and everybody else's badness, from which no growth or moral progress is possible, to encounter Christ at that foetal depth ... and emerge from the trap....

Over the years Lake had identified that the deepest malaise of the human spirit has its origin in the early experience of the individual but now he specified that its universality lies in the shared sense of being in various degrees the 'victim' in foetal dependency.

> The protest of being... the innocent persecuted one at the time of... total vulnerability is... affirmed, and Christ comes alongside in his innocent affliction to share and help in the bearing of those foetal horrors. The protest is given a voice....

Regardless of varying situations every human being has been 'encapsulated' in a precarious order of existence, since all the world's communities are stamped with the character of being made victims, but now there is a way out. When the 'paralyzing, self-limiting foetal agenda' has been consciously 'felt and reliably recognised as the correct one, the pressure to go on insisting on this polarized view of life disappears' (p.66). The whole passage (p.62ff) should be noted with the quotations from Charles Williams.

Lake had often emphasised the tragedy that human wellbeing is thoroughly obstructed by the prevailing malaise, for out of our own suffering as victims we become active in perpetuating the suffering of others, and do so in ways that harm ourselves as much as them. Whereas the foetal experience has driven the infant to blame himself, 'it must be my fault', he learns not long after birth to blame others and protect himself.

> Self-judgment and self-condemnation are damaging, not only because of my cruel alienation and rejection of the victim, but because the adoption of the judgmental attitude diminishes me. I am killing off part of myself. The generous, caring self, in the power of God reaching out to the wretched self to draw it into compassionate closeness, is strangled by hostility and rejection.... I become the victim of my own destructiveness.... Both [the victim and the perpetrator] are aspects of me. It is vital that I recognize that Christ relates to both of these in his saving love. The murderer and the victim are both his beloved. But I am not allowed to forget that I am the murderer. (p.67)

This then is why resistance to conversion and repentance is so great; since the creature who was once obliged to feel that the badness must be 'mine', is now fixated in the conviction that it cannot be me, the fault is 'theirs' (and the Creator's). The religious believer may be compromised in this as readily as the atheist, as Lake pointed out in the words cited below.

How important is repentance?

In bringing my argument towards closure I need to stress again the ontological foundation, established at conception, from which godliness – and penitence – can be developed by the Spirit. This foundation is an experience of assured love to which each can be restored, making it possible for disorder and distress to be gradually overcome in healing, reconciliation and peace. That process, Lake was affirming, 'arises out of being with the risen Jesus, meeting him as the disciples did ... after his resurrection' (p.71). Through discerning that Jesus suffered and died to be with everyone in every situation, alienated human creatures can be reconciled, healed and converted. A 'normal' adult is characteristically upheld by mildly neurotic defences which increase the person's self-content so very often people live 'successfully' in a powerful fortress of independence. For everyone in that position thorough repentance is difficult because the defences are designed to deny that any benefit could come from admitting that 'I myself am at fault'.

If the unborn child was overwhelmed in the womb by feelings of being worthless because rejected by and unacceptable to his mother, that person will later on be strongly disposed to 'sinful attitudes' and 'bad choices' and will also resist the very idea of re-experiencing the dreadful distress – a resistance often reinforced by Christian practices as we have seen already. Yet the recovery of that painful memory is normally the way for such damage to be healed. That is why Lake condemned any 'penitential rigmarole' which disguises the truth of these primitive feelings and seeks instead a pseudo-forgiveness, having prayed in effect, 'will you wipe the negative score card clean, and let it be as though it had never happened?' The result of that 'religious ploy' will be to leave the self split in two and 'full of denials ... condemned to life-long immaturity' (pp.71, 72).

What then is the way forward to true heart-healing? I have stressed that God's presence in Christ crucified and risen is *at the centre*, but also that this perception is intensely hard for the bruised person who has been formed in hardened communities of many kinds. This chapter has had to argue that the Church's witness of corporate holiness in being the Body of Christ is critical at that centre. The world's resistance to discerning and trusting God will not be overcome apart from the Spirit's activity in the Church, so judgment begins there (1 Peter 4:17), that starting from the Church's repentance all may be set free. Because of this there is an urgent need to restore the distinctive eschatological emphasis that Jesus revealed.

Repentance and eschatology

I have urged reform in the Church's life but I do not think those changes will be effective unless we are clearer about the freedom which penitence brings. To clarify this I raise the question whether the Church's present thinking and practice are adequate to enable more people to enjoy that liberation. I have been arguing that the ascended Jesus is truly with his Church, as he promised (Mt 28:18,20; John 14:3) and that this is because God the Trinity, not the Holy Spirit only, is sustaining all who believe. But large parts of the Church do not perceive this to be the case. Many theologians, and of different schools of thought, hold a different doctrine. For example Oliver O'Donovan (*Resurrection and Moral Order*[26]) teaches that although

> God reversed the crucifixion of the Son of man and vindicated the true against the false... that does not alter the fact that the corrupted order had in itself the tendency and the capacity to destroy the uncorrupted, and so to defend itself against all correction or amendment. (pp.94-95)

Whilst there is obvious truth in this, there is also the deeper truth that the events of Good Friday radically changed the human situation. The cross of Christ's humiliation and victory already reveals the Son of Man's participation in God's trinitarian glory as the centurion's words at his dying suggest. Thus the true does 'live alongside the false within the one world', whereas O'Donovan denies this (p.95).[27] In earlier times the fact of Christ's victory was sometimes expressed by the picturesque thought that by the crucifixion of Jesus God tricked the devil into thinking he had won.

The kind of theology I am criticising is, I think, disturbingly ready to concede to the unbelief of the age by turning away from the reality of God's kingly reign where it is hiddenly present in the midst of today's broken world-order. Arguing that the saving events of Christ's life are 'past and future to us' their present power can only be 'secondary to the fact that that they happened, and will happen, then'. Those events can only 'act upon our present in quite another way' because they are 'God's final deed ... in which history is given its meaning' (p.103). In this version of the faith it would seem that the sense of God's immanence must be diminished, but, in contrast to that position, the Church needs to affirm the biblical conviction that God is always attentive to the world and active in it. Why should it be thought that God's presence and authority do not impinge on us as readily as other personal influences do, even when so much of human life remains alienated from him? I remarked on this kind of eschatology in reference to Pannenberg, and its effects are clearly widespread. It is a view which can strengthen the fortress mentality with unfortunate effects on the spiritual wellbeing of church members. It encourages a faith that has little reference to the world as most people experience it. Where Christian faith that relies solely on scripture and the Church's tradition, the believer's witness before agnostics may be unconvincing, especially if he is not sensitive to the initiatives of the Spirit who is leading the newly born-again person to search for the pearl of great value. The best witnesses to those outside the Church, who are being drawn by the Trinity, will point to the spirit, who enables them to discern that Jesus is present. We cannot emphasise too much in relation to eschatology that faith and repentance are to be established in the present, and in relation to the realities in which people share responsibility for the world in its community dimensions and not just in relation to the conduct of individuals.

In addition, the theology I am commending has further significance in reference to penitence and sanctification. The psychological condition of feeling besieged in a hostile and unredeemed world is likely to hold Christians back from deeper self-examination, penitence and growth in holiness, although this may not be at all apparent to themselves. The points I have been making here should now be linked to the spiritual growth transitions and to the defence mechanisms discussed in chapter 2. The fortress mentality is characterised by rigid thinking and by propositional expressions of religious belief, its tendencies being towards the schizoid position of defence which avoids close personal relationships. If by psychological development a person distrusts the immediacy of personal presence he will tend to choose to rely on his own reasoning in isolation from others and to remain subject to unhealed fears. His preference will be to settle matters, whether religious or not, in the mind, which he can make as far as possible a timeless zone where the facts of his embodiment and of living with other embodied people have little impact on what he thinks and decides. When people conduct their lives under the influence of these precepts of the schizoid defence system it becomes virtually impossible for them to repent in the full sense, that is, in a way which involves the faculties of the whole person. While the mind may be sincerely engaged with the conceptual significance of conversion, the centre of personhood, the heart and heart-felt relationships with others, can remain paralysed until emotional healing has begun. For this reason congregational teaching needs to focus on the entire sequence of atonement so that it becomes a matter of experience. The transforming effects of what Jesus endured and finished on the cross are occurring in his direct relationship with every believer and in the fellowship together of those who are being sanctified. This is particularly apparent whenever people recognise that Jesus continues to share the world's suffering.

Solitude and creativity

I do not intend to suggest that only the schizoid disorder makes for these difficulties since all of the disorders are involved, but I have stressed the schizoid as the defensive position towards which humanity tends to gravitate, and the one that is strikingly characteristic of many areas of life in the postmodern age. When any form of 'grand narrative' or supernatural end for the universe is denied, individualism is deepened and it tends to become the prevailing culture – at least of thinking people. But at this point it is necessary to remember that there are features of personhood that may appear similar to the schizoid pattern of defence, but are not pathological. This is because we all need to establish our partial independence and then find the place from which it becomes possible to make critical assessments of ourselves and be ready for change as discussed in chapter 2, section B. Without that standpoint both repentance and adult living remain impossible. Anthony Storr's book *The School of Genius*[28] developed the argument, which he sees to be over against object-relations thinking, that close personal relationships are not 'the main source of life's meaning and satisfaction'. I am sure that is going too far but I agree there is a needed qualification, because God himself can give a stability more secure than that found in human group life alone. Acknowledging the importance of John Bowlby's work on attachment in infancy, Storr pointed to another side of the matter which is of particular significance in the case of

> exceptional people [who] have suffered long periods of solitary confinement without coming to feel that their lives are meaningless…. [A]ttachment theory, in my view, does less than justice to the importance of work, to the emotional significance of what goes on in the mind of the individual when he is alone, and, more especially, to the central place occupied by the imagination in those who are capable of creative achievement. (p.15)

I do accept the positive in that statement, but it surely does not contradict the central thesis of object-relations theory, because the interpersonal life of family and community is the ground upon which every human

person is formed for companionship with the Creator himself. Storr
notes that Donald Winnicott observed that 'the capacity to be alone
in the presence of the mother' is built up as a stage from which the
person is increasingly able to enjoy solitude and through it to develop
in creativity. Behind the ability to tolerate being alone without anxiety
there is the unconscious 'memory' of being safe in the presence of
mother or other supporters.

> [T]he attachment figure has become part of the individual's
> inner world … someone on whom he can rely even though
> the person concerned is not actually present. (p.19)

Storr refers here to the process of introjection, but I have argued that
this psychology has a divine dimension within its human reality

The transcendent element in human agency

Storr himself also points out that the purpose of human life in the
scheme of things goes beyond 'the evolutionary view that man's primary biological task is to reproduce himself'. In the last chapter of the
book, about desiring 'the Whole', he develops the thought that human
creativity does not simply flower through being with other people.
It springs from a transcendent source, which can be absorbed by the
individual. So to make a constructive contribution to society, in either
a simple or a highly distinctive way, a person needs a foundation of individual stability as well as a blend of other gifts and the determination
to follow where they lead. After the dependent relationship has been
established the next main agenda of life is building up personhood
from which increasing creativity can develop. Thus we can agree
with Storr that becoming appropriately independent as individuals is
important for creativity and for sanctity, while there is also the slower
learning to grow towards maturity in spiritual dependency. When the
development of the individual's creativity has become strongly evident, signs of its transcendent dimension are also likely to appear.
Indeed, we find that artists and thinkers often acknowledge that their
creativity seems to come from beyond themselves. Storr includes
a quotation from George Eliot that has many parallels and a much
wider relevance, not least in its similarity to the phenomenon that in
the biblical tradition we know as prophecy. She told J.W. Cross

> that, in all she considered the best writing, there was a 'not
> herself' which took possession of her, and that she felt her
> own personality to be merely the instrument through which
> this spirit, as it were, was acting. (p.198)

Storr was recognising 'a change of attitude in which the subject comes to realise that his own ego or will is no longer paramount, but … must acknowledge dependence upon an integrating factor which is not of his own making' (p.194). He concludes that 'some of the most profound and healing psychological experiences which individuals encounter take place internally, and are only distantly related, if at all, to inter-action with other human beings' (p.202). But if the interpretation I have presented is correct the 'integrating factor' is the personal influ-ence of God forever humanised in Jesus. It is not that interaction with other people is irrelevant, but that God's Spirit is eager to lead all who are willing to be led. Thus the joint divine-human agency goes on in extraordinary diversity, as much outside as within the boundaries of the Church. This universally dispersed activity flows from the presence of the ascended Christ, but it only leads fitfully towards holiness, because it usually occurs in mixed cultures of unbelief and of misguided ideology.

This is eternal life, to *know* the Trinity
With this reminder that Jesus is alive and present and that God works constantly through the particular events of people's lives to give them opportunities of sharing in his communal purpose, I have brought the argument of the book to a close. But, I ask again, is individual and community change on the scale suggested a viable possibility? I have ventured to think, with much reliance on Frank Lake and others, especially Bonhoeffer, that it is. Despite it appearing to be exclusive and super-spiritual in its demands, the way of self-surrender, penit-ence and dispossession is both pedestrian and liberating. That way is not simply set out for us in the scriptural revelation of God in history, but it is also in some sense foreshadowed in the basic patterns of created life at the level of biological nature. As Rowan Williams has written recently,

> [w]hat we say about God as maker of everything and what we say about God who meets us personally in forgiveness and renewal ought to be as closely allied as possible. It is one of the failings of some kinds of teaching that creation and salvation are treated as completely different topics, whereas the Bible seems, again and again, to hold them together inseparably.[29]

I have sought to declare the faith with this in mind, in the hope that Jesus, now risen, ascended and present, who suffered for us and now suffers with us, can be discerned more clearly as the One in whom people can find their place in God's holiness which will be 'eternal life'. Jesus is not only the dependable head that the NT Church knew him to be, but also the person whose hospitality as corporate Christ is bringing all humanity together in one heavenly companionship. In witnessing to the divine holiness the NT Church was gradually discovering that God's plan involved a peculiar eschatology – that 'even in this world we are as he is' (1 John 4:17).

My intention has been to underline the conviction that in the twenty-first century the Church can find restored unity and zeal for the Kingdom through a discipline of diminishing religion. That diminishment, of which Bonhoeffer prophesied, happens spontaneously and therapeutically when believers give their wholehearted attention to God's apparently anonymous presence in the world of today. One corollary is that we should welcome and apply the interdisciplinary studies that show how the Creator promotes his work in every field of interpersonal responsibility. This is where Christianity has a message for the world which has almost been forgotten in these days.

Diagrams

Figure 1. Dynamic Cycle of personhood

THE ONTOLOGICAL MODEL

The sources of personal 'being-itself' and of 'well-being' are
opened by love and care, acceptance and sustenance given by
the source person, who goes 'down' to draw the needy one
into being-by-relationship, and then opens up rich communicable
personal resources. These, responded to, complete the 'input'.
A strong sense of status, and identification motivates a
movement to give out to others. The achievement of this
service is the output.

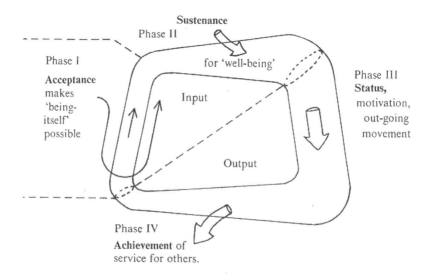

Figure 2. Experiencing the threat of abandonment

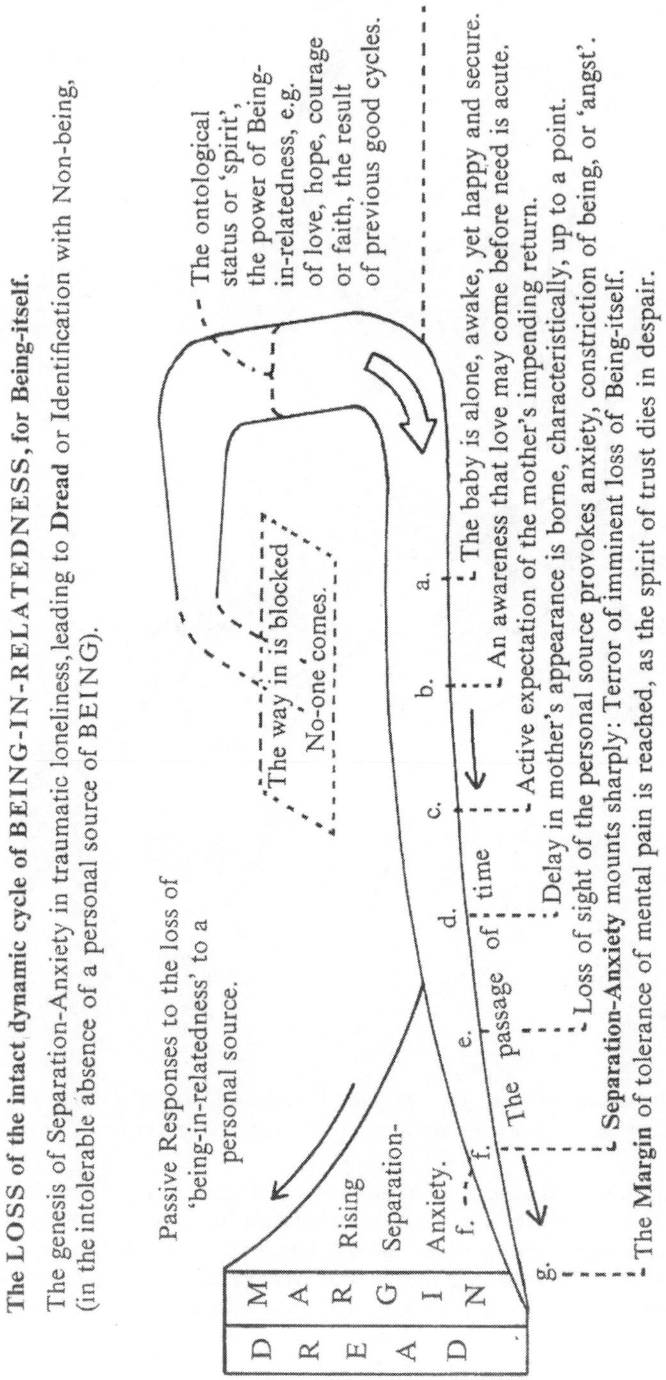

The LOSS of the intact dynamic cycle of BEING-IN-RELATEDNESS, for Being-itself.

The genesis of Separation-Anxiety in traumatic loneliness, leading to Dread or Identification with Non-being, (in the intolerable absence of a personal source of BEING).

Passive Responses to the loss of 'being-in-relatedness' to a personal source.

The ontological status or 'spirit', the power of Being-in-relatedness, e.g. of love, hope, courage or faith, the result of previous good cycles.

The way in is blocked
No-one comes.

D M
R A   Rising
E R   Separation-
A G
I   Anxiety.
D N

f.

g.

The passage of time

a. The baby is alone, awake, yet happy and secure.
An awareness that love may come before need is acute.
b. Active expectation of the mother's impending return.
c. Delay in mother's appearance is borne, characteristically, up to a point.
d. Loss of sight of the personal source provokes anxiety, constriction of being, or 'angst'.
e. Separation-Anxiety mounts sharply: Terror of imminent loss of Being-itself.
f. The Margin of tolerance of mental pain is reached, as the spirit of trust dies in despair.

Figure 3. Severe foetal distress

K.Hale.

*The Persecution of the Foetus: Negative Umbilical Affect and Piercing
Affliction portrayed spontaneously by a 19-year-old girl.*

This drawing is one of a series; in it she pictures herself sitting in a grey, dead hand,
while the feeble hand of the foetus tries to pluck out the thorny twig which twists into
her navel, but cannot. To get away from the body invaded by badness the foetus takes
refuge in the skull. Post-natal life, she felt, was even worse, demanding regression
even into this persecutory womb, which she had become accustomed to coping with
after a fashion. To escape to the moon, seen as a far off good place, would be bliss. It
is identified with the short-lived detachment of the blastocystic phase.

Figure 4. Falling into the worst and defending against it

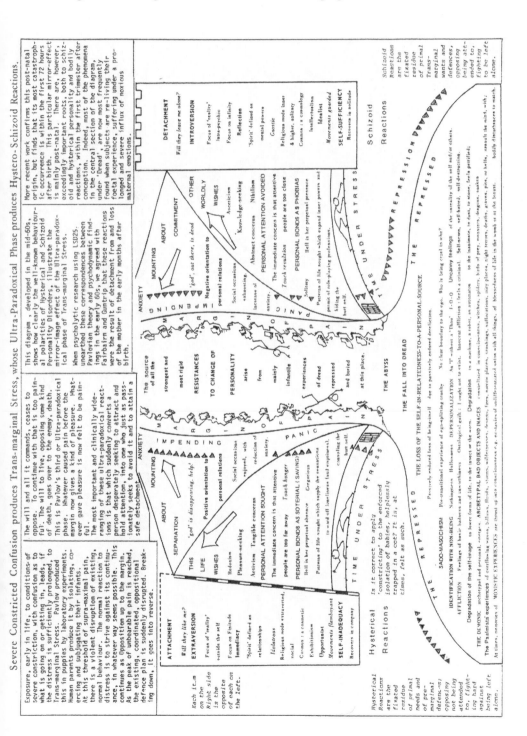

Figure 5. The shape of unhealed humanity

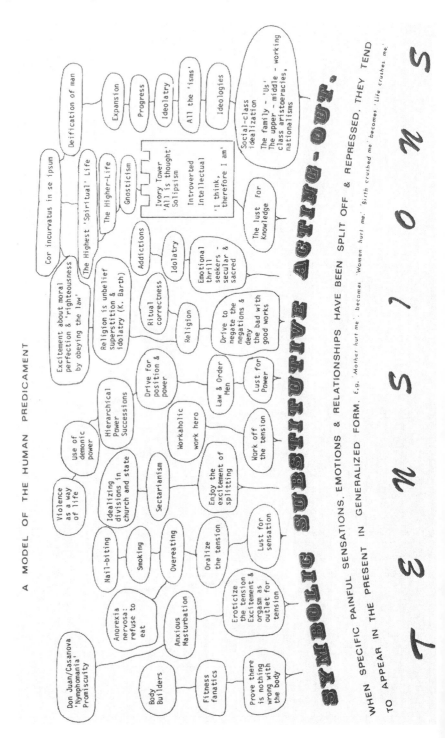

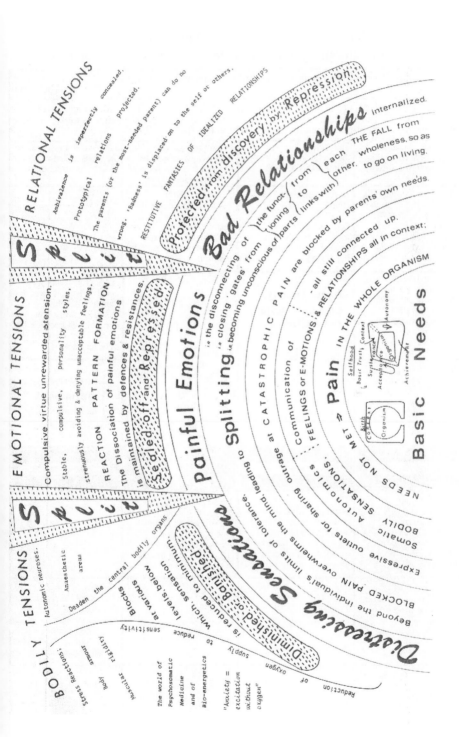

RELATIONAL TENSIONS

Ambivalence is imperfectly concealed.

Prototypical relations projected.

The parents (or the most-needed parent) can do no wrong. 'Badness' is displaced on to the self or others.

RESTITUTIVE FANTASIES OF IDEALIZED RELATIONSHIPS

Protected from discovery by Repression

Bad Relationships internalized.

THE FALL from { from each } wholeness, so as
the funct- { to } other, to go on living.
ioning { links with } of parts

Split

EMOTIONAL TENSIONS

Compulsive virtue unrewarded tension.

Stable, compulsive, personality styles,
strenuously avoiding & denying unacceptable feelings.

REACTION PATTERN FORMATION

The Dissociation of painful emotions is maintained by defences & resistances.

Sealed off and Repressed

Painful Emotions

is the disconnecting of 'closing gates' from {i.e. becoming unconscious of}

Splitting i.e. becoming unconscious of the mind.

leading to CATASTROPHIC PAIN are blocked by parents' own needs.

- all still connected up.

Communication of FEELINGS of E-MOTIONS, & RELATIONSHIPS all in context:

Pain IN THE WHOLE ORGANISM

NEEDS NOT MET →

Basic Needs

Selfhood
(Basic Trust) Context
Acceptance Autonomy
Achievement

Auth Organism

Somatic Autonomic BODILY SENSATIONS

Expressive outlets for sharing outrage overwhelms the limits of tolerance.

BLOCKED PAIN overwhelms the individual's limits or tolerance.

Beyond the individual's limits or tolerance.

Distressing Sensations

Diminished or banished:

is reduced to minimum.

which sensation

Split

BODILY TENSIONS

Autonomic neuroses.

Stress Reactions:

Anaesthetic areas

Deaden the central bodily organs

Body rigidity

Muscular

Blocks various levels below

at which sensitivity to reduce

The world of Psychosomatic Medicine and of Bio-energetics

"Anxiety = excitation without oxygen"

Reduction of oxygen supply

Figure 6. Growth sequence towards spiritual maturity

A Model correlating the Transitional States, 'Active' and 'Passive',
Therapeutic Integration of the Psychodynamic Roots of Depressive,

The Dynamics of Active Religious Character Defences and the Transitions to Actively Passive Openness			
I Positive Dynamic Drives and Motivations	We are dealing, here, not with Breakdown, or ill-health on any level of existence, but with way of moving to a Breakthrough to more abundant health, particularly in the spiritual life.		
In practice, therefore, both positive & negative motivations are at work.	The Active Purgation of 'bad' character traits by moral effort & will.	Trying to beat one's badness gives way to owning its deep roots & allowing God to act.	The Active Purgation of the 'senses' from 'bad' idolatrous attachments
II (a) _Negative Dynamic drives_ compel us to deny and strive against the effects of 'memories' of a 'bad' 'God'. We negate a depressing negation of care by over-reacting.	In reaction against 'badness' on Level IV, the striving is – to deny anger, be mild, to avid sexuality, and to keep up a record of hard work. [1] ⟹	The over-active, restless, never-ending struggle, actively to purge 'badness' out of the character, is now seen to be what it is, & given up. [3]	
II (b) _Negative Dynamic drives_ to deny and yet compensate for hidden separation-panic & covering of sustenance, through enthusiasm in warm 'religious' occasions	**Rage, Anxiety, Lust and Despair** are being 'sat on'.	Reaching down [4] to and reowning the roots of 'depressive' and compulsively compliant personality difficulties.	As persons who need [6] good sensations we can, nevertheless, actively choose good company & godly ways of meeting our need to avid feelings of **Loneliness, Emptiness, & Longings** that feel bottomless.
II (c) _Negative Dynamic_ denial of the death of our ability to relate in a fully human way, with flight into 'introverted modes of 'religion' intensely affirmed.			
III Repressive Layer	Repression Firm		Repression strong
IV (a) _Negative Memories of 'god'_ experienced as 'had', as subjecting a helpless baby to deprivation, with inevitable 'bad' relations & reactions.	The root of depression [2] is in split off & disowned experiences of 'god' as one who provoked rage & anger, fantasy or substitute objects, despair & anxiety. →	These root experiences are re-owned. [5] We offer to God our rage against 'god'. We open our lusts to Him. We come to rest in Christ's work.	
IV (b) _Bad Memories of 'god'_ experienced as allowing or intending desertion or hunger, pain, cold, humiliation & their results.			The roots of these [7] disowned but fixed feelings of painful loneliness and emptiness remain inaccessible. Concealed hurtful deprivations.
IV (c) _Appalingly bad experiences_ of 'god' as callously destructive of trustful 'being' and 'well-being'. Now related by reversed drives. Loving is hell.			

described by St John of the Cross, with the
Hysterical and Paranoid-Schizoid Disorders.

Read across the top, down the left column, then Boxes 1 to 15

Level I Positive Dynamic Drives and Motivations; As I am loved, so I love
Level II The Negative Dynamics; Trying to achieve the opposite of Lev. IV.
Level III The Repression Level; Maintaining the ban on repeats from L. IV.
Level IV Split off memories of bad experiences of 'god' = parental world.

In a 'Passive Night' of the senses the deep roots of compulsive attachments are borne.	The Active Purgation of the religious mind & 'spirit' from contamination by 'lower' elements	In a 'Passive Night' of the spirit we encounter and bear the obstacles to intimate trust & union
We no longer feel our [8] *former satisfactions from this sense-oriented religious style, as if a ligature stopped the flow of feelings. We let them go*		
Reaching down [9] to and reowning the roots of compulsive coveting & envy of 'hysterical' attachments & immaturity. **Dread of Intimacy** *Repression intense*	Being in flight from [11] intimate, whole-person relationships, we can excel at detached, mental or mystical modes of religion	*Our 'higher-life' of* [13] *thought and private devotion dries up on us. We feel our detachment as pain, our excelling as pride. Dread is near* [14] Reaching down to and reowning the roots of 'paranoid' fears & persecutions, and 'schizoid' detachments & revulsions
Aided by the Spirit [10] of Christ we become able to bring to mind primal separation-anxiety, bearing it, and the emptiness.		Trans-marginal layers of primal pain are reached.
	Intense repression [12] *covers the basic injuries which compel flight from a 'god' who annihilates, crushes, and persecutes with ruthless force.*	In loving attention [15] and active abandonment to God in Christ, we endure the pain of having trusted a 'god' who proved to be destructive.

Chapter Notes

Introduction

1. Douglas Knight, 'John Zizioulas on the Eschatology of the Person' in *The Future as God's Gift: Explorations in Christian Eschatology*, ed. David Fergusson and Marcel Sarot (Edinburgh: T&T Clark Limited, 2000) p.189.
2. Rowan Williams, *Lost Icons: Reflections on Cultural Bereavement* (Edinburgh: T&T Clark Limited, 2000).
3. Jacob Needleman, *Lost Christianity*. See ch.1, n.2 and n.19.

Chapter One

1. Charles Taylor, *Varieties of Religion Today: William James Revisited* (Cambridge, MA: Harvard University Press, 2002).
2. Nicholas Lash, *The Beginning and End of Religion* (Cambridge: Cambridge University Press, 1996) pp.36, 37.
3. Sarah Coakley, *Powers and Submissions: Spirituality, Philosophy and Gender* (Oxford: Blackwell,Publishers Ltd, 2002) pp.74, 78, Colin Morris, *The Discovery of the Individual 1050-1200* (London: SPCK, 1987).
4. David Ford, *Self and Salvation* (Cambridge: Cambridge University Press, 1999) p.205.
5. John Habgood, *Being a Person: Where Faith and Science Meet* (London: Hodder & Stoughton Ltd, 1998) pp.58, 60, 62.
6. Nicholas Lash, *Theology on the Way to Emmaus* (London: SCM Press Ltd, 1986) p.143.
7. Richard Swinburne, *The Existence of God*, (Oxford: Oxford University Press, 1979) p.244.
8. Nicholas Lash, *Theology on the Way to Emmaus*, pp.142-145.
9. Nicholas Lash, *Easter in Ordinary: Reflections on Human Experience and the Knowledge of God* (London: SCM Press Ltd, 1988, first published Charlottesville, VA: University Press of Virginia, 1988).
10. William James, *The Varieties of Religious Experience* (London: Longmans, Green & Co, 1902).
11. Nicholas Lash, *The Beginning of the End of Religion*, ch.8: 'Anselm Seeking'.
12. James Mackey, *The Critique of Theological Reason* (Cambridge: Cambridge University Press, 2000).
13. Mike Higton, *Difficult Gospel: The Theology of Rowan Williams* (London: SCM Press Ltd, 2004).

14. Charles Taliaferro, *Consciousness and the Mind of God* (Cambridge: Cambridge University Press, 1994).

15. Wolfhart Pannenberg, *Anthropology in Theological Perspective* (Edinburgh: T&T Clark Ltd, 1985).

16. Richard Norris, 'Human Being' in *Keeping the Faith: Essays to mark the Centenary of Lux Mundi*, ed. Geoffrey Wainwright (London: SPCK, 1989).

17. Simon Parke in *Church Times*, 2nd May, 2008.

18. C.E. Gunton, Bampton Lectures, *The One, the Three, and the Many: God, Creation and the Culture of Modernity* (Cambridge: Cambridge University Press, 1993) pp.30-34.

19. Angela Tilby on 'Thought for Today', BBC Radio 4, 5th December, 2002.

20. Colin Trevarthen's chapter 'The Concept and Foundation of Infant Subjectivity' in *Intersubjective Communication and Emotion in Early Ontogeny*, ed. S. Braten (Cambridge: Cambridge University Press, 1998) provides an introduction and short history of the new movement in development psychology.

21. Colwyn Trevarthen and K.J. Aitken, 'La fonction des émotions dans la compréhension des autres' in *Autisme et regulation de l'action*, ed. R. Pry (Montpellier: Université Paul Valery, 1996) p.11; quoted by Mackey, p.156.

22. Colwyn Trevarthen and K.J. Aitken, 'Self-Other Organisation in Human Psychological Development' in *Development and Psychopathology 9* (1997) p.654; quoted in Mackey p.156.

23. Colwyn Trevarthen and K.J. Aitken, 'Brain Development, Infant Communication, and Empathy Disorders: Intrinsic Factors in Child Mental Health' in *Development and Psychopathology 6* (1994) p.598; quoted by Mackey, p.157.

24. Colwyn Trevarthen, 'Contracts of Mutual Understanding: Negotiating Meanings and Moral sentiments with Infants', *Journal of Contemporary Legal Issues 6* (1995) pp.392, 395; quoted by Mackey, pp.160-161.

25. *Ibid.*, pp.375-376; quoted in Mackey p.161.

26. Op.cit. p.30.

Chapter Two

1. Lake wrote that in Christ "we become able to bear…as Christian adults, the dispiriting crises which in foetal and infant life had shattered the spirit, broken faith, destroyed hope and left love heart-broken" *With Respect: A Doctor's Response to a Healing Pope* (London: Darton,Longman and Todd Ltd, 1982) p.265.

2. *Epworth Review*, 1:2 (May 1974) pp.38-49; cited in *In the Spirit of Truth: A reader in the work of Frank Lake*, ed. Carol Christian (London: Darton, Longman and Todd Ltd, 1991), pp.27-28.

3. Eric N. Ducker, *A Christian Therapy for a Neurotic World* (London: George Allen & Unwin Ltd, 1961) p.80.

4. Howard S. Liddell, *Emotional Hazards in Animals and Man* (Springfield, IL: C.C. Thomas, 1956).

5. Ann Belford Ulanov, *Finding Space: Winnitcott, God and Psychic Reality* (Louisville, KY: Westminster John Knox Press, 2001).

6. Richard Noll, *The Jung Cult: Origins of a Charismatic Movement* (London: Fontana Press, 1996; first published Princeton, NJ: Princeton University Press, 1994).

7. Anthony Stevens. *On Jung* (Routledge, 1990). This passage appears in his chapter on 'Metapsychology: Jung's model of the Psyche', under the heading 'Archetypes and the Collective Unconscious', where Stevens has written: "his

collectve unconscious hypothesis was one of the truly momentous events in 20th-century psychology".

8. C.G. Jung, *Analytical Psychology: its Theory and Practice* (London and Henley: Routledge & Kegan Paul Ltd, 1976) lecture 5, p.184.

9. Alice Miller, *For Your Own Good: The Roots of Violence in Child-rearing*, trans. Hildegarde and Hunter Hannum, 1993 (London: Virago Press, 1987). Originally published as *Am Anfang war Erziehung* (Frankfurt am Main: Suhrkamp Verlag, 1980).

10. Alice Miller, *Breaking Down the Wall of Silence: to Join the Waiting Child*, trans. Simon Worrall (London: Virago Press, 1991). Originally published as *Abbruch der Schweigemauer* (Frankfurt am Main: Suhrkamp Verlag, 1991).

11. Alice Miller, *Thou Shalt Not Be Aware: Society's Betrayal of the Child*, trans. Hildegarde and Hunter Hannum (London: Pluto Press, 1985). Originally published as *Du sollst nichts merken* (Frankfurt am Main: Suhrkamp Verlag, 1981).

12. The book referred to in this passage on p.132 of *Breaking Down the Wall of Silence* is *The Obsidian Mirror* by Louise Wisechild (Seattle, WA: Seal Press, 1988).

13. Frank Lake, *Mutual Caring: A Manual of Depth Pastoral Care*, ed. Stephen Maret (Lexington, KY: Emeth Press, 2008).

14. Roger Moss, *Frank Lake's Maternal-Fetal Distress Syndrome and Primal Integration Workshops* (Oxford: Clinical Theology Association, 1983).

15. Nicholas Lash, *Holiness, Speech and Silence: Reflections on the question of God* (Aldershot: Ashgate Publishing Ltd, 2004).

16. George Steiner, *Real Presences: Is There Anything in What We Say* (London: Faber & Faber, 1989) p.89.

17. Rowan Williams, *Resurrection: Interpreting the Easter Gospel* (London: Darton, Longman & Todd Ltd, 1982).

18. Rowan Williams, *Christianity and the Ideal of Detachment* (Oxford: Clinical Theology Association, 1989).

19. Jacob Needleman, *Lost Christianity: a Journal of Rediscovery* (New York: Doubleday, 1980; paperback edition New York: Harper & Row, 1985) pp.23-28.

20. Kevin Culligan, Ronald Rolheiser and Richard Copsey, *A Fresh Approach to St John of the Cross*, ed. John McGowan (Slough and Maynooth: St Paul's, 1993) pp. 96-100.

Chapter Three

1. Jeremy Young, *The Cost of Certainty: How Religious Conviction Betrays the Human Psyche* (London: Darton, Longman & Todd Ltd, 2004).

2. John Bowker, *The Sacred Neuron: Extraordinary New Discoveries Linking Science and Religion* (London: I.B. Tauris & Co Ltd, 2005).

3. James Alison, *Faith Beyond Resentment: Fragments Catholic and Gay* (London: Darton, Longman & Todd Ltd, 2001) p.39.

4. Pierre Solignac, *The Christian Neurosis*, trans. John Bowden (London: SCM Press Ltd, 1982). Originally published as *La névrose chrétienne* (Paris: Éditions de Trévise, 1976).

5. *Alpha News UK Focus* (February 2008).

6. Op. cit. ch.1, n.13.

7. Not pretending that such unions are marriages, because factually they are not.

8. Elizabeth Johnson, *She Who Is: the Mystery of God in Feminist Theological Discourse* (New York: Crossroad Publishing, 1993).

9. Tom Smail protested to Frank Lake that he should not take the words 'must be born again' to mean re-live your birth. In this he was right, but Lake was justified to the extent that new birth is about awareness and that without psychological growth there is no prospect of the spiritual change of which Jesus was speaking. On this matter I would urge readers to look up the kind words Smail wrote on this matter that are printed by John Peters in *Frank Lake, the Man and his Work* (London: Darton, Longman & Todd Ltd, 1998) p.84. It will be seen that my thesis is presented in the light of theological and psychological considerations on the subject of faith which show that Lake was properly correcting a Christian outlook that had long prevailed. All that has transpired since he died is showing that his insistence on psychological clarity is needed if the Church is to expound the truth of New Testament doctrine. See about atonement below.

10. Charles Marsh, *Reclaiming Dietrich Bonhoeffer: The Promise of his Theology* (Oxford: Oxford University Press, 1994).

11. Karl Barth, *Epistle to the Romans*, trans. Edwyn C. Hoskyns (New York: Oxford University Press, 1968) pp.269, 149.

12. *Captured by the Crucified: The Practical Theology of Austin Farrer*, ed. David Hein and E.H. Henderson (New York: T&T Clark International, 2004).

13. Heinrich Ott, *Reality and Faith: the Theological Legacy of Dietrich Bonhoeffer* (Cambridge: Lutterworth Press, 1971). German edition 1966.

14. Dietrich Bonhoeffer, letter dated 30th April, 1944 found in *Letters and Papers from Prison*, ed. Eberhard Bethge, Bonhoeffer's closest friend, trans. Reginald H. Fuller (London: SCM Press Ltd, 1953). Originally published in *Widerstant und Ergebung* (Munich: Chr. Kaiser Verlag, 1951). This quotation is from the Fontana edition, 1959, p.92. The letter is from the section of the book headed 'Letters to a friend'. These were mainly to Bethge, but also occasionally to others.

15. *Ibid.*, p.91.

16. Dietrich Bonhoeffer, *Ethics,* ed. E. Bethge, trans. N.H. Smith (London: SCM Press Ltd, 1955). Originally published in German (Munich: Chr. Kaiser Verlag, 1949). This quotation is from the Fontana edition, 1964, p.188 and pp.231-235.

17. Harold Lockley, *Dietrich Bonhoeffer: His* Ethics *and its value for Christian Ethics today* (Swansea: The Phoenix Press, 1993).

18. Frank Lake, *Tight Corners in Pastoral Counselling* (London: Darton, Longman & Todd Ltd, 1981) p.60

19. N.T. Wright, *The Climax of the Covenant: Christians and the Law in Pauline Theology* (Edinburgh: T&T Clarke Ltd, 1991).

20. Dietrich Bonhoeffer, *Creation and Fall*, trans. John C. Fletcher (London: SCM, 1959). Originally published in German as *Schöpfung und Fall* (Munich: Chr. Kaiser Verlag, 1937).

21. Dietrich Bonhoeffer, letter dated 5th September 1943, *Letters and Papers from Prison*, ed. Eberhard Bethge, trans. Reginald H. Fuller (London: SCM Press Ltd, 1953).

22. *Captured by the Crucified: The Practical Theology of Austin Farrer*, ed. David Hein and E.H. Henderson (London: T&T Clark International, 2004).

23. Austin Farrer, *A Celebration of Faith* (London: Hodder & Stoughton Ltd, 1970) p.60.

24. Austin, Farrer, 'Thinking the Trinity', published in J.L. Houlden, *Austin Farrer: The Essential Sermons* (London: SPCK, 2008) pp.77, 79.

25. Austin Farrer, *God is Not Dead* (New York: Morehouse-Barlow, 1966) pp.106-

107; quoted by Henderson p.79.

26. That this realisation of God's joint-agency with his human creatures is not new, has been brought out recently, and with particular reference to the theme of my concluding chapter, by Dennis Ngien. His book, *Gifted Response: The Triune God as the Causative Agency of our Responsive Worship* (Milton Keynes: Paternoster, 2008) shows how strongly prominent theologians have affirmed this from patristic times to the Reformation.

27. Austin Farrer, *Lord I Believe: Suggestions for Turning the Creed into Prayer* (Cambridge, MA: Cowley, 1989); quoted by Henderson p.57.

28. Nick Earle, *Does God Make Sense?* (Capetown: Polymathic Publishing, 1998) pp.10, 7.

29. Nicholas Lash, *Easter in Ordinary: Reflections on Human Experience and the Knowledge of God* (London: SCM Press Ltd, 1988, first published Charlottesville, VA: University Press of Virginia, 1988) p.255.

30. John Milbank, *Theology and Social Theory: Beyond Secular Reason* (Oxford: Blackwell, 1990).

31. John Milbank, Catherine Pickstock and Graham Ward, eds., *Radical Orthodoxy: A New Theology* (Oxford: Blackwell, 1997; London: Routledge, 1999).

32. John Milbank, *Theology and Social Theory* (Oxford: Blackwell, 1993) p.359 and 'Postmodern Critical Augustinianism' in *Modern Theology* 7.3 (April 1991) p.225.

33. Steven Shakespeare, *Radical Orthodoxy: A Critical Introduction* (London: SPCK, 2007) p.56.

34. John Milbank, *Theology and Social Theory* (Oxford: Blackwell, 1993), p.206.

35. John Milbank, *The Word Made Strange: Theology, Language, Culture* (Oxford: Blackwell, 1997) p.162; quoted by Shakespeare p.108.

36. John Milbank, *Theology and Social Theory: Beyond Secular Reason*, 2nd Edn (New York: Wiley-Blackwell, 2006) p.xxiii.

37. John Milbank, *The Word Made Strange: Theology, Language, Culture* (Oxford: Blackwell, 1997) p.229; quoted by Shakespeare pp.27.

38. John Milbank and Catherine Pickstone, *Truth in Aquinas* (London: Routledge, 2002), p.111.

Chapter Four

1. Arthur A. Vogel, *Radical Christianity and the Flesh of Jesus: The Roots of Eucharistic Living* (London: Darton, Longman & Todd Ltd, 1996, first published Grand Rapids, MI: Wm B. Eerdmans Publishing Co, 1995).

2. Daniel W. Hardy, *Finding the Church: The Dynamic Truth of Anglicanism* (London: SCM Press Ltd, 2001).

3. John Hull, *In the Beginning there was Darkness* (London: SCM Press Ltd, 2001) p.3.

4. Tom Smail, *Once and For All: A Confession of the Cross* (London: Darton, Longman & Todd, 1998) p.146.

5. David L. Edwards, *Yes: A Positive Faith* (London: Darton, Longman & Todd, 2006).

6. Tom Smail, *Once and For All*, p.134.

7. Colin Gunton, *The Actuality of Atonement* (Edinburgh: T&T Clark, 1988) p.188.

8. N.T. Wright, *The New Testament and the People of God* (London: SPCK, 1992) p.286.

9. N.T. Wright, *The Resurrection of the Son of God* (London: SPCK, 2003) pp.726-728.

10. Tom Wright, *Surprised by Hope* (London: SPCK, 2007).

11. Christina Rees, *The Divine Embrace: Discovering the Reality of God's Love* (London: Darton, Longman & Todd Ltd, 2006) p.152.

12. Christopher Cocksworth, *Evangelical Eucharistic Thought in the Church of England* (Cambridge: Cambridge University Press, 1993) p.191.

13. Gregory Dix, *The Shape of the Liturgy* (London: Dacre Press, 1945) p.243.

14. 1 Corinthians 11:26 (William Barclay's translation).

15. Ronald Rolheiser, *The Shattered Lantern: Rediscovering a felt presence of God* (London: Hodder & Stoughton Ltd, 1994).

16. Daniel W. Hardy, *Finding the Church,* p.221.

17. Christopher Cocksworth, *Evangelical Eucharistic Thought in the Church of England* (Cambridge: Cambridge University Press, 1993), p.202, 204.

18. *Powers and Submissions*, ch.8 'The Resurrection and the "Spiritual Senses"'.

19. Since God seeks to reveal himself to everyone many non-Christian believers come to some awareness of Christ but again without recognising him at first until they are converted.

20. John Foskett, *The Gossip of God's Siblings: the European Pastoral Care and Counselling Movement 1972-2005* (Edinburgh: Contact Pastoral Trust, 2006).

21. Jane Leach, 'Pastoral Supervision: a Review of the Literature' in *Contact: Practical theology and pastoral care* (2006), p.151 on 'Supervision and Support'.

22. Frances Ward, *Lifelong Learning: Theological Education and Supervision* (London: SCM Press Ltd, 2005).

23. *Ibid.*, p.38 quoted in Leach's article.

24. Leach is referring to S. Croft, *Ministry in Three Dimensions: Ordination and Leadership in the Local Church* (London: Darton, Longman & Todd Ltd, 1999), pp.42-43.

25. Mary Travis, 'Supporting Clergy in Postmodern Ministry', *Practical Theology,* 1.1 (2008).

26. Oliver O'Donovan, *Resurrection and Moral Order: An Outline of Evangelical Ethics* (Leicester: Apollos, 1986) pp.94-95.

27. I acknowledge, however, that O'Donovan does so in the context of an argument about Christians adopting practices which he regards as compromising the faith and I regret that I do not have space to give this issue the further attention it calls for.

28. Anthony Storr, *The School of Genius* (London: André Deutsch Ltd, 1988).

29. Rowan Williams, *Tokens of Trust* (Norwich: Canterbury Press, 2007) p.14.

Select Bibliography

Allen, Diogenes. 'Farrer's Spirituality in *Captured by the Crucified: The Practical Theology of Austin Farrer*, Hein and Henderson, eds. T&T Clark, 2004

Bonhoeffer, Dietrich. *Creation and Fall* SCM, 1959

-----. *Ethics*, E. Bethge, ed. Collins, 1964

-----. *Letters and Papers from Prison*. Collins, 1959

Bowker, John W. *The Sacred Neuron: Extraordinary New Discoveries linking Science and Religion*. IB Tauris, 2005

Christian, Carol ed. *In the Spirit of Truth: A reader in the work of Frank Lake*. DLT, 1991

Coakley, Sarah. *Powers and Submissions: Spirituality, Philosophy and Gender.* Blackwell, 2002

Cook, Chris, Powell, Andrew, and Sims, Andrew (eds). *Spirituality and Psychiatry.* Royal College of Psychiatrists, 2009

Cocksworth, Christopher J. *Evangelical Eucharistic Thought in the C of E.* CUP, 1993

Culligan, Kevin. 'John of the Cross and modern psychology: A brief journey into the unconscious' in *A Fresh Approach to St John of the Cross*, John McGowan, ed. S. Paul's, 1993

Dix, Gregory. *The Shape of the Liturgy.* Dacre, 1945

Earle, Nick. *Does God Make Sense?* Polymathic, 1998

Edwards, David L. *YES, A Positive Faith*. DLT, 2006

Farrer, Austin. *Faith and Speculation: An Essay in Philosophical Theology.* A&C Black, 1967

-----. *Saving Belief.* Hodder & Stoughton, 1964

-----. *A Science of God?* Bles, 1966

Ford, David. *Self and Salvation: Being Transformed.* CUP, 1999

Gunton, Colin E. *The Actuality of Atonement: A Study of Metaphor, Rationality and the Christian Tradition.* T&T Clark, 1988

Habgood, John. *Being a Person: Where Faith and Science Meet.* Hodder & Stoughton, 1998

Hardy, Daniel. *Finding the Church: The Dynamic Truth of Anglicanism.* SCM, 2001

Hartt, Julian N. and Wilson, W. McF., 'Farrer's Theodicy' in *Captured by the Crucified*, Hein and Henderson, eds. T&T Clark, 2004

Henderson, Edward Hugh. 'The God who Undertakes Us' in *Captured by the Crucified*, Hein and Henderson, eds. T&T Clark, 2004

Higton, Mike. *Difficult Gospel, The Theology of Rowan Williams.* SCM, 2004

Johnson, Elizabeth A. CSJ. *She Who Is: the Mystery of God in Feminist Discourse.* Crossroads Publishing, 1993

Jung, Carl. *Analytical Psychology, its Theory and Practice.* Routledge & Kegan Paul, 1982

Knight, Douglas. 'John Zizioulas on the Eschatology of the Person' in *The Future as God's Gift.* Fergusson and Sarot, eds. T&T Clark, 2000

Lash, Nicholas. *Theology on Dover Beach.* DLT, 1979

-----. *Theology on the Way to Emmaus.* SCM, 1986

-----. *Easter in Ordinary: Reflections on Human Experience and the Knowledge of God.* 1988

-----. *The Beginning and End of Religion.* CUP, 1996

-----. *Holiness, Speech and Silence: Reflections on the question of God.* Ashgate, 2004

Lake, Frank. *Clinical Theology.* DLT, 1966

-----. Abridged edition of the same, Martin H. Yeomans, ed. DLT, 1986

-----. *Tight Corners in Pastoral Counselling.* DLT, 1981

-----. *With Respect, A Doctor's Response to a Healing Pope.* DLT, 1982

-----. *Mutual Caring: A Manual of Depth Pastoral Care,* Stephen Maret, ed. Emeth Press, 2008

Lockley, Harold. *Dietrich Bonhoeffer, his Ethics and its value for Christian Ethics today.* Phoenix Press (Swansea), 1993

Mackey, James P. *The Critique of Theological Reason,* CUP, 2000

Marsh, Charles. *Reclaiming Dietrich Bonhoeffer, The Promise of his Theology.* OUP, 1994

Millbank, John. *Theology and Social Reason: Beyond Secular Reason.* 1990

Miller, Alice. *Thou Shalt Not Be Aware.* Pluto, (1985) 1990 2nd ed

-----. *For Your Own Good: Hidden Cruelty in Child Rearing and the Roots of Violence,* Hildegarde and Hunter, trans. Hannum Virago Press, 1987

-----. *The Untouched Key: Tracing Childhood trauma in Creativity and Destructiveness,* Hildegarde. and Hunter, trans. Hannum Virago Press, 1990

-----. *Breaking Down the wall of Silence: To Join the Waiting Child,* Simon Worrall, trans. Virago Press, 1991

Moltmann, Jurgen. *The Trinity and the Kingdom of God: The Doctrine of God.* SCM, 1981

Needleman, Jacob. *Lost Christianity, a Journey of Rediscovery.* Harper & Row, 1980

Ngien, Dennis. *Gifted Response: The Triune God as the Causative Agency of our Responsive Worship.* Paternoster, 2008

Noll, Richard. *The Jung Cult: The Origins of a Charismatic Movement.* Fontana, 1996

Norris, Richard. 'Human Being' in *Keeping the Faith: Essays to Mark the Centenary of Lux Mundi,* G. Wainwright, ed. SPCK, 1989

O'Donovan, Oliver *Resurrection and Moral Order: An outline for evangelical ethics* Apollos 1986

Ott, Heinrich. *Reality and Faith.* Lutterworth Press, 1971

Pannenberg, Wolfhart. *Anthropology in Theological Perspective,* J. O'Connell, trans. T&T Clark, 1985

Prestige, G.L. *God in Patristic Thought.* SPCK, 1952

Rees, Christina. *The Divine Embrace: Discovering the Reality of God's Love.* DLT, 2006

Rolheiser, Ronald. *The Shattered Lantern: Rediscovering a felt presence of God.* Hodder & Stoughton, 1994

-----. 'John and human development' in *A Fresh Approach to John of the Cross,* John McGowan, ed. St Paul's Press (Slough), 1993

Shakespeare, Steven. *Radical Orthodoxy: a Critical Introduction.* SPCK, 2007

Smail, Tom. *Once and For All: A Confession of the Cross.* DLT, 1998

Storr, Anthony. *The School of Genius.* Andre Deutsch, 1998

Taliaferro, Charles. *Consciousness and the Mind of God.* CUP, 1994

Taylor, Charles. *Varieties of Religion Today: William James revisited.* Harvard University Press, 2002

Trevarthen, Colwyn (with K.J. Aitken) 'La function des emotions dans le comprehension des autres' in *Autism et regulation de l'action*, R. Pry, ed. Universite Paul Valery (Montpellier), 1996

Ulanov, Ann Belford. *Winnicott, God, and Psychic Reality.* Westminster John Knox, 2001

Vogel, Arthur. *Radical Christianity and the Flesh of Jesus:The Roots of Eucharistic Living.* DLT, 1996

Williams, Rowan. *Resurrection: Interpreting the Easter Gospel.* DLT, 1982

-----. *Lost Icons: Reflections on Cultural Bereavement.* T&T Clark, 2000

-----. *Tokens of Trust: An Introduction to Christian Belief.* Canterbury Press, 2007

Wilson, William McF. (with Hartt) on 'Farrer's Theodicy' in *Captured by the Crucified.* T&T Clark, 2004

Wright, N.T. *The Climax of the Covenant: Christ and the Law in Pauline Theology.* T&T Clark, 1991

-----. *The Resurrection of the Son of God.* SPCK, 2003

-----. *The NT and the People of God.* SPCK, 1992

-----. *Surprised by Hope.* SPCK, 2007

Young, Jeremy. *The Cost of Certainty: How religious conviction betrays the human psyche.* DLT, 2004

Index

Lightning Source UK Ltd.
Milton Keynes UK
24 March 2010
151805UK00002B/2/P